PRAISE FOR INCLUSIVE TALENT MANAGEMENT

'We are truly in the age of diversity, but we still have so much to do in creating inclusive working environments and cultures to give opportunity, build voice, and drive value from that diversity. Stephen and Danny are truly amongst the foremost thinkers and practitioners on diversity in all its forms and provide a thorough and practical review of where we are, and what we need to do. The time is now, and we must make progress. This book will challenge and guide us, and it's then up to all of us to make it happen.'
Peter Cheese, CEO, CIPD

'Thought-provoking and practical – the book every executive who cares about people should consider reading.'
Antonio Simoes, Chief Executive Officer, HSBC Bank

'Diversity is not separate from talent, it *is* talent. With their brilliant book, Stephen Frost and Danny Kalman enable us to walk the talk. A must-read for leaders who want to benefit from 100 per cent of the talent pool and make a difference in the world.'
Iris Bohnet, Professor of Public Policy, Harvard Kennedy School, and author of *What Works: Gender equality by design*

'Inclusive talent management is imperative to the success of any company that aims to compete in today's global competitive environment. Thanks to their unique professional backgrounds and pragmatic perspectives on the subject, Stephen Frost and Danny Kalman provide us with a very insightful overview of what smart inclusive talent strategies could look like for your company.'
Dominique Turpin, President, IMD International

'This book challenges all organisations to review their talent management strategy and provides practical suggestions on how to change their approach to enhance diversity and inclusion. All those in leadership or talent management roles will relate to the issues raised and benefit from considering the proposed solutions to meet their future talent needs.'
Stephen Pierce, Chief HR Officer, Hitachi Europe

'A must-read for HR professionals and for those in roles promoting diversity and inclusion. I particularly like the checklists in part two of the book as they give an excellent nudge in what steps to take in implementing a talent strategy underpinned by a mindset of diversity and inclusion.'
Ann Pickering, HR Director, O2 UK

'Danny and Steve's challenging new book analysing inclusive talent management (and why it remains such a tough nettle to grasp) should be essential reading for anyone wanting to take part in a mature debate over how we can start to challenge the norm, and unlock talent in its broadest sense.'
Gary Theobald, Head of HR & OD, Health Education England

'Steve and Danny lay out the commercial imperative for inclusivity and diversity as a cultural norm. From Darwin to Gladwell to McDonald's, they show that nature might have the answers, how Talent Wars are totally avoidable and a diverse workforce is the only one that can navigate a volatile future. Great storytelling, belief-shifting data, practical advice and a passion for their subject make it a must-read for any CEO, business owner, manager and maybe even HR professionals!'
Roger Philby, CEO, The Chemistry Group

'I found this book interesting and learned a lot. A compelling and well-written book with some humour to boot.'
Tim Sarson, Partner, KPMG

INCLUSIVE
TALENT
MANAGEMENT

STEPHEN FROST
DANNY KALMAN

INCLUSIVE
TALENT
MANAGEMENT

How business can thrive
in an age of diversity

KoganPage

LONDON PHILADELPHIA NEW DELHI

Publisher's note

Every possible effort has been made to ensure that the information contained in this book is accurate at the time of going to press, and the publishers and authors cannot accept responsibility for any errors or omissions, however caused. No responsibility for loss or damage occasioned to any person acting, or refraining from action, as a result of the material in this publication can be accepted by the editor, the publisher or the author.

First published in Great Britain and the United States in 2016 by Kogan Page Limited

2nd Floor, 45 Gee Street	1518 Walnut Street, Suite 1100	4737/23 Ansari Road
London	Philadelphia PA 19102	Daryaganj
EC1V 3RS	USA	New Delhi 110002
United Kingdom		India

© Stephen Frost and Danny Kalman 2016

The right of Stephen Frost and Danny Kalman to be identified as the authors of this work has been asserted by them in accordance with the Copyright, Designs and Patents Act 1988.

ISBN   978 0 7494 7587 1
E-ISBN 978 0 7494 7588 8

British Library Cataloguing-in-Publication Data

A CIP record for this book is available from the British Library.

Library of Congress Control Number

2016943591

Typeset by Graphicraft Limited, Hong Kong
Print production managed by Jellyfish
Printed and bound in Great Britain by CPI Group (UK) Ltd, Croydon CR0 4YY

For Peter James Simpson

CONTENTS

FIGURES

ABOUT THE AUTHORS

STEPHEN FROST

Stephen founded Frost Included in 2012 and works with clients to embed inclusion in their decision making through both system redesign and leadership development. From 2007 to 2012 Stephen designed, led and implemented the inclusion programmes for the London Olympic and Paralympic Games as Head of Diversity and Inclusion for the London Organising Committee (LOCOG). From 2004 to 2007 he established and led the workplace team at Stonewall, growing the Diversity Champions programme to the largest of its kind in the world with over 600 members. He also established the Stonewall Leadership programme which has now developed hundreds of corporate LGBT leaders and the Workplace Equality Index which is now a standard benchmark across hundreds of organisations worldwide.

He was a Hertford College Scholar at Oxford and a Fulbright Scholar at Harvard. He was elected recipient of the 2010 Peter Robertson Award for Equality and Diversity Champions, named a 2011 Young Global Leader by the World Economic Forum and recently voted one of the top 20 influential LGBT people in the UK. He is a Fellow of the Chartered Institute for Personnel and Development and the Royal Society of Arts.

He teaches Inclusive Leadership at Harvard Business School and is an Adjunct Lecturer at Sciences Po in France. He serves as an adviser to the British Government, the White House, KPMG, the International Paralympic Committee and several other organisations. Stephen is author of *The Inclusion Imperative: How real inclusion creates better business and builds better societies* (Kogan Page, 2014) and is a frequent conference speaker.

DANNY KALMAN

Danny Kalman's expertise is supporting organisations to adopt an inclusive talent management strategy. He strives to ensure they have the right people in the right place at the right time to maximise business results.

Danny was Director of Global Talent at Panasonic Corporation from 2008 to 2013. He was instrumental in the development and implementation of their global talent management policies and procedures. Danny was responsible for leading a more systematic approach in the identification and development of Panasonic's key personnel.

Prior to this Danny worked as the first non-Japanese HR Director of the company's European operations. He was responsible for HR staff in 15 countries, worked closely with the Business Domains in Japan and was a Board Member of Panasonic Europe.

Since April 2013 Danny has advised high-profile organisations on their talent strategies. He is an ICF accredited coach, speaks regularly at conferences on talent management and has led leadership development programmes in the UK, Africa, Asia and South America. His extensive experience of working within a Japanese culture has led to him being appointed as a consultant with Deloitte, supporting the leadership development of their Japanese clients.

Danny is co-author of *Make Your People Before You Make Your Products: Using talent management to achieve competitive advantage in global organizations* (Wiley, 2014).

ACKNOWLEDGEMENTS

Steve would first and foremost like to thank Danny, who challenged him to write this in the first place. I am very grateful to all the friends, colleagues and clients who allowed me the time and space to write and supported me on the journey. The f(i) team and people who inspire me and who I learn from – Carly Grover, Johan Jensen, Irfaan Arif, Gina Badenoch, Dawn Fraser, Phoebe Miles, Tinna Neilsen, Manuel Wachter, Jonathan Ashong-Lamptey. Mel Richards and colleagues at KPMG including Melanie Richards, Hilary Thomas, Margaret Stephens, Gareth Williams, Alex Holt, Bernard Brown, Nigel Slater, Kru Desai, Iain Moffat, Karl Edge, Stewart Hastie, Linda Ellett, Chris Hearld, Ben McDonald, Tim Payne, Chris Sheryn, Guy Warrington, Justin Zatouroff, Melissa Allen, Claire Warnes, Ashley Thomas and Claire Harvey. Iris Bohnet at Harvard, David Boehmer at Heidrick & Struggles, the Young Global Leaders at the World Economic Forum and everyone who has helped make this happen. Mum and Emma in particular who conscientiously read the manuscripts, as well as Stefan Reichenbach, Tim Sarson, Mike Innes, Katherine Cowan, Andrea Coomber, Paola Cecci Domingo, Bruno Sánchez-Andrade Nuño, Johan Jensen, Belinda Parmar, Mary-Frances Winters who have all helped with proofreading and suggestions for case studies and inclusion of latest research. Not forgetting Steve Humerickhouse and the Forum on Workplace Inclusion gang, Lora Solis for the Pomodoro technique and the other Young Global Leaders/ Saudi crew that helped get this over the line!

Danny would like to thank Steve for providing the opportunity to write this book with him. So many family members and friends have provided invaluable support by giving hours of their time to read the manuscript at different stages in its development. They provided ongoing suggestions and encouragement; Annette Kurer, Barry Stillerman, Emma Rees, Fiona Crutchfield and Hilary Baker deserve particular mention. Danny's wife, April, daughter Bianca, son-in-law Dan and mother-in-law Tess requested regular updates as the book evolved. A special thank you to Danny's grandson Dylan for providing welcome distractions. To all of them Danny says thank you.

Danny and Steve would both like to thank the team at Kogan Page for their patience, advice and counsel on the journey – Katy, Lucy, Megan, Christina and Helen – as well as Sue Brooks and all the interviewees. The enthusiasm and encouragement of so many people to see this come to fruition made the effort worthwhile.

All errors and omissions remain our responsibility entirely.

FOREWORD

This book is about the benefits of including diversity in our people decisions, and the dangers of not doing so.

People make sub-optimal decisions because their approach is based on colleagues and information that they themselves select. Their biases cloud their decision-making. So why would diversity be the primary answer to that? Why not better executive education, better governance, or better processes?

The answer is because we are inherently biased. In an age of diversity, we still prefer sameness to difference. This is an observation, not an accusation. The executive education we might choose, the governance we put in place or the processes we enact will be deemed 'better' if they are more to our own liking. That's the problem.

Managerial failure is in no small amount due to unconscious (or possibly conscious) biases. Biases are one of a range of reasons for poor decision-making. We are not denying the complexity and multi-variable nature of organisational decision-making in the 21st century. We understand that diversity in the absence of other good practices does not necessarily lead to success. But there has been insufficient focus on bias to date and insufficient focus on diversity as the solution.

We are in the midst of fundamental demographic and technological change that we can barely comprehend. It is these revolutions that provide this book with its urgency and platform.

Demographically, increasing populations in certain regions, ageing and declining populations in other parts of the world, and changing workforces, work places and work patterns are causing the globe to pivot from west to east and north to south.

Technologically, the explosion in data has led to near-ubiquitous information but this has not necessarily resulted in greater knowledge.

Allowing us to select what we consume more than ever before has simply indulged our biases and created new invisible siloes to compound demographic segregation.

In this sense, whilst technological and demographic change offer us unprecedented opportunity, this will only be realised with inclusive leadership. In the absence of such leadership, physical segregation of people, and siloes in our minds, will triumph. This is to the detriment of all of us.

It is in the midst of this revolution that diversity is still too often seen as separate to talent. This segregated mindset has deep historical routes but, most troubling of all, current technological and demographic trends are reinforcing siloes and segregation.

There remain 'recruiters' and separate 'diversity recruiters'. Why isn't everyone responsible for the recruitment of diverse talent? There remains a discourse of the 'other' and we seek to fix 'them' rather than 'us'. How are diverse candidates defined? How can it be that so few talented minorities have made it to the top of our organisations?

Leadership is required now more than ever to ensure alignment, common purpose and integration. It's never been more important to challenge the still commonly held assumption that inclusion is about being nice to people or avoiding hurting their feelings. Inclusion is self-interest as well as collective interest. Leadership is the vehicle to change understanding of diversity from a zero-sum game to enlarging the pie for everyone.

Above and beyond a business case for inclusive talent management, there is value in having an inclusive working culture and environment in which everyone's contribution is valued and appreciated. This just makes for a more happy and productive workplace, where we still spend the majority of our time.

The first half of this book gives us the reasons for our current predicament, and the second part gives us the how-to's. The focus on recruitment, development, staff retention and leadership offers us not only hope, but also a practical way forward.

This book is urgent and required reading for anyone in a leadership or decision making position, anyone who manages people and for anyone who cares about the future of our global economy and society.

Helena Morrissey,
Chief Executive Officer, Newton Investment Management,
and Antonio Simoes,
Chief Executive Officer, HSBC Bank

Figure 0.1 Organisations featured in the book

	Chapter							
	1	2	3	4	5	6	7	8
Accenture						●		
AIG					●			
Arctic Shores					●			
AT&T								●
Avanade					●	●		
B&Q			●					
BAE					●	●		
Bank of America							●	●
Barclays							●	
Big Lottery					●			
Bouygues					●			
BP					●	●		
Burson-Marsteller							●	
Civil service (UK)					●			
Credit Suisse					●		●	
Deloitte	●		●		●			
Deutsche Bank							●	
Deutsche Telecom		●						
Edelman							●	
EY	●							
Facebook		●	●	●	●			
FCO						●		
Fuji Film				●				
Genesis Housing							●	
Gild					●			
Goldman Sachs			●			●	●	
Goodlife			●					
Google	●	●	●	●	●		●	
Grant Thornton								●
Hitachi			●			●		●
HSBC	●		●	●				
IBM							●	
Kimberly-Clark					●			
Kodak				●				
KPMG	●		●		●	●	●	●

Figure 0.1 *continued*

				Chapter				
	1	2	3	4	5	6	7	8
L'Oréal				●				
Lloyds Bank					●			
LOCOG	●	●	●	●	●	●	●	●
McDonald's			●					
Microsoft							●	
Mitie					●			
National Grid					●			
NHS					●	●	●	
Nokia				●				
O2					●	●	●	●
Oxfam			●					
Panasonic			●		●	●		
Penguin Random House					●			
Photobox						●		
PWC	●							
Rank					●			
Red Hat							●	
Rio Olympics					●			
Royal Mail					●		●	●
SAP					●			
SAS							●	
Shell					●			
Simmons & Simmons					●			
Singapore Airlines							●	
South West Trains					●			
Southwest Airlines							●	
Staffordshire Police					●			
Swiss Air				●				
Swiss Re							●	
Tate Gallery					●			
Telus					●			
Unilever							●	
Virgin Money					●			
Volkswagen					●			
Zappos							●	

(CHALLENGE)

in an age of **diversity**
the addiction to **likeness**
=
homogeneity

PART ONE

THE FIERCE URGENCY OF NOW

The words of Martin Luther King Jr are as relevant today as they were when he said them in 1968. 'We are now faced with the fact that tomorrow is today. We are confronted with the fierce urgency of now. In this unfolding conundrum of life and history, there *is* such a thing as being too late. This is no time for apathy or complacency. This is a time for vigorous and positive action.'

This book highlights a simple contradiction in the way we manage our people and run our organisations that is too often overlooked – we are addicted to sameness in an age of diversity. That is fundamentally an unsustainable position to be in.

At one extreme, terrorists kill difference in the most unspeakable ways. At the other end of the spectrum, we all have our own prejudices and biases that orientate us towards people we like and agree with. Therein lies danger too.

Have you ever wondered why certain decisions were made? Have you ever been frustrated at the promotion of someone who is less able or diligent but performs better in a 'hands-up' culture? Have you ever been exasperated at the intransigence of the organisation and decided to vote with your feet, rather than take on the status quo?

If the answer to any of these questions is yes, then this book is for you.

Moreover, if you have colleagues who would answer no, or who would not even recognise the legitimacy of the questions in the first place, then this book is for them too. Because this is a book for people who believe that the only way to make our organisations work better, and therefore serve society better, is for the people within them to be organised according to their talent and skills.

Why isn't this the case already?

We'll answer this question during the course of the subsequent chapters, but here are seven potential answers to be pondering right now:

Because even though we claim to understand the business case for it, diversity is still seen as a 'nice to have', rather than a core component of strategic advantage.

Because vested interests get in the way.

Because we have an idealised view of what talent is and if people don't fit that image we reject them, even though they may add more value.

Because we make emotionally based decisions, then post-rationalise them as logical.

Because we dislike change.

Because we are afraid to challenge the norm.

And most of all, because we are fundamentally dishonest about our so-called like of diversity. The truth is, we prefer people similar to ourselves. An emotional connection, likeness and comfort, trump meritocratic diversity every time.

We undertook a number of interviews with organisations from different sectors that revealed how a handful of courageous and dedicated professionals are attempting to tackle these issues. We will share real insights, rather than proclamations of intent, throughout the book.

Read the chapters that follow as a series of observations, rather than accusations – we will be challenging, and give you the opportunity to get out of your comfort zone.

In Chapter 1 we assess the current situation in organisations, and how they have unconsciously adopted homogeneous talent management (talent management that fails to account for or benefit from difference) as their default way of managing people. We define diversity and talent at the end of the chapter.

In Chapter 2 we analyse how this situation arose with reference to history and bias. This is important context for the pages that follow. Chapter 3 looks at demographic and technological megatrends that are shaping our future world, before exploring aspects of diversity world wide. Chapter 4 proposes an alternative way to manage our people and run our organisations. We call it inclusive talent management.

1

HOMOGENEOUS TALENT MANAGEMENT

THE SEARCH FOR THE SAME PEOPLE

All over the world, chief executive officers (CEOs), human resources directors (HRDs), talent directors and other professionals are obsessing about talent. Talent consistently ranks in the top three priorities for CEOs, worldwide. They are rightly concerned with finding the people who will be able to best contribute to their business and so help their business grow and compete. It's about three main variables – whom can we recruit? Whom can we promote into the right positions? And whom can we keep?

The problem is that most of them are obsessing about the same people. At most, they are focused on a small group of similar people. They are all busily, and often unconsciously, engaged in homogeneous talent management (HTM).

Homogeneous talent management is talent management that fails to account for or benefit from difference. Ever since the publication of *The War for Talent* in 1997,[1] HTM has prevailed. As a strategic business challenge, and a critical driver of corporate performance, the prevailing logic has been to compete for the best talent in a limited pool. The assumption is that demand will outstrip supply.

Michael Porter, of Harvard Business School, said that strategy was 'about deliberately choosing to be different'.[2] Yet in an edition of *Harvard Business Review* in 2015 there was a flyer for the bestselling business strategy book *Clear Blue Ocean*.[3] It proclaimed how over 3.5 million copies had been sold and it had been translated into 43 languages.

There is something deeply ironic about offering an insight to the mass market – the credentials the book was using to further its sales are precisely those that will diminish its impact. If 3.5 million people all pursue the same strategy then any competitive advantage will be quickly eroded.

There is also a deep irony in the analysis of the average CEO, HRD or talent director. If differentiation is the key to competitive advantage then why are they all looking for the same people?

In 2015 a total of 477 of the top Fortune 500 global companies were run by male CEOs.[4] Malcolm Gladwell also found that 58 per cent of Fortune 500 company CEOs were over 6 feet tall, compared with 14.5 per cent of the United States (US) population. Furthermore, 3.9 per cent of the general US population of adult men are 6 feet 2 inches or taller, but among Gladwell's CEO sample a whopping 30 per cent were 6 feet 2 inches or taller.[5]

The lack of diversity at senior levels with regard to women, disabled people, gay people or ethnic minorities can be somewhat explained with reference to history, discrimination and cultural patterns. But how do we explain the exclusion of short people? How do we explain the relative absence of white men who happen to be below 6 foot?

In a US study researchers followed thousands of people from birth to adulthood. Holding all other variables constant (such as gender, age and weight) they concluded that an inch of height is worth $789 a year in salary.[6] That means that a person who is 6 feet 2 inches tall, but who is otherwise identical to someone who is 5 foot 5 inches, will make on average $7,101 more per year.

COMPETING IN A SELF-LIMITED POOL

Porter's Five Forces of competition are instructive here.[7] At the heart of the so-called 'war for talent' is competition between rival groups (organisations) for the 'best' talent. An obvious example would be the 'Big 4' professional services firms, Deloitte, EY, KPMG and PwC. Should one partner leave one firm for a rival, he or she is put 'on gardening leave' for up to a year in order to neutralise their competitive risk to the firm they are leaving. So intense is the competition between them for their star performers that anyone leaving is often immediately ostracised by their current colleagues before being welcomed into their new firm. Yet all four firms fish in the same, relatively small pool.

Similarly, in Olympic Games organising committees, a standard job description required 'previous Games experience'. The amount of highly talented people without 'previous Games experience' was substantial. This means that the 'Big 4' firms and the biggest event organisation on the planet all deliberately limit the size of the talent pool they are competing in.

In addition to competition for talent between existing rivals, there also exists the threat of new entrants. Obelisk is a legal services provider started in 2010 by Dana Denis-Smith, an ex-City lawyer. It was founded to answer the challenges faced by businesses due to an increased volume in legal work and the cost pressures that resulted from the financial crisis. Denis-Smith built the business around home-based ex-City lawyers, mainly women, who left the profession to care for their families and stepped completely outside the labour force. At Obelisk, women can choose the hours they work, with no minimum or maximum required. Obelisk contracts them back into businesses, law firms and other professional-services organisations offering clients more affordability through the flexibility of the model. Obelisk is taking market share from the established legal big boys as a consequence of their refusal to change their existing culture.

When London 2012 challenged the Olympic Games norm by emphasising local recruitment and the employment of local talent, it threatened the vested interests of the 'Games circus' – those professionals who would otherwise and in normal circumstances travel from employment at one Games to the next almost seamlessly. The London 2012 bid had been based on including local people and refreshing the Olympics' 'licence to operate'. Had London 2012 not adopted this approach, it would have endured even tougher treatment at the hands of the British press and politicians, who were concerned with holding the Games accountable to its promises.

Closely related to the threat of new entrants is the threat of substitute products or services. In addition to new players like Obelisk, technology is also a game-changer. London's black cab drivers are world-famous for 'the

Knowledge' – a demanding test of London's complicated geography which is required in order to gain a licence to operate. Cabbies pride themselves on the high bar to entry and the talent required in order to be a London cab driver. None of them anticipated the arrival of Uber. Now with GPS technology, a smartphone and a car, many people can sidestep the knowledge requirement and become a transport provider.

On one side is the bargaining power of buyers (ie the recruiter). In some instances this can be significant. For example, Google enjoys the current luxury of approximately 400 candidates applying for every vacancy.[8] On the other side there's the bargaining power of suppliers (ie the candidate). The word candidate assumes an unequal relationship from the start – that the organisation holds all the cards and the candidate is passive. However, candidates can bargain more than they often realise. When it comes to salary, men do it rather better than women. This is partly because they are, on average, more money driven, partly because of temperament, partly because of ego. Research suggests that women are far more likely to argue on behalf of others but when it comes to their own interests they often defer.[9]

DIVERSE TALENT DOESN'T FIT HOMOGENEOUS CULTURE

While candidates are infinitely diverse, and bring different (needed) skills to the door of organisations, the organisational response is often crude. How often have you heard people obsess over 'fit'? Will he/she 'fit' into our existing culture? Even when recruiters are looking 'for women', they are often looking for women who will 'fit' into the existing (male) culture.

The response to the real and pressing talent management challenges of recruitment, development and retention is often a cookie-cutter one size fits all approach that fails to maximize the benefits of diversity. A flaw in the 'war on talent' that has been largely unanswered until now is that there is often plentiful talent; we simply unconsciously (and sometimes consciously) decide to ignore it.

Let us now look at what lessons we can learn from the world around us. First, we will look at lessons the natural world can offer us, followed by lessons from the financial markets, as shown in Figure 1.1. Finally, we will

Figure 1.1 Ecosystems, financial systems and people

System	Ecosystem	Financial system	People system
Diversity benefits	Biodiversity increases productivity and resilience	Diverse portfolios mitigate risks, and increase resilience	Mitigates groupthink, correlated with higher financial performance
Diversity costs	Cost of conservation	Potentially lower short-run returns	Potential conflict (if unmanaged)
Importance	Each species, no matter how small, has an important role to play in the ecosystem = basis of human existence	Avoids system contagion and economic crises, maintains growth and standard of living	Can improve decision making, market and social relevance and mitigate social exclusion

apply those lessons to looking at people, and reframing what we really mean by 'talent'.

ECOSYSTEMS, BIODIVERSITY AND EXTINCTION

Ecosystems are communities of interacting and co-dependent organisms situated in a particular environment. In his 1859 book *On the Origin of Species* Charles Darwin postulated the need for diversity in the ecosystem in order to sustain life. This is a fact often overlooked by the focus on the more famous (and clichéd) 'natural selection' and evolutionary biology aspects of the book. But in *On the Origin of Species* you will read that Darwin discussed how a field with distantly related grasses would be more productive than a field with a single species of grass. In other words, diversity (and not just specialisation, as is often assumed) is a key ingredient of productivity.

DIVERSITY CAN BE MORE PRODUCTIVE

Darwin's theory has been proved in more modern studies. Marc Cadotte from the University of Toronto grew 17 different plants in various combinations of one, two, or four species per plot, as shown in Figure 1.2.

Figure 1.2 Modern-day Darwin grasses experiment

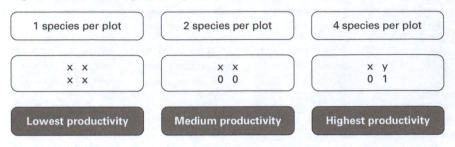

He discovered three things that are of interest to us. One, multi-species plots produced more plant material than single species plots. Two, plots filled with plants that were distantly related to one another were more productive than those that were closely related. For example, a plot containing *goldenrod* and the closely related *black-eyed Susan* was less productive than a plot with *goldenrod* and the more distantly related *bluestem grass*. Finally, species that were furthest apart in evolutionary terms produced higher yields than those that were closer together. He concluded, 'If you have two species that can access different resources or do things in different ways, then having those two species together can enhance species function. What I've done is account for those differences by accounting for their evolutionary history.'[10]

Marc explained:

> What's going on isn't mysterious. Distantly related plants are more likely to require different resources and to fill different environmental niches. One might need more nitrogen, the other more phosphorus; one might have shallow roots, the other deep roots. So rather than competing with one another they complement one another.

SAMENESS CAN BE A KILLER

The importance of these different plants is seen in today's conservation efforts and the widespread recognition that if we don't preserve or enhance our ecosystem, it won't support human existence. In other words, we have implicitly signed up to the notion that biodiversity is important. If those bugs and bees don't thrive and pollinate other plants then the entire food chain will collapse. At its core, biodiversity is a risk mitigation tool for human survival.

Take the case of Chilean fish farms. In 2007 a virus killed millions of salmon that were being farmed in Chile's fish farming industry, the second largest in the world. With hindsight, three variables stand out as significant. One, they were being farmed at much higher density than is the case in Norway or Scotland, and this made the transmission of the disease via sea lice all the more potent. Two, the proximity of Chilean fish farms was far more co-located than in the case of other countries, again allowing disease to spread faster. Three, the salmon were treated with a high level of similar antibiotics, which made the farmed salmon more vulnerable to disease in the long run. In other words, this created sameness made them more vulnerable to a single threat. The World Economic Forum concluded, 'Chilean farmed salmon suffered from a viral disease in a homogeneous environment.'[11] When the farms had to be shut down, thousands became unemployed and the costs rose into millions of dollars.[12]

Conversely, we can increase resilience by taking advantage of 'eco-system services' – the services ecosystems provide us humans with, from agriculture and tourism to fisheries and medicine.[13] The value of biodiversity can be seen in relation to our resilience to disasters such as floods. Upland habitat restorations have increased flood resilience, for example the Pumlumon Project in Montgomeryshire, Wales or the Culm Grassland in Devon, England. Culm is a grassland sponge structure that is excellent for soaking rainwater for slow release, thereby mitigating the risk of flood. 'Biodiverse landscapes are species rich habitats such as grasslands, wetland and upland bogs that act as giant sponges, absorbing and holding water and slowing down water runoff.'[14]

It is the biodiversity (species richness, lots of specialists) that creates resilient structures. It was the lack of biodiversity (caused through the use of strong antibiotics) that exposed the salmon farm to catastrophic risk.

GOING DODO

The International Union for Conservation of Nature (IUCN) has highlighted the plight of the lemur. Ninety-four per cent of all lemurs are under threat, with more than a fifth of all lemur species classed as 'critically endangered'.[15] The reasons vary from hunting for their meat, to habitat destruction in their native Madagascar. They have suffered in particular from illegal logging activity and increasingly from Chinese investments, including road construction. The disappearance of lemurs creates a reduction in biodiversity and a reduction in our future options.

A 2015 report led by the universities of Stanford, Princeton and California, Berkeley analysed extinction rates for vertebrates by assessing fossil records.[16] They concluded that vertebrates were disappearing at a rate 114 times faster than 'normal'. In 2014 a report by Stuart Pimm, a biologist at Duke University, warned mankind was entering a sixth mass extinction event. Stuart claimed that the current rate of extinction was more than 1,000 times faster than in the past. All these authors conclude that the Earth has entered a new period of extinction, and humans could be among the first casualties.[17]

Sir Ken Robinson, the former Education Adviser to the British Government, famously gave a warning and a lesson in humility. If all the insects were to disappear from the planet tomorrow then all life as we know it would be gone within 50 years. However, if all human beings were to disappear from the planet tomorrow then in 50 years' time all life as we know it would be thriving.[18]

SOLUTIONS

The authors of the aforementioned extinction reports conclude that salvation is still possible but it requires intensive and rapid conservation action. Back to our plots of grasses, we could actually use the evolutionary distance between plants to predict future productivity. If plant species disappear and the Earth becomes less productive, plants will draw even less carbon from the atmosphere, possibly increasing the rate of climate change. But if we use the diversity data to inform replantation efforts and conservation strategies, we could pick which combinations of species to introduce to have the most productive effect.

Marc's experiment of different species in different plots reminds us of Darwin's original observation; increased biodiversity leads to greater productivity. Conversely, the Chilean fish farm reminds us that a lack of diversity lowers resilience and can have catastrophic consequences. Consider the application to people and organisations. As we will discuss in Chapter 4, increased diversity of people can be correlated with increased productivity and financial performance. The human equivalent of the Chilean fish farm is witnessed in everyday 'groupthink' and intolerance of different perspectives. Groupthink is the tendency of humans to agree with each other in order to prevent conflict. It is something we will explore in more detail in the next chapter. It can lower organisational resilience and increase the organisation's exposure to risk.

The professional services firm KPMG has placed beehives on the roof of its London offices to support the fight back of the bees. Others are encouraged to re-plant wild flowers and other vegetation to re-create bee-friendly habitats. There are things that can be done. All is not lost, not yet.

FINANCIAL MARKET VOLATILITY, MONEY AND RISK

Just as there are lessons for talent management from the natural world, so too can we learn from recent financial events. On 8 June 2009, in the year following the 2008 financial crisis, Jean-Pierre Landau, Deputy Governor of the Bank of France, said:

> Increases in complexity did not come with (corresponding)... diversity. On the face of it, market participants looked more and more different in their legal status, investment strategies, and business objectives. It has now become apparent that, behind these veils of diverse colours, there was a profound uniformity in the approach to risk, its measurement, its management, as well as in the drivers of risk appetite. This uniformity had very destabilizing consequences.[19]

THE DANGERS OF SAMENESS

The principles of biodiversity and the dangers of sameness can also be applied to the financial system. The financial system allows the transfer of money between savers (and investors) and borrowers. An analysis of the 2008 economic crisis shows that one of the major contributory factors was the proverbial 'all eggs in one basket'.

It was a logical consequence of capitalist endeavour (some may say greed) that financial institutions pursued an increasingly homogeneous set of strategies based on increasingly specialised products that offered the best returns. From a purely marginal returns perspective, it would be illogical to do otherwise. However, when those baskets let the eggs fall, they smashed. There was an insufficient number of other baskets with other eggs in to keep the wheels turning. And none of the eggs were hard-boiled; they were all of the same type and smashed at the same time.

Prior to 2008 many financial institutions were creating above average returns from an increasingly specialised product portfolio. They were running similar businesses, with similar people, competing over similar talent, paying similar wages.

Many banks were taking large positions in structured credit products based on the same underlying asset classes. They were fishing in the same pool for short-term credit and applying similar risk mitigation methodologies.

The most obvious one was the capital ratio risk model, whereby a bank could leverage up to a certain amount based on the probability of a shortfall. They were all relying on the same credit ratings that were being calculated in the same way and assurances were given that a fact was a fact, based on statistical significance with 95 per cent confidence probability. However when the 5 per cent probability arose, the US sub-prime mortgage bubble burst – the lenders all pulled out in the same manner at the same time.

Most calculations were based on a series of assumptions and a series of probabilities. However, the danger arose when banks that are supposed to be in competition with each other made similar assumptions that tranches of collateralised debt obligations were safe based on their AAA credit rating. This was a perfectly logical thing to surmise and it was based on the work of incredibly intelligent people.

However, in the pursuit of ever-higher returns and stretching ratios to the maximum, these assumptions failed to acknowledge that the ratings were based on precarious assumptions about default risk, house prices, and cross-correlations among the risks of the underlying assets. As the World Economic Forum concluded, 'Financial companies also kept large inventories on their balance sheets, and ultimately suffered substantial losses – failing to recognize that there would be a penalty on sameness and a prize for diversity.'[20]

THE HERD

A senior employee gave a presentation to the executive team at Lehman Brothers over two years before the crisis. He criticised the current strategy and presented some suggested amendments to the strategy. He was shut down in conversation in the meeting and then fired in March 2005. The two leaders at the top didn't want to hear what he had to say.[21] This example of groupthink and failure to tolerate difference now stands out as a critical milestone on the journey to Lehman Brothers' eventual collapse.

In a 2010 report the World Economic Forum investigated what the financial sector could learn from other sectors about managing risk.[22] The report concluded that 'Regulators thought nationally, not globally, until it was too late; firm, product and trading strategies became complex yet homogeneous, leading to a stampede once positions did deteriorate.'

Sameness is very seductive. When a rival institution is on to a winner, the shareholder of another firm will call its executives and ask them why they are not following the same path to financial enlightenment. An example of this is how in the lead up to the 2008 financial crisis the demarcation between financial institutions became blurred. Retail banks began behaving like investment banks and hedge funds, in order to more efficiently recycle their capital (create larger returns). This actually reduced the diversity of the players in the market. In effect the retailers created a shadow banking system, whereby they copied many of the activities of their investment banking cousins. Even insurance companies began offering products traditionally only available through investment banks. This rush to sameness created a critical source of systemic risk.

It is easy to understand how a herd mentality can take over. In the face of expert 'best practice', intense competition and the desire not to be left behind, professionals succumb to intense shareholder pressure to keep up and to follow a 'proven' profitable path or course of action. However, while a herd mentality is understandable it is also deeply dangerous. The World Economic Forum stated, 'Institutions should avoid crowded business strategies and vary modelling assumptions for risk management. Boards, executives and investors should think for themselves rather than implementing me-too strategies and obsessing with benchmarks.'[23]

This sameness was not only at the institutional level. In his 2013 book *The Hour Between Dog and Wolf* John Coates analysed behaviour on the trading floor. He described, in vivid detail, the 'inner biological storm' that takes place in the bodies of traders as they are making decisions:

> On a winning streak we can become euphoric, and our appetite for risk expands so much that we turn manic, foolhardy and puffed up with self importance. On a losing streak we struggle with fear, reliving the bad moments over and over, so that stress hormones linger in our brains, promoting a pathological risk-aversion, even depression, and circulate in our blood, contributing to recurrent viral infections, high blood pressure, abdominal fat build up and gastric ulcers.[24]

A key lesson from the trading floor is that people prone to risky decisions can create tremendous value, but they can also be delusional and take grave risks. Another is that if these people are all similar in outlook, the consequences can be catastrophic. A healthy body can tolerate a problem in one organ. But if there is multiple organ failure, the body is in trouble. Classical economics assumes rational man. Yet we know that people are deeply irrational, and even traders make decisions based on the emotional – and the biological.

There appears still to be a high degree of monoculture in the trading floors of New York, Tokyo and London. The culture is very selective and diversity in many senses is minimal. On a recent visit to a couple of trading floors at competitor banks, Steve couldn't help reflecting that their environments were remarkably similar (even down to the same type of pot plants), their strategies seemed remarkably similar and the people executing them seemed remarkably similar.

SYSTEMIC RISK

Professor Simon Levin, from Princeton University, studies complex systems. These involve large numbers of component parts and occur in nature and finance. Their importance is only recently understood in terms of, for example, how diseases spread, or how a vaccination campaign could meet with success or failure. He identified that in order for a complex system to be robust, a critical ingredient was heterogeneity.

In complex systems, strong non-linear patterns can emerge, often without warning, and they can magnify underlying conditions leading to cataclysmic changes. Think of it as the financial equivalent of an earthquake, such as the run on a bank. The resilience of a system (such as an economy) is largely dependent upon heterogeneity – the ability to adapt, as per Darwin's work, and the ability to come up with new solutions in response to change. A lack of diversity equals a lack of options. Sameness creates future selection bias. This is a situation in which competitor banks found themselves during the dark days of 2008. This is the financial equivalent of the Chilean fish farm.

Consider the big variables in any system: time, space and scale. If people all act at the same time, if they are all co-located, and if the stakes are high, then the system is exposed to significant risk.

SOLUTIONS

We have come to accept that diverse financial portfolios are a way to mitigate risk in the financial system. For example, banks are now subject to capital reserve controls, meaning that they have to maintain a 'buffer' in terms of any over-exposure in their lending. Governments have imposed walls between the retail and investment parts of institutions to limit 'contagion' in the event of a repeat of 2008. This 'forced diversity' is in deliberate response to created sameness. It is an anti-sameness strategy.

One of the best things financial institutions could do is actively avoid 'best practice', as shown in Canada in 2008. Canadian banks proved to be comparably resilient during the crisis. On the whole, Canadian banks demonstrated the value of a more diversified and devolved strategy in avoiding the contagion that ripped through the US and UK banking sectors.

Financial institutions could actively encourage diverse and contrasting approaches towards modelling risk. They could actively cultivate 'ruffing' (inviting challenge in meetings to interrogate a proposed course of action) and vigorous debate when determining business strategies. Regulators could encourage variation in institutions' risk management approaches by increasing capital charges for systemically crowded high-risk/high-return business strategies. However, just as sameness in strategy is to be avoided, so should sameness in regulation. Complete regulatory convergence is also a risk.

What we learn from finance is akin to what we learn from nature – diversity is correlated with decreased risk and increased resilience. Homogeneous systems are less resilient than diversified ones. Homogeneous strategies based on a narrow definition of highest returns can be incredibly successful in the short term, but catastrophically disastrous in the medium to long term.

THE LIMITATIONS OF HOMOGENEOUS TALENT MANAGEMENT

If we review our conclusions from ecology and finance and apply them to people, what do we discover?

Fifty years ago, the average life expectancy of a Fortune 500 company was 75 years. Now it is 15 years and declining. Are companies facing extinction like the lemur? Only 61 companies that were in the Fortune 500 in 1955 still remain. The extinction rate is 88 per cent. In 2014 CNBC proclaimed '10 years to a mass extinction event in the Fortune 500'.[25]

As previously mentioned, when Marc grew his 17 different plants he found that combinations of plants that were distantly related to one another were more productive than combinations of plants that were closely related. Applying that to a team, the obvious answer is to forego *black-eyed Susan* in favour of *bluestem grass* in order to improve productivity when mixed with *goldenrod* (who let's say is already in the organisation, a lifer and doesn't want to leave). However *black-eyed Susan* performed 'better' at interview and the manager in the department knows her from his previous job. Even though *bluestem grass* would add more value to the organisation, make it more productive, more competitive, more differentiated and help build the team's resilience in the face of change, the organisation chose *black-eyed Susan*. Why?

When faced with the need to diversify its product portfolio to mitigate risk, a fund manager decided to concentrate his investments in a fund that was performing particularly well. Furthermore, when the regulator got involved, it imposed additional regulations that further narrowed the investment strategies available and by default increased the specialisation of the product selection even more.

Applying that to a team, the regulator, in an effort to decrease the chance of risky hires, has unintentionally narrowed the talent pool. Instead of supervising the process according to the nature of the skill set needed, we have imposed our own (biased) view of what good looks like and screened out diverse candidates. We have displayed a lack of tolerance for different approaches in the same way that the Lehman bosses fired an employee who dared to offer a different strategy. Why?

In both examples, sameness is very seductive. In the first example, emotional ties are at play. The candidate is known to a current employee, and there is an emotional bond, as well as trust. Even though the other candidate may objectively be a better addition to the team, the organisation decides to recruit the sub-optimal candidate for emotional reasons. These will be fed back and justified in a logical fashion.

In the second example, fear is at play. The hiring manager is afraid of the unknown, in much the same way as the regulator. Just as the regulator cannot know more than product managers in individual organisation, a hiring manager cannot know more than the candidate about the candidate's own abilities and skills. Going against the herd requires courage. In view of this, the hiring manager 'plays safe', even though this course of action could be quite the opposite, compounding systemic risk.

DIVERSITY TRUMPS INDIVIDUAL ABILITY

In his 2008 book *The Difference*,[26] Scott Page ran various tests to establish the Diversity prediction theorem. We'll discuss this in more detail in Chapter 4, but for now consider this. Using models and logic Page showed how diversity can trump ability. Furthermore, collective ability is dependent upon diversity in addition to individual ability. In other words, diversity among a group or team trying to solve problems is more important than any individual excellence within that team. This flies in the face of HTM.

In nature, the most evolved species (supposedly us) are dependent on every part of the ecosystem. Each piece plays its part. HR fails to realise that people systems are not so different from ecosystems. Just as in nature, in organisations too there is a talent food chain. Every player is important and when diversity is diminished it diminishes the resource base for future growth, productivity and risk mitigation.

TECHNICAL FIXES TO CULTURAL PROBLEMS ARE UNSUSTAINABLE

Furthermore, just as in finance, HR tends to apply technical fixes to cultural problems. HR too often prioritises process over reason. One of the reasons HTM persists is because of how we have been educated. Highly educated people in senior corporate positions tend to have a quantitative bias. These people tend to assume they are rational and objective. However, if we accept the basic premise that diversity is infinite (see below) and that people are in fact irrational, cultural creatures, then applying logical, technical HR strategies to manage them will be highly inefficient and ultimately fail.

An example would be women on boards. Actually it's not about women, it's about cognitive diversity to increase the resilience of boards and improve their decision-making abilities, but more on that later. Take gender as a proxy for cognitive diversity. The solution has tended to be 'find women'. But by applying a quantitative method to a cultural problem, we have found the women most like men and most able to 'fit' into male culture. The women that are most likely to put themselves forward, most likely to respond to a hands-up culture are precisely those who are most similar to the existing men. So what about diversity?

When it comes to our people, we have yet to apply the principles of biodiversity or financial diversity to talent. While a great deal of thought has been given to preserving biodiversity through conservation efforts, and even more work has been put in latterly to rethink our approach to risk management in the wake of the financial crisis, we still haven't seriously considered risk and diversity when it comes to our people.

We still have an idea of what 'good' looks like, and it isn't diverse. As we discussed earlier in this chapter, most CEOs are over 6 feet tall, male and white. Most promotions go to extroverts over introverts. Most graduate recruitment processes discriminate against brilliant young talent that doesn't have a degree (either by choice or lack of financial means).

This means that we are in effect staring down the barrel of the gun. In failing to learn from the extinction of the Dodo, in failing to learn from what happened from financial specialisation and contagion, we are putting all our talent eggs in the same basket.

WHAT IS DIVERSITY?

There are 7.3 billion of us on this planet and each one of us is unique, determined by our individual DNA. A survey of HR practitioners reveals a strong focus on demographic diversity, most notably gender. So for many organisations 'diversity' is reduced to 'gender'. Rather than 7.3 billion talent permutations, we settle for two, men and women.

Diversity means 'a range of different things'. In one sense, diversity is simply our individual physical make-up, such as gender, ethnicity, age, disability and sexual orientation. Even with this limited definition of diversity, physical make up can change over time. Obvious examples include women becoming pregnant, or people becoming disabled. While only women can become pregnant, if we live long enough we all eventually become disabled. Less obvious and less common examples would include people who undergo gender reassignment, or some other major life-changing event.

However, diversity is also cultural, socio-economic, religious and linguistic. The difference in language can be profound, even within relatively small geographies such as the United Kingdom. In the UK there are literally hundreds of dialects of English, not to mention the significant cultural differences between the UK and USA, both majority English speaking countries. On one level Switzerland and Northern Ireland are not particularly diverse. However, Switzerland has four official languages; and in Northern Ireland your religion can be the salient individual characteristic that will determine your life and career trajectory.

How a person looks is one of the principal factors in discrimination. 'Lookism' has only recently been taken seriously, but how attractive we perceive people to be may in fact be the number one factor in whether someone gets hired or not. Physically attractive people are portrayed as positive stereotypes and are often shown in adverts as reliable and successful people. The reverse is true for people considered to be unattractive, who are given negative connotations.

If you compare brain scans of male and female brains at rest an interesting pattern emerges. In the female brain there is a whirr of activity with neurons working overtime at 3 am, while she is asleep, as she processes the day's activities and plans for tomorrow, analysing and re-analysing events. In the male brain, nothing is going on. He is at rest, and the neurons are taking a break too.[27] While of course we exaggerate for effect, this is statistically true and the differences in male and female brains are sufficient that gender can indeed act as a proxy for cognitive diversity. In recent research it has been shown that women have greater connectivity than men between left and right brain hemispheres, proving the stereotypical multi-tasking ability.[28]

Or take the example of how people view the same object differently. To some, the Confederate flag in the United States is a symbol of the different cultural heritage of the southern United States, a struggle in the face of overbearing government. To many more, it is a symbol of racism and the pro-slavery Confederacy that predates the Union.

Ultimately, diversity is a combination of a person's physical DNA, their life experience to date and the social context they find themselves in – nature and nurture, or raw materials, location and education. This leads us to a more sophisticated understanding of diversity, rarely articulated within corporations. Diversity, ultimately, is cognitive difference. In this sense diversity is infinite – 7.3 billion permutations of homo sapiens.

DO WE LIKE DIVERSITY?

In Old French, diversity also had the distinct honour of meaning 'repugnant'. This is, truth be told, how many people still view it.

Most people will, in public, claim they like diversity. When Londoners are polled about why they live in London, one of the top reasons they give is its diversity. Whenever Steve gives a class he often ask the students if they like diversity. In front of fellow classmates, almost everyone raises their hand in the affirmative. People want other people to think that they like and value diversity.

However, if we ask the question anonymously the response is often different from our publicly stated views. A professional services firm in Ireland was considering setting targets for gender representation in the firm. Publicly, most partners said it was a good idea. However, when voting was conducted using anonymous keypads, it turns out 69 per cent of them were against. The majority male audience did not want targets for increased female representation, even though it was incredibly low and getting worse, and even though they said they did.

If we ask a question privately, we get an even more divergent response to the publicly stated one. If we ask people to consider, privately in their own head, their closest friends and family, a more homogeneous picture emerges. When asked to name their top five friends, students more often than not name people of the same gender and ethnicity. There is increasing incidence of sexual orientation diversity but declining religious diversity and still very little inclusion of disabled people.

If we ask professionals to consider their partner or spouse (or, if it's not going so well, the partner they would like to have) we tend to find evidence of another 'half' that reinforces the world view of the individual being asked. Isn't love about making us whole, complete? Isn't the very idea of love to reinforce our sense of self and find a 'partner' who has a similar world view?

If we ask people where they live, it tends to be according to affordability and/or neighbourhood choice. 'Nice' neighbourhoods tend to be euphemisms for neighbourhoods where 'people like me' live. Where I feel safe.

So even though people claim to like diversity, a brief analysis of the facts of whom they love, who their friends are and where they live suggests something rather different. We call this cognitive dissonance, or the intention/action deficit. It's not an accusation (though much corporate diversity work presents it in such a way), it's just an observation. But it is an important one, and it has ramifications for the rest of this book.

If we are honest about it, most of us dislike diversity, as evidenced in our actions as opposed to our proclamations. We prefer sameness because it is easier to live with than difference. That's one reason why most CEOs in the USA are tall white men.

WHAT IS TALENT?

A partner at a professional services firm said what many people refrain from saying – talent can be seen as one of those meaningless management euphemisms for, essentially, paid labour. Talent may indeed be over-used as a term, but do we really understand what we mean by it and why it is important?

Talent means good people with ambition and potential. Talent refers to the aptitudes of different people matched to the needs of an organisation. Talent management strategy is the attraction, deployment, development, reward and retention of people in specific strategic positions or projects. The value of it comes in the development of a culture of opportunity for all employees in order that the organisation can achieve its business goals and objectives.

Talent used to be viewed as an audience; fish that were simply waiting to be caught. Now we view talent as a community, an ecosystem, fish swimming all over the global talent pool that are harder to catch. Talent 1.0 focused on succession planning, Talent 2.0 on the attraction of 'star' CEOs and executives, and Talent 3.0 on the attraction of high-potential and specialist individuals. Only now is Talent 4.0 catching up with the world around us, focusing on talent management in a multi-generational, multi-cultural, mobile, high-expectation, networked, information-transparent global environment.[29]

Nazia Mahmood, Mariam Namagembe and Alison Taylor are three fictitious women's names invented by British government researchers in 2009. They were then placed at the top of three separate but identical CVs/resumes and mailed out to real job vacancies in the UK marketplace. What happened? Alison received one response per nine letters mailed. Nazia and Mariam received one response per sixteen letters mailed.

In this experiment, identical CVs presented with different names received wildly different responses. Yet on the evidence presented all were of equal 'talent'.

The report authors concluded, 'The key strength of the correspondence test based on applications to vacancies... is that there are no plausible explanations for the difference in treatment found between white and ethnic minority names other than racial discrimination.'[30]

Applicants with a 'white sounding name' were 29 per cent more likely to succeed. While this only applied to the initial recruitment stages, it was that all-important foot in the door. Candidates were denied access to a range of jobs in a range of sectors across British cities as a result of having a name associated with an ethnic minority background.

Researchers have labelled this an 'ethnic penalty' in the labour market. Aside from the moral and ethical issues raised by this experiment, it lays bare the inefficiency in HTM processes. (See Chapter 5 for a practical solution from the British civil service.)

BIAS AND GROUPTHINK

Up to 98 per cent of brain activity is unconscious.[31] Much of this activity is low order maintenance activity, such as repair, processing food and so on. Part of it, however, is high order activity that actually determines our behaviour.

When we answer a question in a group setting about whether we like diversity, we consciously decide to answer in the affirmative. That could be because it's what we actually consciously believe, or it could be because we are socially conditioned to say so. We are socially conditioned to believe that racism is bad and diversity is good. In recent years, in the West, we have become socially conditioned to the idea that homophobia is bad and equal marriage is generally a good thing.

But when we make hiring and promotion decisions, we are still being influenced by the unconscious brain.[32] This causes bias. We all have implicit biases based on our individualised life experiences to date and the social context we find ourselves in. We are all deeply flawed creatures. Even though we think we are objective, we are the opposite. This is important – not only are we biased, we don't even recognise it. Rather than mitigating it, we proceed as though we are objective and so compound it.

Ironically, we actually learn this behaviour. As children we often interpret things literally. So, for example, a child may point at a wheelchair user in the supermarket and ask why they are in the chair. The parent responds by reprimanding the child for 'being rude', as we have become socially conditioned to refrain from asking personal questions. In the United States, hiring managers consistently fail consciously to ask race-based questions for fear of incurring litigation. We'll explore more on bias in the next chapter and how to mitigate it in Part Two.

Talent is ultimately about the best skills in the best body and mind matched with the right opportunity. Unfortunately, so much other stuff gets in the way. We usually don't acknowledge that and continue with our own illusion of objectivity that we are the right selectors to determine the right candidates.

When diversity is understood as cognitive difference, the practical question for professionals is, why do we persist in separating it from talent? Diversity is talent. Talent is diverse. Yet, of the organisations we surveyed for this book, the vast majority had segregated talent management and diversity functions. Diversity is a reality. So separating it from talent seems rather strange. It's akin to entering a new market but not wanting to countenance hiring locals to assist you. Inclusion is a choice and, as we will see in the next chapter, it's a choice many of us are not even aware we are rejecting.

Time and time again we see the consequences of groupthink, homogeneous talent management and the intolerance of diversity. Diversity is not without its own costs and problems of course, but they can be managed, as will be discussed in Part Two. What remains is a body of evidence that sameness in ecosystems, in financial markets and in people practices has led us astray. There is a seductive pull from sameness. This is understandable, but increasingly hard to justify, given the consequences.

KEY TAKEAWAYS

1 Biodiversity in nature is correlated with increased productivity. Reduced diversity lowers resilience and threatens ecosystems.

---

2 Diversity in financial markets is a critical tool to mitigate risk and increase resilience. The homogenisation of strategies and products exposes the system to systemic risk and was a key driver of the 2008 financial crisis.

3 Homogeneous talent management systems in current HR thinking ignore the plentiful evidence from nature and finance in terms of the value of diversity. They are not fit for purpose.

4 Diversity is a combination of a person's physical DNA, social context and life experience. Gender and other demographic aspects are in one sense simply proxies for cognitive difference.

5 Talent is infinite and comes in all shapes and sizes. However, because we are biased we don't always recognise it and therefore we fail to incorporate it.

NOTES

1 Michaels, E *et al* (1997) *The War for Talent*, HBS Press.

2 Porter, M (2004) *Competitive Strategy*, Simon & Schuster.

3 Chankim, W and Mauborgne, R (2005) *Blue Ocean Strategy*, HBS Press

4 www.catalyst.org/knowledge/women-ceos-sp-500

5 Gladwell, M (2006) *Blink*, Penguin.

6 Gladwell, M (2006) *Blink*, Penguin.

7 Porter, ME (2008) The five competitive forces that shape strategy, *Harvard Business Review*, January.

8 Conversation with Google colleague.

9 YSC (2014) Cracking the Code: A gender intelligent approach to developing corporate leaders, KPMG, 30% Club.

10 University of Toronto (2013) Productivity increases with species diversity, just as Darwin predicted, Science Daily, 13 May, www.sciencedaily.com/releases/2013/05/130513152830.htm

11 World Economic Forum (2010) Rethinking Risk Management in Financial Services Practices from other Domains, World Economic Forum.

12 *New York Times* (2008) Salmon virus indicts Chile's fishing methods, New York Times, 27 March, www.nytimes.com/2008/03/27/world/americas/27salmon.html

13 Beattie, A and Ehrlich, PR (2004) *Wild Solutions*, 2nd edition, Yale University, p. 223.

14 Beattie, A and Ehrlich, PR (2004) *Wild Solutions*, 2nd edition, Yale University, p. 223.

15 www.bbc.co.uk/news/science-environment-33096260

16 http://advances.sciencemag.org/content/1/5/e1400253.full

17 www.bbc.co.uk/news/science-environment-33209548

18 Robinson, K (June 2006) Do schools kill creativity?, Ted Talks Subtitles and
    Transcripts, Ted.com

19 Landau, J (2009) Complexity and the financial crisis, www.bis.org/review/
    r090806c.pdf

20 WEF (April 2010) *Rethinking Risk Management in Financial Services*, WEF

21 Conversation with Binna Kandola (June 2015).

22 WEF (April 2010) *Rethinking Risk Management in Financial Services*, WEF

23 WEF (April 2010) *Rethinking Risk Management in Financial Services*, WEF

24 Coates, J (2012) *The Hour Between Dog and Wolf*, Fourth Estate.

25 www.cnbc.com/2014/06/04/15-years-to-extinction-sp-500-companies.html

26 Page, S (2008) *The Difference*, Princeton University Press

27 Presentation by Barabra Annis at Novartis, June 2013.

28 www.theguardian.com/science/2013/dec/02/men-women-brains-wired-differently

29 Turner, P and Kalman, D (2014) *Make Your People Before Making Your
    Products*

30 www.natcen.ac.uk/media/20541/test-for-racial-discrimination.pdf

31 Conscious thought – Am I thinking what I'm thinking?, Being Human online
    community, 31 March 2013.

32 As for the unconscious brain, read Vedentan, S (2010) *The Hidden Brain: How
    our unconscious mind elects presidents, controls markets and saves our lives*,
    Random House

2

HISTORY – HOW A SEGREGATED MINDSET EVOLVED

How often have you heard an HR director or CEO espouse their 'support' for and belief in 'diversity' – but 'not at the expense of talent'? In other words, there is an innate assumption that the two are diametrically opposed. In order to 'do diversity' one must necessarily take a 'hit on talent'.

It is this segregated mindset that is the main inhibitor to inclusive talent management. And it can be very hard to shift. Certainly the $8 billion US corporations have spent on training every year in the first decade of the 21st century has made little impact.[1]

In order to understand how we shift this mindset we need to confront two major factors. The first is collective history and our personal life experience in it. We'll explore how this segregated mindset evolved in the first place through colonialism, Western literature and the civil rights movement. The second factor is personal bias.

A useful framework to analyse these concepts and to check our learning is the Diversity and Inclusion Maturity Model©, which we will discuss later in this chapter. Colleagues in organisations worldwide have found this a useful tool to assess whether their organisation is a Diversity 101, 2.0 or 3.0 organisation – and then what they can do about it.

COLONIALISM AND THE CONCEPT OF THE 'OTHER'

It was Edward Said who popularised the idea of the 'other' using the example of imperial Britain and its increasing understanding of self in relation to its colonies around the world.[2] Said wrote his famous book *Orientalism* in 1978; in it he laid out the created dichotomy between the rational West (Occident) and the illogical or inferior East (Orient). In his own words,

> Orientalism is a style of thought based upon an ontological and epistemo-logical distinction made between 'the Orient' and 'the Occident'. Thus a very large mass of writers, among whom are poets, novelists, philosophers, political theorists, economists, and imperial administrators, have accepted the basic distinction between East and West as the starting point for elaborate theories, epics, novels, social descriptions, and political accounts concerning the Orient, its people [and] customs.

In other words, he brought to public attention how much of Western thought had been predicated on the idea of what we are not. For too long, diversity has been seen as the 'other', largely by a comfortable, homogeneous group of decision makers who are in positions of power. Critically, many of the 'minorities' that constitute the 'other' define themselves in this sense too, and thus partake in their own exclusion. Scholars such as Michel Foucault and Simone de Beauvoir have written extensively on this.

Jean-Jacques Rousseau, one of the key Enlightenment thinkers of the 18th century, labelled the part of the earth between the tropics as the 'torrid zone'. Even as recently as the 1990s Swissair had an advertisement for Africa that advertised its wild animals and was completely devoid of people. In the Rwandan genocide of 1994, in which nearly a million people died in a hundred-day period, the headline in the British newspaper *The Sun* was BRITS FLEE JUNGLE BLOODBATH. This treatment of the 'other' reinforces stereotypes and further embeds a segregated mindset.

MODERN INTERPRETATIONS OF 'THE OTHER'

A person's definition of other people is a key part of what defines their own being and own identity. For example, in many Western societies, white men think their way of doing things is 'normal' and minorities accept it as so. In each sense, their understanding of the other side reinforces their own situation. White people don't often consider 'race' in relation to themselves, only in relation to 'others'.[3]

In many Western societies, when a white male commits an atrocity, such as Timothy McVeigh and the 1995 Oklahoma bomb[4] or Adam Lanza and the school shooting at Newtown in 2012,[5] they are labelled 'crazy guys'. When a Muslim male commits an atrocity, such as the Tsaernaev brothers in Boston 2013[6] or the two men who hacked a British soldier to death in London in 2013,[7] they are labelled 'terrorists'. In some ways, a white terrorist would be the most disturbing of all for the majority, acting completely outside the constructed norm, which is why we call them 'crazy' instead.

In a London 2012 Olympics and Paralympics board meeting in 2008, a male member of the LOCOG Board made a homophobic comment that Steve overheard. The man in question appeared to be far more comfortable with a 'camp' gay head of department (conforming to norm) than he was with a 'masculine' gay head of department (challenging his perception of gay people). Norms and stereotypes are key determinants not only of our behaviour, but also of our beliefs.

Take socio-economic situations, or 'class', for example. Many lower socio-economic groups, or 'working class' individuals will purposely self-limit in order to avoid feeling uncomfortable. Steve's mum is a classic example of this. Even though she is very intelligent, has worked hard, becoming the first person in her family to reach university, and became a professional teacher, she is still bound by her working class roots. When she was offered an upgrade on a recent flight, she turned it down because she would feel 'more comfortable' in the main cabin.

NORMS

We all live within constructed norms. In many corporations it is just 'normal' that the executives are predominantly older white men.

As long as diversity remains 'the other' it is doomed. The decision-making powers and associated resources will never be focused on it. It will never be 'the norm'. Sarojini Sahoo, an Indian feminist writer, builds on the work of De Beauvoir, by asserting that women can achieve self-actualisation by 'thinking, taking action, working, creating, on the same terms as men; instead of seeking to disparage them, she declares herself their equal.'[8] That's one way to challenge a norm.

The legacy of slavery and the civil rights movement casts a long shadow over corporate America, which in many ways is still failing to deal with the fallout. Brent Staples is a columnist for the *New York Times*. He is brilliantly intelligent, holds multiple degrees and is very kind to strangers. But when he walks down the road at night, people tend to cross over to avoid him.

Brent is black. He would say that's merely one aspect of his identity, but it's one that people see before they see the rest of him. And the stereotype is that when walking down a street late at night black = danger. Black = to be avoided. And so people cross the road.

Ask any black colleague in a Western context and they may well tell you that in spite of being just as smart, just as capable, they are much more likely to be followed by a security guard in a department store. Or more subtle occurrences, such as never being asked to taste the wine in a restaurant.

Brent learned to whistle Vivaldi.[9] It could have been any classical music, but its familiarity to white people gave reassurance, a non-verbal signal that he was one of them, that there was no danger. He tried this on multiple occasions and the whistling often reduced his stereotype threat, sometimes even generated a smile. People didn't cross the road.

In the French Jura mountains there is a fascinating and deeply moving museum that honours the memory of those murdered in the 1940s Nazi occupation. In Le Musée de la Résistance et de la Déportation de Besançon there is a quote on the wall from George Santayana that is the first and last thing visitors see. It says, 'Those who do not remember the past are condemned to live it again.' History gets us halfway to understanding our own mindset. There is a rich, deep and complex history to our own arrival on the planet and our own sense of self. Layered on top of this, and correlated with our lived experience, is our own bias.

BIAS

Bias is the inclination or prejudice for or against one person or group, especially in a way considered to be unfair. It can be measured by our association with opposing factors, such as day and night, men and women, English and French. Only by understanding and then appreciating our own bias can we possibly comprehend our own individual lens on the world. And how we see the world is not necessarily how others see it. Appreciating our own bias is the start of seeing the world through different lenses, to get a richer, more accurate picture of what's really going on.

TYPES OF BIAS

The main type of bias pertinent to talent management is unconscious bias. We are cognisant of only about 2 per cent of our brain's activity.[10] Around 98 per cent of the activity in our personal 'headquarters' that controls our thoughts and our actions passes through our unconscious.

Recently, leading corporations have begun to educate their people on unconscious bias because of the massive inefficiency it may be generating in what they do. People are paid to do things they are good at, but they are only using a proportion of the already tiny 2 per cent of their cognitive capacity. Furthermore, their actual thoughts and thus actions may be taking place without the checks and balances of conscious reasoning. The cumulative effect of this in thousands of team members is inefficient, and in many ways terrifying.

Most people, even those in charge of millions of dollars of investment, are not aware of their own unconscious biases. A simple way of starting to make people more conscious of them is to explore the gap between what a person states they believe in and what the facts actually suggest they do believe in. We call this cognitive dissonance.

For example, with executives worldwide we ask them if they believe in the business case for diversity (see Chapter 4). They usually answer in the affirmative. (It often varies depending on whether the answer is public or private). However, when we ask them to describe their partner, their friends and where they live, the actual evidence suggests they strongly prefer sameness to diversity, as discussed in the previous chapter. Even though they

Figure 2.1 Types of bias pertinent to talent management

Type of bias	Definition	How it affects decision-making
Unconscious bias	Bias that we are unaware of and that happens outside of our control	Decisions are made instinctively without thought or deliberation
Cognitive dissonance	The state of having inconsistent thoughts, beliefs or attitudes	Decisions are based on behaviours and attitudes, often to reduce tension and avoid conflict
Confirmation bias	The tendency to interpret new evidence as confirmation of one's existing beliefs	Prevents us from considering important information when making a decision
First acceptable option	Feeling compelled to some degree of making a quick decision	Deciding before considering other possibilities
Groupthink	Tendency of humans to agree with each other in order to prevent conflict	Decisions are based on similar or the same thinking
Framing bias	Taking into account contextual features of a situation	Base decisions on interpretation of the background to a situation
Egocentricity	Viewing everything in relation to oneself and being self-centered	Decisions are made on how the person making the decision sees things and not from others' points of view

claim to support, even advocate, the diversity business case, the way they live their life suggests they prefer to associate with people like themselves.

Stereotypes are a cognitive shortcut we use to cope with information overload. In the information age, they are becoming even more of a crutch. However, when a person receives undue focus (perhaps because they are a minority and stand out from the norm) they can exhibit behaviours that confirm our previously held assumptions. We call this confirmation bias. By observing what we expect, this leads us to ignore evidence that contradicts our preconceived notions.

When this works in a positive sense, it is known as the halo effect – favourable first impressions influence us most. Evidence is then interpreted in the light of those beliefs. If we find a candidate attractive, we are more likely to think they are intelligent and good for the job, confirming our initial impression of them. When it works in a negative sense it is often known as negative stereotyping or 'horns', hence the 'horns and halo' effect.

There is a first 'acceptable' option problem – once an acceptable option is found the search for and evaluation of potentially better options ceases. We also sometimes call this a 'technical fix'. There can be an escalation of commitment – even in the face of failure people often demonstrate strong commitment to an action. And anchoring causes us to weigh one piece of information too heavily in making a decision. As humans we like to avoid harm, and can be reluctant to make a decision where there is a trade-off between benefit for the majority and increased harm for the few.

Our role within the group further affects bias. The impact of group membership can be significant. It tends to reduce a person's feeling of responsibility for a particular decision. People will make decisions in groups that they would not normally make. Often, groups tend to make riskier decisions than members acting separately, as apportionment of blame is spread more widely. This is known as the herd instinct – we are more likely to fall in with a decision that everyone else is in favour of. We witnessed this to spectacular effect in the 2008 financial crisis, detailed in Chapter 1.

Finally, we would point out framing bias – the language used will affect the decisions taken. For example the number of jobs 'saved' as opposed to the number of jobs 'lost'. 'Diversity training' is often framed so poorly, leading most people to suffer confirmation bias – they thought it would be preachy and compliance-based, and they seized on the elements that were like that and then concluded that it was all like that. The reason most diversity training fails is because it fails to acknowledge history and bias. By failing to fully appreciate the cynical perspective most attendees come from, it then reinforces their view.

You can assess your own bias in ten minutes. Just Google 'Harvard IAT' and take a test. The test measures your implicit association, for example women with housework, men with cars. Or white people and safety and black people and crime. You can take the test for a number of diversity criteria and the results may surprise you.

A student of Steve's who had dedicated his career to women's rights came to class distraught one morning. He shared with the class the results of his IAT and it demonstrated a significant gender bias in favour of men. Our accumulated life experiences and identities run very deep. 'Terrorists' are currently mostly thought of as predominantly Arabic people. When a white person commits an atrocity they are thought to be a lone wolf 'murderer'.

EGOCENTRICITY AND TRUST

By appreciating our own lens on the world, and the way we evaluate people, recruits, promotion candidates, peers, bosses and team members, we can begin to understand our own egocentricity. When we work with executive teams we ask them to write down on a piece of paper, confidentially, if they view themselves as below or above average compared with the other group members.[11] Invariably, the majority of the group in male-dominated Western-based executive teams all think that they are above average, which of course is statistically impossible.

We tend to trust people who look like us, talk like us and share common reference points with us. We tend to distrust those that are different. In Darwin's grassy fields, we would prefer the similar species and reject the distantly related species, even though including them would be more productive. Egocentricity and trust are more powerful reasons for segregated thinking.

You may have wondered why so many people whose performance is average or mediocre end up in positions of authority in companies and organisations. One of the main reasons is our own illusion of objectivity. Consider the cumulative effect of all the biases detailed above. Then consider that most people are not even aware they exist, let alone what theirs (or others) might be. Most people, and certainly most men, would not be aware that men tend to return a head-hunter's call in two attempts. On the other hand, women require up to seven calls to make the same response.[12] This is because when it comes to even the most important positions, we think that our selection decisions are a good deal more rational than they actually are.[13]

History, and our own life experience within it, our collective and individual biases plus factors such as trust, short-termism and stress mean that a segregated mindset prevails. One way to determine the level of that segregation is to use the Diversity and Inclusion Maturity Model©.

THE DIVERSITY AND INCLUSION MATURITY MODEL©

Progress on talent management to date has been mixed, limited largely by segregated thinking and the fact that diversity without inclusion doesn't work. The main organisational diversity paradigms are detailed in Figure 2.2. It is virtually impossible to propose a complete synopsis of organisational change/diversity programmes in the last two decades, but from trialling this model in organisations worldwide we believe Figure 2.2 to be a fair summary, and hopefully recognisable to many existing practitioners. The terms will be explained as we progress through the chapter.

Figure 2.2 The Diversity and Inclusion Maturity Model©

Paradigm	Diversity 101 'Diversity for diversity's sake'	Diversity 2.0 'Diversity for social responsibility'	Inclusion 3.0 'Diversity as business strategy'
Definition	Programmes designed to raise awareness of difference	Programmes designed to draw out the benefits of difference	Integrated systems designed to embed the benefits of difference
Origins	Colonialism, nature versus culture, civil rights movement	Shareholder pressure, HR and marketing functions and corporate social responsibility	Recognition of unconscious bias, egocentricity and leadership deficit
Education method	Diversity training, compliance-based business case	Diversity workshops, up to date business case	Structured conversations, original interventions, evidenced business case
Leadership approach	Top down, authority led, compliance driven	Top down, authority led, auditing approach	Bottom up, top-level support, creative group leadership, peer review
Delivery mechanisms	Equalities team, equality impact assessments	Diversity team, needs assessments	Whole organisation, benchmarking and information sharing
Measurement	Quotas, legal reporting	Voluntary targets, corporate social responsibility reporting/PR	Target zones, high frequency, real time reporting and individual accountability

DIVERSITY 101

'Diversity 101' programmes originate from the 1960s civil rights era, but can more recently be traced back to 1990s 'equal opportunities' programmes in the UK and 'affirmative action' programmes in North America. They tend to educate the general workforce in an organisation about the existence of diversity, usually gender and ethnicity. They were designed to raise awareness of difference, contribute to rectifying past injustices and in many contexts provided a useful window for employees into otherwise unknown minority worlds.

In some ways, they are more watered-down versions of equal opportunities and affirmative action programmes. They are designed to be less offensive to the status quo and in that sense do not really challenge the existing paradigm. They offer a variety of initiatives anywhere on a scale of action from awareness raising of minority issues amongst the majority to actually creating opportunities for minorities in terms of jobs and training programmes.

Diversity 101 programmes are typically run by an 'equalities team' sitting somewhere in HR or the back office of an organisation. In many cases they are the 'office' for affirmative action programmes, government reporting and any outreach activities to minority groups. Mandated by the organisation to ensure compliance with legal requirements such as equal gender pay reporting, they can assist with employment tribunals and workforce equalities/ legal compliance training. In many cases, they have an important role to play, and in many cases they were essential creatures of their time.

LANGUAGE

Language can be incredibly important. 'Politically correct' language emerged in the 1960s as an understandable response to derogatory and downright dangerous language regarding minorities. However, political correctness (PC) has subsequently acquired a derogatory meaning itself, slammed by tabloid journalism for its supposed contribution to unjustified minority advancement and the limiting of free speech. However, as Gary Younge of *The Guardian* observed, PC has been attacked and misused by 'those who realise they are never going to win arguments about equality if they tackle their opponents head on'.[14]

We are not advocating the death of political correctness, or total support of it. We are advocating a language that needs to be one the majority of people in the organisation understand, which doesn't reinforce cliques, be they academic elites or a homogeneous crowd of diversity practitioners. In his discussion paper, Ziauddin Sardar concludes: 'The terminology used... needs to be accessible to the wider world and owned by the public.'[15]

Consider the widespread use of the terms 'male privilege' and 'white privilege' in US academic and professional circles. There is overwhelming theoretical and empirical data to support these terms, but how useful are they in practice? To label many straight white men 'privileged' is probably factually true, but does it lead to greater inclusion? It does the exact opposite on two counts. One, it probably offends and repels the more sensitive straight white men who might have been otherwise supportive of an inclusion programme. Two, it probably offends and further repels the diversity-disliking less sensitive straight white men who are now running even further away from the tent. In the London 2012 Organising Committee, one of the key 'target groups' was white working class young men who were fast becoming one of the lowest-achieving and hardest to reach groups. They were male, they were white, but they were far from privileged.

DIVERSITY TRAINING DOESN'T WORK

Diversity programmes, diversity officers and public relations (PR) all point to the now widespread acceptance of the need to 'do something'. The problem remains that so many of these initiatives ignore bias, rendering most of them ineffective and possibly even counterproductive. In addition to a time and cost element, so many of the 101 diversity initiatives can be framed poorly. They attack self rather than role or behaviour (see Chapter 8) and are therefore rejected. As long as some white men are told that they are culturally incompetent, they will probably continue to refrain from listening.

Today, in many professional environments, Diversity 101 programmes are alive and well. Due to a fertile combination of increasing legislation and economic bounty in the 2000–08 period, there now exists a myriad of programmes and job positions. Training, diversity weeks, affinity groups, compliance questionnaires, equality impact statements and monitoring forms have become commonplace. Initiatives have sprung up and budgets have been allocated. But, as Frank Dobbin has concluded, 'Diversity training doesn't work.'[16] The fact that so much diversity infrastructure was scaled back following the 2008 economic crisis tells us a lot about the depth of these programmes and the organisational commitment behind them.

Many corporations, governments and international organisations have rushed to develop 'diversity programmes' without really considering their relevance to the organisation other than pacifying the reporting requirements of government, and increasingly of shareholders. This is not a good starting point for actually adding value to the business. So many are poorly understood initiatives, just about sold in to sceptical Chief Executives, that have a cost requirement to them. This cost has to be small enough so as not to raise opposition, large enough to actually achieve something (usually an 'event' or 'training') but usually ends up being too small to make any significant impact.

THE NEGATIVES OF DIVERSITY

Increased diversity can actually increase conflict. 'Relational demography' demonstrates that people like to associate with people like themselves.[17] Diversity 101 programmes can lead to lower motivation, commitment and happiness in the job. Other negative effects of diversity can include lower team cohesion, lowered likeability of each other and increased emotional conflict.[18] At a national scale it can include 'ethnic fractionalisation' which can actually undermine GDP growth.[19] Diversity 101 has nothing to say about this. For that reason alone the notion of a 'diversity officer' in an organisation could be analogous to creating a 'conflict officer' or a 'lower-growth officer'. The absence of focus on inclusion is profound.

THE LIMITS OF 101 APPROACHES

Diversity 101 programmes are problematic on two counts. First, they don't really challenge the existing paradigm and therefore fail to impact the very injustices they purport to address. They are tolerated by authority precisely because they don't effectively challenge it. Second, they lack support and buy-in from the majority. Well-meaning attempts to support minority groups have unfortunately often led the majority of people who feel they do not fit into one of 'those groups' to run fast in the other direction. Furthermore, people often do not want to associate with those groups, even if they are defined as such.

The real issue for many people outside the 'target groups' is that they feel Diversity 101 programmes are an intervention where non-merit-based selection criteria (ie demography, or superficial inclusion) trump ability and they feel that is intrinsically unfair. Advocates of Diversity 101 programmes have been unsuccessful in countering this claim. As we started this chapter, how often do you hear a chief executive proclaim their support 'for diversity' but not 'at the expense of quality'?

Diversity 101 policies fail because they are a superficial solution to what are in fact systemic problems. For example, the lack of women in senior positions is a systemic problem. Demand-side causes include male (and female) discrimination in hiring and promotion decisions, unconscious bias and implicit associations. Supply-side constraints include childcare, access to information and confidence levels. Yet the Diversity 101 policy response to date has been 'diversity training', which men, in particular, resist attending.

Many practitioners have realised the shortcomings of Diversity 101 approaches. Many have realised that pigeon-holing people and conducting 'equality impact assessments' takes the work further away from the mainstream current in an organisation, rather than advance the cause of equality. It's analogous to poorly designed foreign aid programmes. No matter how many millions are spent on aid, they remain a fraction of the flows the other way from unequal terms of trade. Even the most well-designed diversity programme will fail to shift the trajectory of the organisation if it remains removed from where the real profit and loss incentives or other strategic levers of the organisation actually lie. It's time to stop the diversity aid programmes and focus instead on the terms of trade.

It is important to state the debt we all owe to many Diversity 101 practitioners. Many of these people are heroes and trailblazers hailing from the civil rights era and to whom we owe a great deal, for trying to make a difference rather than not, for caring rather than ignoring. This book is merely one example of many current interventions that are standing on the shoulders of giants. Without the work done by many Diversity 101 practitioners there would be no platform on which to build. However, the best legacy we can build on that platform is to remain relevant to today's realities. Compliance will always be needed, but we cannot rely on Diversity 101 to deliver inclusive talent management.

DIVERSITY 2.0

Diversity and inclusion programmes have evolved to embrace other differences such as socio-economic or geographic, at national and international scales. These marketing-friendly programmes can be grouped into 'Diversity 2.0' programmes to reflect their better relation to current realities. Laura Liswood's book *The Loudest Duck*[20] is a move in this direction and critics have suggested it is on the road to becoming a more successful Diversity 2.0.

Diversity 2.0 programmes are better designed to draw out the actual benefits of difference, which are increasingly well documented. Rather than compliance-based training, which is soul destroying for many employees, Diversity 2.0 policies offer workshop-style events with an opportunity to ask (as well as be told) and a more up-to-date business case as to why a busy employee should sacrifice an hour of their day to learn about diversity.

Some more progressive organisations have definitely moved on from Diversity 101 to embrace 2.0 policies and programmes. They use them in their PR and corporate social responsibility reporting. They use them in their graduate recruitment, mindful that they are now competing with new kids on the block such as Facebook and Google for talent that is increasingly mobile. There are needs assessments (responding to business requirements) rather than 'equality impact assessments' and audits and there may even be a genuine desire at the top of the organisation to make Diversity 2.0 a part of their brand, marketing or overall corporate responsibility programme.

EVOLUTION, NOT REVOLUTION

However, Diversity 2.0 is still a linear progression from Diversity 101. While 2.0 programmes acknowledge many of the shortcomings of the 101 approaches, they are still defined and constrained by them. They still make their employees attend training, costing substantial amounts of money for unquantifiable results. The approach is still top down – practitioners go to bed each night praying for the day the 'top team get it' and diversity receives an appropriate mention in the chief executive's speech.

Worse still, Diversity 2.0 programmes are seductive for the busy chief executive wanting easy results, a couple of paragraphs for the annual report and to avoid changing their own behaviour or current strategy. They are technical fixes to cultural problems. While there is now a plethora of online statements from leading corporations proclaiming their embracing of all things diverse, we know that this is often still far from the reality within those same organisations.

MENTORING

Diversity 2.0 talks a lot about mentoring. As discussed in Sheryl Sandberg's book *Lean In*,[21] mentoring can be a great initiative, focused on cracking the unwritten code and helping minorities advance. Dasgupta has written of the need to increase the visibility of successful women in organisations and to increase the prevalence of mentoring relationships.[22] This can be worthwhile, but when mentoring becomes about helping minorities 'blend in' we are left wondering what happened to leveraging the benefits of diversity and different perspectives? Making women learn more stereotypically male traits actually reduces diversity, which is a somewhat ironic goal for a diversity programme.

At a World Economic Forum seminar a female chief executive behaved in a more stereotypically 'male' fashion than her male counterparts on the panel. There persists a 'uniform' of shoulder-pads and pearls, which still seems more appropriate to many than women simply being themselves. Of course, if people want to wear shoulder-pads and pearls, or genuinely feel it is professionally appropriate to do so, then fantastic. But if women are doing so under duress, consciously or unconsciously, this is, well, unfortunate.

QUOTAS

Diversity 2.0 practitioners are currently wrestling with the issue of quotas. Their frustration is understandable. Ignoring the business case completely (see Chapter 4), organisations have made excruciatingly slow progress toward including minorities, especially in senior positions. It is not surprising now, therefore, that the largest and most powerful 'minority' group of all has had enough. 'Women on company boards' is now a hot topic everywhere in Western professional life. Lobbyists have mobilised, alliances have been formed and the race is under way. But the race for what?

The '20% by 2020 Women on Boards' group proposes 20 per cent of board places for women.[23] In the UK the 30% Club was founded with a target of 30 per cent and is now active in several countries. Viviane Reding, EU Commissioner, proposes 40 per cent of board places for women by 2020.[24] Norway, outside the EU, has already imposed 40 per cent as a requirement for Board composition among its top firms.[25]

The argument against quotas

(Gender) quotas may crowd out other marginalised ethnic or socio-economic groups. By reserving certain positions for women, there may be fewer positions open for candidates that are also under-represented. Men may also be negatively affected. This can increase the number and vociferousness of those opposed to diversity generally – and fuel confirmation bias amongst the antagonists.

Quota requirements are not always implemented. There is some evidence of quota avoidance in Norway by organisations not in support of the law. Ahern and Dittmar (2010) provide observational evidence that after the quota legislation was passed in Norway, more firms chose to become private instead of public limited firms. In addition, they show that more Norwegian firms chose to register in the UK rather than in Norway. While they are not empirically able to attribute these moves directly to the quota law, the evidence is quite suggestive.[26]

Quotas are in many ways a rearguard action, a crude, insensitive intervention and another barrier to the free flow of talent. Quotas can reduce women's incentives to invest. If women believe their path toward advancement has been made easier with a gender quota it may become internalised as a 'subsidy' and reduce their drive and/or confidence.[27]

They can also introduce uncertainty into promotion decisions and bring into question whether a promotion was merit-based or quota-based. This can undermine genuinely merit-based promotions and new hires. Unsurprisingly, many talented 'minority' candidates are therefore among the fiercest opponents of quotas. Quotas can actually further the stereotype that might be preferable to combat,[28] remove goodwill or individual agency in colleagues and nullify the competitive process evident in merit-based selection.

The argument in favour of quotas

However, how 'merit-based' is merit-based selection in practice? For example, a competent assertive woman is more likely than a man to be viewed as 'bossy and aggressive', whereas a man exhibiting the same traits would be more likely viewed as 'normal'. Furthermore, the man would be rewarded for acting to stereotype, whereas the woman would be penalised for stepping outside her norm.[29]

If we assume that IQ and talent is equally split amongst the sexes, and we have no reason or evidence to suggest otherwise,[30] then, in an ideal world, power and decision making would be reflective of that talent. The fact that it is not highlights the imperfections and malfunctions in the structures we have created to govern ourselves. Since the structures are imperfect, we can remedy them through an intervention, namely quotas.

Take the example of women in the UK Parliament. A century ago the Parliament was 100 per cent male. In 1919 Nancy Astor became the first female Member of Parliament; but even after women won the franchise there were only 16 female Members of Parliament elected in 1929 (about 2 per cent). It increased incredibly slowly until 1997 when the Labour Party under Tony Blair won a landslide election victory, including the use of all-women shortlists in many constituencies to select Labour Party candidates. This policy was controversial, and denied many capable men the right to stand, but the number of women in Parliament doubled overnight from 60 to 120 (about 18 per cent).

Today, Members of Parliament are still about 75 per cent male but the injection of a cohort of talented women has achieved tipping point, provided role models and improved the scope and quality of debate. Rachel Reeves, former Shadow Chief Secretary to the Treasury and herself a product of an all-women shortlist, is regarded as one of the finest politicians and economists of her generation. She points out that not only would she have been denied opportunity without the Labour Party's policy, but also half of the Members of Parliament under 30 are now women.[31] Change has indeed been initiated.

To the extent that quotas influence existing norms, or create new norms, they can be an effective short-term shock to correct a structural imbalance. They can create role models and help an organisation achieve 'tipping point'[32] sooner. We know that one of the main incentives for minority progression in organisations is the presence of other minorities at similar or more senior levels.

The problems start when quotas are positioned as an alternative to the free flow of talent in the long run. Over time they become counterproductive, like subsidies, giving fuel to the enemies of diversity, and increasing superficial inclusion among minority groups whose career trajectory, and subsequently life chances, veer even further off course from that of the majority. Subsidies have a cost, and they are another technical fix that is ultimately unsustainable.

'DIVERSITY' AS SELF-INTEREST

One of the biggest problems with existing diversity 'initiatives' to date is that they appear self-interested. They care, or are perceived to care, more about the group that stands to directly benefit, rather than the greater good. Take the gender debate, for example. The exclusion of race, sexuality, disability and other diversity characteristics from the discourse advocated by so many women leads many others to wonder what their real motive is. Worse still, sometimes 'other causes' such as race or disability can often be viewed as competing for airtime with the main programme. Does it really come down to a zero-sum game of female advancement at the expense of others?

In Steve's graduate school class the women, fed up of male-dominated conversation, decided to present together at the front of the room.[33] They had emailed each other in advance of class and were ready to go up to the front as one group. However, they had forgotten about the one woman who was a wheelchair user and who could not go up the steps to the front of the room. This female wheelchair user had even been excluded from the preparatory emails, suggesting that the ignorance was present from the beginning. Did the other women not see a female wheelchair user as a 'woman'?

THE LIMITATIONS OF 2.0 APPROACHES

Many organisations will only support demographic or 'niche' causes because it helps their marketing. They still view such activity as little more than reputational risk mitigation. They will happily market to a segment of the diverse community, but ignore the fact that the power of diversity is not just market-based.

A good example would be the lesbian and gay market. Their above average spending power and disposable income in many Western markets is widely documented. While companies are happy to exploit this, there is not always a matched commitment to lesbian and gay rights. Even in the United States, exploitation of the lesbian, gay, bisexual and trans-gender (LGBT) market came much earlier than support for civil rights measures such as equal marriage.

We could learn from history. The Suffragette movement is rightly celebrated as an example of successful positive social change. However, the negative experience for black women is conveniently forgotten in the retrospective historical analysis. While white women in the United States won the vote in 1920, black women did not fully gain the right until 1965. A movement has to make progress – but it should be progress that does not harm another human's ability to make similar progress. The challenge is to identify what builds rather than what diverts, to walk the line between the strategic and the tactical with a preference for the former whenever possible.[34]

Diversity is about infinite difference and real inclusion is about bringing those differences together to add value. Superficial inclusion is about bringing token diversity together, intervening at a personal scale and assuming the work is done. This is true for minority groups who stick together and ignore the challenge, as well as for majority groups who maintain the status quo.

Diversity and inclusion are both necessary in order to add value to the purpose of an organisation. Real inclusion involves strategies designed to add value by embedding infinite diversity in existing infrastructure, intervening at a systemic level, where decisions are actually made. That is in some ways harder work, but essential for real value to be harnessed.

Diversity 101 and 2.0 have offered contributions to empowering different groups but now offer largely superficial solutions to systemic problems, and are stuck in a zero-sum game world. They are technical fixes. Real inclusion strategies start in a different place and focus on achieving systemic change, and enlarging the pie, to add value for everyone.

INCLUSION 3.0

We argue for a very different diversity and inclusion. Instead of additional programmes, with associated additional costs, we focus on the removal of barriers that already exist – subtracting rather than adding 'initiatives'. It is about the removal of barriers to allow a more efficient functioning of the market for talent. It is about setting people free, not lumbering them with more protocol that adds little value and that many resent, diverting them from the day job and often lowering morale in the process. You don't need to sugar-coat Diversity 101 policies or 2.0 programmes to achieve change. It's as much about the barriers you remove, as about the decorations you add.

Real inclusion strategies are detailed in Part Two of this book. They integrate diversity considerations into existing infrastructure. This not only costs less than creating new (often ineffective) infrastructure, it actually embeds the benefits of difference where the decisions are made, through the line, in the hands of middle management.

Inclusion 3.0 starts from the premise that people want to do 'the right thing', they just need some practical tools, rather than to be lectured to. When people are working alongside difference everyday and it is part of business as usual, people adapt. That adaptive process is messy and it can be painful. But it is a reality check-in with the world outside. Ultimately, it is a necessary adaptation for survival.

LET'S TALK

Inclusion 3.0 strategies permit conversations, including difficult and seem-ingly facile conversations, such as how disabled colleagues go to the toilet or survive a business trip, or how Muslim colleagues can attend team drinks in a bar. 3.0 programmes offer original interventions such as guest presenters, celebrities, events, competitions and rewards and allow mass participation rather than limited participation in a top-down training programme. One of the most liberating, and effective, strategies employed in 3.0 organ-isations is the power of peer review. Nothing affects individual professional behaviour more than reputation amongst colleagues. Peer review is a far more powerful tool for encouraging 'the right thing' than any training session. By sharing information, gaining the curiosity of colleagues and positioning diversity and inclusion as desirable goals, people can actually take up the baton willingly.

3.0 strategies are real time and relevant. With high-frequency, real-time reporting, people can gain up-to-date information that they find both interesting and useful. When this is coupled with individual accountability it can produce focused behaviour, strong enough to counter the effects of unconscious bias. There may be a resource constraint to the frequency and depth of this information-sharing, but it can be integrated into existing systems in recruitment, procurement and customer databases. What gets measured gets actioned, but in the past there was no consensus to support the measurement in the first place.

Inclusion is not about inter-personal conflicts, individual demography or individual psychology as much as it is about understanding and then working with the existing power structures, status and hierarchies evident within an organisation. The challenge for leaders is to improve collective intelligence and hence improve overall group performance. It is necessary to have an honest and insightful understanding of the current dynamics – more diversity could be a threat, real or perceived, to the status quo. It doesn't matter how many women's leadership programmes you have, if men don't want women leaders because they perceive them as a threat in a zero-sum game, then diversity initiatives will be unsuccessful. A dose of realpolitik is required.

ZERO-SUM GAMES AND ENLARGING THE PIE

One argument is that men do not want to relinquish power and share with women. No matter how good the business case, it is meaningless if men are not prepared to give something up. But why position diversity and inclusion as a zero-sum game where one faction wins and one faction loses? While that can be true, it is not always so. Assuming guilt in colleagues, before they can prove their innocence, has been characteristic of diversity programmes being rebuffed by the status quo to date.

So how do we remove the perception amongst the majority that it is always a zero sum game? Patricia Daley, a Geography Professor at Oxford University, recalled how upon being appointed to Jesus College she entered the Senior Common Room. The other (white, male) professors assumed she was one of the staff serving drinks rather than the new tutor with a distinguished academic record. This wasn't just about ignorance, it was about comfort levels. It is simply harder work to engage people who are different from you. But how was her presence taking away from them? They still had their tenured positions, tea at four o'clock, generous pension allowance and stimulating students in class every week. Patricia Daley was the new African Studies Professor, a new role, a new resource for the college and its students and a breath of fresh air in the Senior Common Room.

Of course it's not always that straightforward. What about a male colleague losing out on a promotion to a female colleague? For her to be promoted he has to forego the promotion. If she is more qualified than the male counterpart, then it's a case of merit-based selection, as in the case of Rachel Reeves we mentioned earlier in this chapter. If she is less qualified than the male colleague, then it's a case of positive discrimination and unsupported by Inclusion 3.0 theory. If, however, this is a successful organisation, growing, adapting, progressive, diverse and inclusive, there may well be multiple opportunities for both parties to seek promotion in the near future.

What about when people do need to sustain loss? What about when a majority group does have to concede ground? If and when they give something up, we need to work hard to articulate how they get more in return. The framing of the conversation is crucial. Some average performing men in an organisation we had worked with were dismayed at female promotions in their place. But the men were average performers. They had assumed promotion was their right and a norm. No one had pointed out that average performers don't get automatic promotion.

Because the women were in a minority they stood out and attracted disproportionate criticism, even though they had done nothing wrong. Again, the example of women in Parliament is instructive. A controversial policy still only resulted in a quarter of Members of Parliament being women – women were not taking over, they were catching up.

With this window ajar, it is then the responsibility of the practitioner to advance a more intelligent and coherent argument for inclusion, such that the status quo listen. It is the responsibility of the practitioner to emphasise change, which is hard but palatable, over loss, which will be rejected. Deutsche Telekom has set clear gender diversity targets for 2020. In achieving them, it is highly probable that capable men will lose out in promotion. On an individual level, we don't have an answer. Only by taking a wider view can we evaluate the collective benefits, which may be more than the sum of the parts. Moving the conversation from 'zero sum' to 'enlarging the pie' is the responsibility of the inclusive leader.

Consider the example of inclusive design in enlarging the pie for everyone. For no additional cost, it is possible for architects to design venues accessible to all. Ramps instead of steps, lower urinals in the men's bathroom, automatic doors that are energy efficient to boot. Facilities that work not just for disabled people, but also for mums and dads with buggies, older people, younger people, 'able bodied' people who have temporarily broken their leg skiing, operational people who have to move equipment around and prefer level access. This is real inclusion, when everyone benefits, when people understand it doesn't always have to be a zero-sum game.

PEOPLE ARE HUMAN, FALLIBLE AND WANT TO HAVE FUN

Diversity doesn't have to be worthy and dry. The decision to replace the popular Jon Stewart (an older, white Jewish North American man) with Trevor Noah (a younger, black South African man) to host the US's Daily Show, went down well with critics. Yet Police in the UK still know twenty words they are not allowed to use for Diversity 101 reasons and they are walking on created eggshells, resenting the imposition of training. We know that people perform better when they can be themselves. Think of the conversations, the infinite creativity unleashed. Inclusion 3.0 is liberating. Of course there is a requirement and a necessity for professional standards. But we are adults, and we know the rules.

In some ways, adults consciously and unconsciously work against inclusion. From the end of childhood onwards we collect baggage that we assume is the 'right way' to conduct ourselves in professional life. However, while maintaining respect, it might be helpful for us to revert to childhood curiosity in order to better engage with people who are different from us. Genuine curiosity is to be welcomed, encouraged and celebrated. Clearly and intentionally disrespectful behaviour is not. The corollary is that those who perceive themselves to be in the minority and the target of the alleged discrimination need to distinguish between positive and negative intent. That is an individual responsibility, not something taught in the classroom.

We all have implicit association biases and prejudices. That is natural and normal. We all exhibit unconscious bias. We will tend to hire people in our own image because they seem a 'good fit' or they 'get it'. In one sense, we cannot fight human nature. People want to associate with people like themselves. After two decades of Diversity 101 and 2.0 policies, many are more convinced of this than ever before.

However, it is increasingly a precondition of successful modern life that we do exactly the opposite. Diversity 101 policies are compliance driven and repel more people than they convince. Diversity 2.0 programmes are marketing driven and relatively superficial answers to systemic problems. 2.0 companies increasingly believe their own hyperbole. It is now time to intellectually and emotionally engage with a new way of seeing inclusion in business, for the sake of business, as well as society at large.

Knowing history and being aware of our biases will equip the professional to have a much richer view of talent. What we have come to learn from our work across the world, with hundreds of organisations and thousands of professionals, is that it's very hard to change people (minds); you have to change their environment (systems) in order to change their behaviour.

KEY TAKEAWAYS

1 An appreciation for our collective history provides a richer context to practise talent management. Reflecting on your own life experience to date will help you to place yourself within that history and better understand your own perspective in relation to others.

2 A self-awareness around individual bias will also help you make more accurate decisions. Additionally, it will help you to recognise and be aware of bias in others.

3 Diversity 101 is a compliance-based approach to talent management. Well intentioned, it has its roots in the civil rights movement but it is limited by its own centricism and lack of value-add.

4 Diversity 2.0 is a marketing-based approach to talent management. Well intentioned, it is more akin to corporate social responsibility, stakeholder management and marketing than to any serious value-add talent management programme.

5 Inclusion 3.0: Both compliance and marketing are important contributory factors to talent management but in themselves are insufficient. Only by accounting for history, bias and exercising leadership through a 3.0 approach to real inclusion can the professional and the organisation realise inclusive talent management.

NOTES

1 Dobbin, F, Kalev, A and Kim, S (2011) *Try and Make Me: Why corporate diversity training fails*, MIT Sloan.

2 Said, E (2003) *Orientalism*, Penguin, 1–3, Chapter 5.

3 Shroyer, A (2015) White fragility is racial violence, Huffpost Impact, 18 September.

4 Fox News (19 April 2015) Timothy McVeigh viewed Oklahoma bombing as failure, www.foxnews.com/us/2015/04/19/timothy-mcveigh-viewed-oklahoma-city-bombing-as-failure-docs-show.html

5 Katersky, A and Kim, S (21 November 2014) 5 disturbing things we learned about Sandy Hook shooter Adam Lanza, Abc News, http://abcnews.go.com/US/disturbing-things-learned-today-sandy-hook-shooter-adam/story?id=27087140

6 Bergen, P (18 May 2015) The lasting mystery of the Tsaernaev brothers, CNN http://edition.cnn.com/2015/05/16/opinions/bergen-tsarnaev-brothers-mystery/

7 *Guardian* (19 December 2013) Lee Rigby killing: Two British Muslim converts convicted of murder, www.theguardian.com/uk-news/2013/dec/19/lee-rigby-killing-woolwich-verdict-convicted-murder

8 See, for example, Sahoo, S (2009) *The Dark Abode*, Indian Age Communication.

9 Powell, JA (2014) *Health and Racial Equality in Turbulent Times: Implicit bias examined*, Haas Institute for a Fair and Inclusive Society.

10 Leading cognitive neuroscientist Michael Gazzaniga in his book *The Mind's Past* claims that 98 per cent or more of all brain activity is unconscious.

11 This is something also conducted by Binna Kandola and we are grateful to him for the conversation in Madrid, June 2015.

12 Interview with Norman Broadbent.

13 Gladwell, M (2006) *Blink*, Penguin UK.

14 Younge, G (2000) The badness of words, *Guardian*, 14 February.

15 Saardar, Z (2008) *The Language of Equality*, Equality and Human Rights Commission.

16 Professor Frank Dobbin, as cited in http://donaldclarkplanb.blogspot.co.uk/search?q=Dobbin and also quoted to me by Victoria Budson, Executive Director of Women and Public Policy Program at Harvard Kennedy School on 17 April 2013. Victoria Budson also reminded me, while we were discussing the limitations of diversity training, that Martin Luther King said, 'I have a dream', not 'I have a gripe.' Diversity training seems to be mired in the gripe/moan/blame/compliance culture that is self-defeating. Compliance will only ever create the minimum. According to Hansen (2003) $8 billion was spent annually on diversity training in US corporations in this period. That's a lot of input. We are yet to be convinced of the output.

17 See, for example, Riordan, CM (2000) Relational demography within groups: Past developments, contradictions and new directions, *Research in Personnel and Human Resources Management*, **19**, pp. 131–173.

18 See, for example, Mannix, EA and Neale, MA (2005) What differences make a difference? The promise and reality of diverse teams in organizations, *Psychological Science in the Public Interest*, **6** (2), pp. 31–55; van Knippenberg, D. and Schippers, M.C. (2007) Work group diversity, *Annual Review of Psychology*, **58**, pp. 515–541.

19 Phillips, K (14 February 2013) Can female leaders mitigate negative effects of diversity? The case of National Leaders' Women and Public Policy Program Seminar, Cambridge MA.

20 Liswood, L (2010) *The Loudest Duck*, Wiley.

21 Sandberg, S (2013) *Lean In*, WH Allen (especially the sections on career jungles, as opposed to career ladders).

22 Dasgupta, N (18 April 2013) Thriving despite negative stereotypes: How in-group experts and peers act as social vaccines to inoculate women's self concept and achievement, WAPPP Seminar.

23 www.2020wob.com/learn/why-gender-diversity-matters

24 Viviane Reding, European Commissioner for Justice, Fundamental Rights and Citizenship, conversation at Davos meeting, January 2012.

25 Norway passed a law in 2006 requiring 40 per cent of boardroom seats to go to women (or men in the rare cases where women predominate).

26 Ahern, K and Dittmar, A (2010) *The Changing of the Boards: The value effect of a massive exogenous shock*, Mimeo, University of Michigan.

27 Coate, S and Loury, G (1993) Will affirmative-action policies eliminate negative stereotypes? *The American Economic Review*, 83 (5), pp. 1220–1240.

28 Mona Lena Crook researched the issues of quotas in political life. She concluded that they too often act as a fix for more structural problems. For example, 'Gender quota policies result in the election of more women, but only those who will reinforce rather than challenge the status quo.' As we discussed above with reference to 101 superficial inclusion, the idea that women can only represent 'women's issues' is worrying. Men are seen as advocates of general issues – why not women or other minorities? Women and minorities are diverse within groups as well as between. Crook, ML (2008) Quota laws for women in politics: Implications for feminist practice, *Social Politics*, 15 (3), pp. 345–368.

29 Conversation with Iris Bohnet, March 2013.

30 This quotas example is based on gender but other minorities could be applied. A recent controversial article by an HKS doctoral student suggested that IQ was in fact different among different ethnic groups. IQ varies between and within groups according to a multitude of factors, but for the purposes of this book the differences are statistically insignificant, as well as morally debatable.

31 Conversation with the author at her home, while on maternity leave, 24 May 2013.

32 Gladwell, M (2000) *The Tipping Point*, Barnes & Noble.

33 Leadership Class, MPP programme, Harvard Kennedy School, Fall Semester 2002.

34 Another example would be gay marriage vs civil partnership.

3

THE FUTURE – DIVERSITY IS LOCAL, INCLUSION IS GLOBAL

We called the first part of the book 'The fierce urgency of now' to highlight how accepting or rejecting difference will determine future business fortunes. The first two chapters focused on where we are now and why talent management is in its current state. We now analyse future trends and realities pertaining to talent.

Demographic and technological change is altering the way we live our lives, but the way we work is lagging behind. Dealing with a changing world is a professional responsibility. An inclusive mindset is a resource than can help you handle that change.

We have shown how current homogeneous talent management (HTM) processes fall short. But if they fall short in the present day, they will fail even more spectacularly in the future. Inclusive talent management (ITM) will move from 'nice to have', to 'strategic prerequisite'. Early adopters of ITM will gain competitive advantage.

It is now widely accepted that we are living in a VUCA world – one that is volatile, uncertain, complex and ambiguous. We explored volatility in the natural and financial worlds in Chapter 1. Uncertainty is seen in the geopolitical situation in Ukraine, the Greek debt crisis, the future of the European Union (EU) and the potential for mass outbreak repeats such as SARS or Ebola. The lack of predictability is seen in volcanic eruptions, tsunamis, stock exchange falls, combined with a lack of understanding of issues and events, three centuries after the supposed Age of Enlightenment. Complexity manifests itself in the chaos and confusion that permeates organisations struggling to make sense of the changes around them, let alone take advantage of them. Many organisations simply lack the capacity to comprehend what is going on and, rather than take soundings from external experts, they struggle on in ignorance. Finally, ambiguity is a daily reality – the potential for poor decision making in the absence of information, or the inability to piece together complex pieces of information in order to maximise the potential of a situation or gain a competitive advantage; confusion between cause-and-effect.

Of course many people, and HTM processes in general, ignore these realities. That is fine for an antique shop that creates value from preserving the past, but it is wholly inadequate for organisations facing the future.

Chapter 3 explores the need for ITM to mitigate the negative effects of global demographic and technological change as well as attempt to take advantage of the opportunities they present. It outlines the complex localisation of diversity around the world as a resource to be taken advantage of, rather than a reality to be ignored, tolerated or merely 'incorporated'.

DIVERSITY IS A REALITY

Whether it's the different status of women in the Middle East and United States, the extent of immigration in Japan versus France or the different work styles of Millennials and baby boomers, diversity is a reality. ITM policies thrive in this reality, seeking out difference as a resource and a competitive advantage.

Three demographic trends will elevate the importance of diversity still further.

RISING POPULATION IN AFRICA AND ASIA

First, the global population will rise from 7.3 to 8.3 billion people over the next decade,[1] but that growth will be geographically uneven. Growing population will, on balance, benefit Africa and Asia. This is set to be their century – a different and larger supply of labour, larger (and new) markets and more diverse customers for firms outside those regions.

Africa's population is expected to double by 2050, whereas Europe's and East Asia's will shrink. The average age in Japan is 54 while in Nigeria it's 21. Nigeria's population is expected to exceed that of the US by 2045.[2] In North Africa and the Middle East youth unemployment is the highest in the world at 27.2 per cent (more than double the global average). This is particularly urgent as more than half of the population is under 25. As CNBC reported, 'the demographic youth bulge represents one of the greatest opportunities as well as one of the greatest challenges faced by the Arab world'. The youth population in the developing world is at an all-time high (1.6 billion children and 1.0 billion young people). The developing countries' labour force is projected to add nearly one-half billion workers over the next decade.

The global supply of graduates from emerging countries will increase from 54 per cent in 2015 to 60 per cent in 2025. This will mean that the southern hemisphere will become the major source of technical talent. Already, the 10 largest economies in Asia (China, India, Indonesia, Japan, Malaysia, Philippines, Singapore, South Korea, Taiwan and Thailand) spent an estimated $399 billion on research and development (R&D) in 2011, significantly more than Europe's $300 billion.[3]

AGEING WORKFORCE AND POPULATION IN THE WEST AND PARTS OF ASIA

Second, the global share of older people (aged 60 plus) increased from 9.2 per cent in 1990 to 11.7 per cent in 2013 and is projected to increase to 21.1 per cent by 2050.[4] Some countries and organisations are preparing better than others. China has for many years invested heavily in the education of its people to the extent that by 2030 there will be more educated people of working age in China than in North America and Europe combined.

Twenty-seven per cent of the population in Europe is over 65 and this is the fastest growing population segment. For both governments and employers an ageing workforce presents a number of different challenges. In many countries legislation is already in place eliminating a compulsory retirement age. Even though governments know they should invest in youth, politically they often prioritise older voters, who are more likely to vote. Wealth resides increasingly in the hands of older people and investment in young workers is starved.

An ageing population rewrites the rules on retirement and what talent looks like. It's not simply a case of older experience versus younger entrepreneurs because often Millennials have more technological experience than older workers and are setting the agenda, while 'silver surfers' are ever more entrepreneurial and creating new markets and second careers. With more active older workers there is the potential for conflict arising from oversupply of labour for limited jobs. Millennials are facing significant youth unemployment and baby boomers are working longer for many reasons, including the absence of state pensions.

Already a number of organisations in the finance and retailing sectors are giving employment opportunities to older generations. One example is the UK's chain of DIY stores, B&Q, which decided to target older people to work in their stores as they would have more DIY experience than those from a younger generation. The more traditional mindset of 'getting rid' of your older workforce in order to focus on the younger generations will need to change.

DECLINING BIRTH RATES

Third, a declining birth rate in several countries exacerbates regional differences between them, and Africa and Asia. A declining birth rate raises serious questions for Western-based organisations in terms of their own recruitment, and also in terms of competition from growth regions benefiting from a demographic dividend.

The picture varies from country to country but it's particularly acute in Germany, Japan and South Korea. Europe's population is projected to decline from 739 million in 2011 to 709 million in 2050. Russia's population is projected to decline by 10 million between 2010 and 2030. The projection for less developed countries' population is to increase from 5.9 billion to 8.2 billion by 2050. The birth rate in Germany and Japan is below replacement levels, yet Japan is still resistant to immigration. Something has to give.

Most of Europe and East Asia will see their labour force decline. The labour force in Japan is forecast to shrink from 66 million in 2013 to 40 million in 2060 (a decline of almost 40 per cent), and China and South Korea's decline is expected to be 17–18 per cent. In Europe, Greece, Portugal and Germany will see their labour forces decline by over 20 per cent. The birth rate in Germany is currently 1.4 children per family and as a result they are facing both a declining and ageing population. As a consequence these countries may not be able to sustain their desired growth.

Europe, Asia and Latin America will need to mobilise and attract people not currently in the labour force, whether unemployed or underemployed, simply to meet the demand from employers. In addition, these regions will need to continue to welcome higher immigration. It is calculated there is an annual flow globally of 2.4 million immigrants from less developed countries. As has been widely reported, such a flow of immigrants brings political and social challenges but for many countries they are a vital supply of labour.

The International Monetary Fund (IMF) has projected that Africa will continue to have the fastest growing regional economy. Seven out of the world's 10 fastest growing economies are located in Africa. People are living longer, having fewer children and consequently the fastest growing age segment is the over 65s. The world is pivoting from West to East and North to South.

TECHNOLOGY MEGATRENDS

The three population megatrends are compounded by technological megatrends that are changing the way we work. Information technology (IT) is transforming the workplace. It's become almost a cliché now to reference technology but few people really appreciate its transformative impact. We will discuss three trends – the replacement of professionals with technology, the failure to effectively generate knowledge, and the importance of inclusion to avoid thinking in silos.

TECHNOLOGY WILL REPLACE PROFESSIONALS, NOT JUST WORKERS

Much has been written about technology replacing lower skilled jobs, but new research highlights the impact on the professions. Professor Richard Susskind and Daniel Susskind's book *The Future of the Professions* explains how 'increasingly capable systems' – from telepresence to artificial intelligence – will bring fundamental change in the way that the 'practical expertise' of specialists is made available in society.[5]

As IT and machines take over many of the tasks previously seen as the 'domain' of professionals such as doctors, accountants and lawyers, this creates fundamental talent management questions. If the general public can make their own will, self-diagnose an illness using online information and complete their own tax affairs as opposed to seeing an accountant then the prospects for the professions look grim. More people signed up to one of Harvard's online courses in one year than the number who have attended their courses in their entire 377 year history.

Technology is not only transforming the workplace, it is redefining what the workplace actually is. It is providing access to learning previously only available to the 'privileged few', allowing more flexibility to the way we obtain information and questioning the way we see the role of specialists and the services they offer.

The Susskinds challenge the 'grand bargain' – the arrangement that grants various monopolies to today's professionals. They argue that our current professions are antiquated, opaque and no longer affordable, and that the expertise of the best is enjoyed only by a few.

TOO MUCH INFORMATION, TOO LITTLE KNOWLEDGE

We are living through a fundamental (as opposed to incremental) techno-logical revolution. Technological change can be viewed on a continuum from Data, then Information, to Knowledge. However, as ex-NASA data scientist Bruno Sánchez-Andrade Nuño argues, we are still missing the third knowledge stage.[6]

The data revolution has led to exponentially diminishing costs for gener-ating, storing and processing data. Very roughly speaking, every five years these costs are one order of magnitude cheaper, and we have one order of magnitude more. Silicon Valley is pushing this trend as part of the elastic business model: more data to profile and optimise advertisements and operations.

Processing all that data generates lots of useful information and content. As such there is a race for optimising, customising and contextualising the user experience based on usage data. As technology optimises to our behaviour, we get smaller and smaller pieces of information in a constant stream. Facebook feeds, Twitter feeds, news aggregators – less and less friction to consume a river of bite-size content made specifically for us. This contextual information is inherently biased as it is profiled just for the individual. We get what we like, in very effective silos, far away from a comprehensive view of the world's happenings. And we get an infinite buffet of catchy bite-size content that displaces any other appetite for richer content.

For the first time in human history we have instant access to virtually any topic, and most of the content we consume would be considered utterly irrelevant just a few years ago. How often are you subjected to pictures of your friends' food/children/new dress on Facebook? We are drowning in information, but we are drowning in shallow waters.

With ever-decreasing friction to access information, and ever-refined personalisation of that we consume, we are getting further and further away from genuine knowledge. Knowledge creation is the deliberate process of concentrating, filtering and absorbing information and constructing logic, the underpinnings that explain the information we get. It requires deep dives with lots of information; it requires focus and energy. Knowledge creation is hard, slow and messy – as consumers, we don't like that.

Here is where talent management comes in – without leadership information does not become knowledge. The information remains ubiquitous, shallow and biased. According to Bruno, knowledge creation only works if the incentives for creation and management are aligned with the core values of an organisation. For example, consulting firms could enforce a strict process, since they need to get their consultant up to speed very quickly. Human resources could force cross-functional collaboration.

THE RISE OF THE MACHINES

Beyond human talent management, machines are starting to undertake 'learning' in the same way. Algorithms optimise their inner 'neural networks' to create abstract layers of representations to explain and predict. They can do, better than us, tasks we always thought needed human understanding, like disease diagnosis, driving cars, understand multilingual conversations in a noisy room.

We are letting technology drive this process and insufficiently managing it. We get an optimised view of the world and our networks, driven by an infrastructure that favours herd behaviour and shallow constant streams processed by machines that are actually learning. As Bruno says, 'There is a risk we are leaving our brains out of the process. I look around and see personalised social streams polarise fluid mobs of likes and retweets... Ochlocracy is a word we'll start to hear more and more.'[7]

We are not seeing the knowledge revolution because machines are living the knowledge revolution, while we get distracted with social media. Talent management is needed to bring different (biased) people together to create knowledge and applied solutions to our global and local problems. We need to rethink how technology can support thinking, not replace it.

Technological change raises important practical and moral questions. In an era when machines can out-perform human beings at most tasks, what are the prospects for employment, who should own and control online expertise, and what tasks should be reserved exclusively for people? It is in this context that organisations that refuse 'flexible working' are starting to look completely out of touch.

The consequences of the demographic and technological trends we have discussed include segregation – both physically and mentally. Physically, we are moving to be with people like us. Bill Bishop's 2004 book *The Big Sort* chronicles the rise of a divided USA.[8] The plethora of choice that the American consumer has enjoyed for the last few decades has resulted in them choosing to live with people like them. And so in the proverbial melting pot of the USA, with all the immigration that has occurred, people are more segregated residentially, politically and socially than ever before. Mentally, the consequences of information selection is that we only consume what we believe in and we filter out challenge.

TALENT MANAGEMENT IMPLICATIONS

Leading professional services firms, banks and other major graduate recruiters are already suffering at graduate recruitment level because would-be candidates prefer Teach First[9] to accountancy. Much has been made of the 'Millennial mindset' but the implications for talent management are already stark.

There are several high-profile 'shortages' of talent, for example science, technology, engineering and mathematics (STEM) subject areas, coding and engineering. Even if industry persuaded more of its existing target audience to consider employment, they would still be short of talent. We now have to engage 'non-traditional' demographic sectors for purely economic reasons. Hence Google aiming coding classes at women, the drive to greater flexible working to attract returners and the attractiveness of multiple linguists to allow labour mobility.

The demographic dividend lowers the cost of labour and new markets open up. But increased competition results and offshoring is now established. Migration is needed to fill the demographic gap in developed countries, but without inclusive policies it will contribute to existing social and workforce problems.

Offshoring is a fact of modern corporate life. India has dominated these markets, capturing 65 per cent of the information technology outsourcing and 43 per cent of the business process outsourcing markets.[10] Today, India has more technology workers than any other country, and China is on track to pass the United States as the country with the largest number of R&D workers.[11]

For many organisations, offshoring is not simply a cost-reduction exercise. Offshoring, and entering new markets, can open up new perspectives and gain new insights that can be transferred around the organisation. Given reduced economic growth in the West, organisations seek to be players in the fastest growing areas of the world. Over the next decade, nearly 80 per cent of the world's middle-income consumers will reside in emerging economies.[12]

There remains, however, a growing Chinese managerial and executive talent gap.[13] In a study conducted by McKinsey, researchers found that although nearly 50 per cent of the engineers in Eastern European countries such as Hungary and Poland are suitable to work for multinational companies, only

10 per cent and 25 per cent of those in China and India, respectively, could do so.[14]

Many of the organisations we spoke to are now recognising and then leveraging this locally rooted global diversity to boost core competencies, for example great customer service, technological innovation and local market insights. These and other competencies can be found in their staff and the ability to take advantage of this creativity is key to the success of the organisation. Through trust and respect for staff at a local level, organisations can better develop the business by understanding the needs of their local customers through local eyes.

DIVERSITY IS LOCAL

Organisations need to make the most of local differences and include them in their global mindset if they are to truly gain competitive advantage. In Chapter 1 we defined diversity as being 'a combination of a person's physical DNA, life experience and social context'. Around the world, combinations of these exist and are accepted to wildly differing degrees. We'll briefly examine twelve aspects relating to talent management – language, age, gender and gender identity, flexible working, ethnicity, religion, sexual orientation, disability, veterans, socio-economic status, expatriates and internal/external pipelines.

The picture is mixed in many countries, for example some African countries such as Liberia or Rwanda are global leaders in gender equality, but many Middle Eastern countries are starting from a very low base, such as Saudi Arabia. In some countries diversity is not even part of the discussion, for example LGBT rights in much of the Middle East. In many instances compliance (Diversity 101) is the driver for disability inclusion and in others marketing and stakeholder relations (Diversity 2.0) the driver with, for example, veterans outreach in North America and Europe. In a few instances there is genuine leadership (Inclusion 3.0), for example with gender in Canada or flexible working in the EU.

In the US the emphasis tends to be on racial minorities (and ethnic minorities/immigrants in Canada). Organisations have a very direct approach to diversity and inclusion, set quantitative targets and use management incentives to reach them. But the USA and Canada are in some ways very different. Many US corporations are driven by a Diversity 101 mentality that is compliance-based. A focus on race and gender alone can produce tokenism in the absence of leadership and cause resentment on both sides, leading to a sometimes adversarial relationship between employee and employer. Canada has a more European, ambiguous approach.

Europe is at a crossroads with globalisation, the disruptive impact of new technologies and the slow pace of the recovery of the European economy all providing challenges for organisations. In Europe there is more emphasis on internal persuasion and more focus on attracting and retaining female staff. But as a region it has the most advanced legislative protection for minorities anywhere in the world.

In Latin America there is a complex mix of strong influence from the Catholic Church combined with a progressive social agenda from many governments. This mix of conservatism and liberalism is also seen throughout Asia Pacific. China is comparatively progressive on gender, compared with Japan and South Korea, which continue to massively under-utilise their female talent. A resistance to immigration in Japan contrasts with Singapore, which is also nudging forward on other issues such as LGBT inclusion. However, resistance to immigration is growing in Singapore in spite of it being a mainstay of the economic model. In Asia generally there is much more of a laissez faire approach with the mindset that diversity and inclusion will evolve naturally.

Africa is also a mixed picture, with female leaders spearheading change across the continent, compared with an avowed opposition to LGBT and minority rights in some countries such as Uganda and Nigeria. In the Middle East, post Arab Spring, the biggest issue is how to employ a massive youth population. In Saudi Arabia, for example, the main focus is giving local nationals more access to employment and promotion opportunities.

In most countries worldwide, the main emphasis is on gender. Women are in one sense the largest 'minority' and the largest pool of inefficiently used talent. However, if diversity is infinite a focus on just female identity will ignore as much as it includes.

Mercer, in its 2014 report *Diversity and Inclusion: An Asia Pacific perspective*,[15] highlighted variances pertaining to talent planning in that region. The ageing population in Japan and Australia is a key concern but this is not the case in India and China. Flexible working is seen a high priority in Australia but is of little concern in Japan. Of the 355 organisations surveyed by Mercer in 11 countries gender was a key theme for over 90 per cent of organisations in Australia, India and Japan but only 53 per cent of organisations in China thought it important.

A 2009 report commissioned by the Society for Human Resource Management, *Global Diversity and Inclusion: Perceptions, practices and attitudes*,[16] surveyed 500 executives and researched the diversity readiness in 47 countries. The report noted that organisations have come to understand that different demographic and social groups think and communicate differently. This factor needs to be taken into account when new staff from diverse backgrounds join an organisation so that they can be truly integrated into the workforce.

Let's look at some of the critical aspects of diversity on a global scale that affect talent management practices, starting with language.

LANGUAGE

Mandarin is the language spoken by most people on the planet. While 14 per cent of the global population speaks Mandarin, they are overwhelmingly based in one country, China. After Mandarin, it's Spanish at 6 per cent, English at 5 per cent and then Hindi and Arabic around 4 per cent each.[17] English, in particular, is more geographically porous, an international language of business. Online, English and Mandarin dominate, but the web is giving voice to an ever more diverse range of languages. This is important in view of the fact that up to 90 per cent of the world's 7,000 languages are predicted to be extinct by the end of the century.[18]

It is predicted that the five most spoken languages in 2050 will be Chinese, Spanish, English, Hindi-Urdu and Arabic. The United States is destined to become the largest Spanish-speaking country by 2050 and many of its students now learn Mandarin as a compulsory high school class. Superintendent Romain Dallemand argues that 'Students who are in elementary school today, by 2050 they'll be at the pinnacle of their career. They will live in a world where China and India will have 50 per cent of the world GDP. They will live in a world where, if they cannot function successfully in the Asian culture, they will pay a heavy price.'[19]

From a talent management perspective it's important to establish a common language. Of course, on a local level, it's acceptable, even desirable, to speak the native language, but for those organisations that have a global reach an agreed common language is a key to success. A lack of language skills has a direct impact on a country's ability to attract inward investment. Take Brazil, where only 11 per cent of its population has the ability to communicate in English.[20] Like China with Mandarin, the vast majority of Portuguese speakers worldwide reside in the one country of Brazil. According to the Californian Company Global English Corporation, Brazil is number 70 in the level of fluency in English out of 78 countries in which it works.

Many organisations have realised that their ability to harness the skills and experiences of their staff, such as the language and cross-cultural skills, could give them a competitive advantage over other organisations in their sector. Take firms in New York, which has a huge immigrant population. Many people struggle with speaking English so organisations that employ multi-lingual staff can work more effectively and be more productive in such communities.

AGE, MILLENNIALS AND MULTI-GENERATIONAL CHALLENGES

There are now five generations in the global workforce: Traditionalists (born before 1946), baby boomers (1946–64), Generation X (1965–76), Millennials (1977–97) and Gen Z (born after 1997). Many organisations are struggling to build inclusive cultures when it appears these groups all have different aspirations and attitudes towards work.

As a result of when they were born, each generation has been influenced by the historical, cultural, technological and economic circumstances they experienced. Each generation will have different skills and experiences to offer to their organisation and the challenge will be to leverage these for the benefit of the organisation, the team and the individual.

A flexible approach to learning and development activities will be necessary as each generation will have preferences for their learning styles, for example, Millennials are more likely than baby boomers to be comfortable with e-learning. Beyond the technology stereotype, Millennials also prefer face-to-face and authentic conversation and learning to top-down training.

Managers will need to understand the different expectations each generation will have and to be able to recognise the different talent they have in their team. Having a mindset to appreciate the diversity they have and leverage the different skills and experiences will be key as to whether the team will be able to achieve their goals – see Chapter 8 for more on leadership style.

The intergenerational debate can descend into cliché. People are first and foremost individuals of varying ages and may transcend created groupings. Treating people as individuals, rather than simply groups, is more efficient. However, a key talent issue is that Millennials are setting the global agenda in terms of technology, social media and culture, yet they are not in control of organisations. This is a warning to those organisations that are run by baby boomers refusing to let go, they are steering a very different course.

Google and Facebook appear to be successful because of their homogeneity – friends and colleagues closely related in age who all pursued a single vision. But dig a little deeper and it becomes apparent that Larry Page and Sergey Brin at Google brought in Eric Schmidt and Mark Zuckerberg brought in Sheryl Sandberg (who herself was mentored by Larry Summers). There is age diversity at the core of the successes of these companies.

A 2015 Deloitte survey[21] interviewed 7,800 graduate Millennials from 29 countries and found striking similarities – a belief that business should have a positive impact on society and the need to be innovative. Millennials want to work for an organisation with a strong sense of purpose and expect their leaders to be inspirational, strategic and have strong interpersonal skills.

Another report[22] surveyed 40,000 respondents in 18 countries and found that Millennials care about social impact and welcome opportunities to get involved in projects/activities that contribute in some way to society or their local community. Millennials want to work for an organisation that has a reputation for making a social contribution so that they can feel proud of their employer. Female Millennials in particular seek out employers with a strong record on diversity and inclusion. Diversity and inclusion programmes can have a social impact, so embedding these principles is another way to attract and engage the generation soon to be in charge.

GENDER AND GENDER IDENTITY

Gender is a salient diversity issue for most organisations. They see it as the biggest pool of talent they are currently under-utilising, as well as one of the easiest to measure. Women account for just 16 per cent of members of executive teams in the USA, 12 per cent in the UK and 6 per cent in Brazil.[23]

A study by Korn Ferry of 2,360 companies globally found that those with one or more female board members have delivered higher average returns on equity, lower gearing and better average growth.[24] The study also looked at the composition of boards in Asia and one of its conclusions was, 'the composition of a board should reflect that organisation's target market – and its customer base. Organisation that rely solely on men to make strategic decisions on products, innovation and growth are short-changing themselves on the fiscal and cultural benefits that women in leadership bring'. In the Asia Pacific countries of China, Hong Kong, India, Japan, Malaysia, New Zealand, Singapore and South Korea, women account for less than 10 per cent of directors. More than 50 per cent of boards in India, Japan, New Zealand, Singapore and South Korea have no female directors at all.

A growing number of top management recognise the importance of women as leaders and are implementing new policies, development programmes and other initiatives to create an environment where women can thrive. However, the understanding, let alone policies, aimed at transgender people is extremely limited to pockets of Western Europe, North America and countries such as Thailand and Argentina. Transgender people are those that identify with a different gender to their birth gender. For example, a person born male that identifies as a woman may undergo transition 'male to female', or 'M2F'. Understanding that how a person identifies is often more important than how they present is important in order to include them and allow them to work efficiently.

Christian Mattey served ten years in the British Army as a woman and has undergone treatment and now wants to serve on the front line as a man.[25] This directly challenges the gender segregation policies still in place in the Army, for example not allowing women to serve in certain combat roles such as infantry battalions and armoured regiments. Private Mattey is now a recruiter for the Royal Engineers and the Army is supportive of his continued service.

The World Economic Forum's 2014 report on *Global Gender Gap*, however, paints a rather gloomy picture of progress made on gender equality.[26] It showed that in nine years of measuring the global gender gap there has only been a small improvement in equality for women in the workplace.

There are big regional variations, with companies in Europe and Central Asia occupying 12 of the top 20 positions in the index. However, in such countries as Japan, China, India and the Middle East there is still much room for improvement in giving women equal opportunities. Klaus Schwab, founder and ex-chairman of the World Economic Forum, said, 'Achieving gender equality is obviously necessary for economic reasons-only those economies who have full access to all their talent will remain competitive and will prosper. But even more important is that gender equality is a matter of justice.'

FLEXIBLE WORKING

Men and women want to have more flexibility in their working lives in order to achieve work–life balance. Organisations recognise that to keep their talents or to be able to recruit those with specialist skills they need to have a more flexible approach. In Chapter 1 we discussed Obelisk, proof of what happens when traditional HTM process remain steadfast. In Germany the term *Rabensmutter*[27] still prevails – the notion that women who return to work after childbirth are somehow bad mothers to have 'flown the nest' and abandoned their little ones. Contrast this with recent moves in the United States where two of the 'Big 4' professional services firms are now run by women.

A classic response to the childbirth and maternity needs of mothers is to allow more generous paid leave. However, research suggests that there may be a negative correlation between paid leave and the gender pay gap. In Austria, where women are entitled to 42 weeks of paid maternal leave, the gender pay gap is 23 per cent. In Belgium, where women only receive 11 weeks of statutory leave, the gender pay gap is much smaller at 7 per cent.[28] Of course there are other factors at play, but a solution may be in shared paternal leave where men are also paid to get involved in childcare and the burden shifts away from being exclusively on the mother. The UK has followed Scandinavian countries where this has long been the norm. A more inclusive policy has allowed both mothers and fathers greater flexibility. It's important to note that flexible working is often wrongly categorised as a female issue. Men are increasingly seeking balance in their work too.

Oxfam had a specific need for staff with certain skills at certain periods of time. It introduced a part-time response and resilience team of staff who are contracted to work six months a year. These are highly skilled and experienced staff who are on call to be deployed to emergencies around the world. Their range of skills include public health engineers, emergency food security specialists, logistics experts and programme managers. This allows a more inclusive recruitment approach appealing to people who have other commitments, and for whom working 50 per cent of the year suits their circumstances.

ETHNICITY

Ethnicity is, by definition, dependent upon context. In many Western societies white people are the majority and 'ethnic minorities' tend to be people of an African, Caribbean or Asian heritage. In the United States, African Americans and Native Americans are acknowledged to have suffered the most severe historical discrimination and therefore there is now a focus on them in particular. However, 'Latinos' are numerically the largest minority group in the US today, reflective of immigration from South America, Mexico in particular.

It is traditionally assumed that the 'ethnic minority' is to be the target or beneficiary of HTM/Diversity 101 processes, and this is true in many of the above contexts. However, in Asia Pacific white people, expatriates, are the 'minority'. In Singapore expatriates constitute 35 per cent of the population, whereas in Dubai and other Gulf cities the proportion is 95 per cent of the working population.

Ethnicity is therefore contextual and also dependent on locale. In the US history has led to more overt racism and a more deliberate response. In the UK racism also exists, it is just more subtle. For the London 2012 Olympic and Paralympic Games, the immediate local talent pool was majority minority (Black British and Bangladeshi Asians in particular) in a majority white country where ethnic minorities make up only 12 per cent of the population.

RELIGION

Freedom of conscience is a fundamental human right and enshrined in the Universal Declaration of Human Rights. However, a person's ability to exercise their religion varies wildly according to geography. In many UK workplaces it is common to have prayer rooms and/or faith facilities to allow people to express their faith during the working day. In France, the secular work culture dictates the opposite.

In addition, there is often a real and/or perceived conflict with LGBT (see below). Gay rights and religion are often positioned as a zero-sum game. Same-sex relationships are often positioned as running counter to religious teaching. Charles Radcliffe, of the Office of the United Nations High Commissioner for Human Rights (OHCHR), says:

> In this case, the conflict between the rights of LGBT people on the one hand and culture, tradition and religion on the other is a false one. Protection of one need not be at the expense of the other. The key is to bring the debate back to the rights of individuals including the right to define their own beliefs, values and culture for themselves.[29]

In other words, religion is 'not monolithic, nor can [it] override individual freedoms'.[30]

LGBT

Lesbian, gay, bisexual and transgender people exist worldwide but the main determinant of their inclusion in the workforce is the extent to which they can be 'out'. In other words, the prevalence of openly LGBT people is more a measure of inclusion than it is a measure of diversity.

In many countries there has been a phenomenal rate of progress in the rate of inclusion of LGBT people in society in the last decade. In the Americas, Argentina, Brazil, Uruguay, Mexico, USA and Canada have all legalised same-sex marriage and most countries offer legal rights. In Europe, 14 countries recognise same-sex marriage, including Ireland where a national referendum gave a clear result in favour from a majority heterosexual electorate.

Yet in other regions there has been either a lack of progress or regression. In Africa only South Africa has equal marriage and constitutional protection for LGBT people and even there violence against gay women is common. In Asia, no country awards equal marriage rights except Israel.

Iran, Mauritania, Saudi Arabia, Sudan and Yemen still maintain a statutory death penalty for homosexuality and 71 countries criminalise same-sex couples. In total, 2.79 billion people live in countries where being gay can lead to prison or death, compared with 1.3 billion people who live in countries with some form of legal protection against LGBT discrimination.[31]

Many organisations have acquired talent through being LGBT-friendly, even in challenging operating environments. For example, HSBC lit up its Hong Kong headquarters in the rainbow flag colours for Pride, Goldman Sachs was involved in the Pink Dot celebrations in Singapore and major Fortune 500 companies publicly supported the push for same-sex marriage in the United States, including companies that had formerly opposed it. However, even companies that score 100 per cent in the Human Rights Campaign Corporate Equality Index have only about 50 per cent of LGBT employees out at work.[32] It's about culture, not just 'check the box' polices.

Companies run into difficulty when the geographical variations come into conflict with each other. For example, Coca Cola, McDonald's and VISA all sponsored the Sochi Olympic games in Russia. Russia ranks bottom in a European league table of LGBT equality[33] and there are real issues of homophobia in society and the workplace. Yet these same sponsors all supported the legislative drive for same-sex marriage in the United States.

DISABILITY

Similar to LGBT, disability statistics are often more a measure of inclusion than a measure of diversity. Whether and to what degree someone defines as being disabled is intrinsically related to his or her environment. In the UK the social model of disability is commonly accepted, whereby disability is defined in relation to being enabled or disabled by external factors, from steps versus ramps to inclusive or exclusive policies. In the US and many European countries there is more emphasis on a medical model, whereby people are defined as 'having' a disability, rather than 'being' disabled. There, the emphasis is more on individual solutions to disability, with the individual adapting to the environment.

Again, both extremes could be more effectively integrated whereby it is both an individual responsibility as well as a collective responsibility to improve accessibility. Unlike with LGBT and gender, there have not been the same improvements in disability inclusion. This is disappointing given that globally one in five people has a disability, and most of us become disabled over time.

MILITARY VETERANS

In the United States in particular, military veterans are increasingly seen as a targeted group for workforce integration. Demobilising from frontline service is a challenging process yet clearly such individuals have unique skill sets to offer. Many may be disabled but not identify as such.

Recognising the importance of transferable skills and matching them to suitable roles has been the key in the success of Deloitte's policy of recruiting ex-service women and men from the military. Their Military Transition Talent Programme was established in 2012 and currently has over 150 ex-military and reservists working for them in the UK. Seven have made partner. Chris Recchia, a former Army captain and now partner in their risk advisory business, said: 'I am acutely aware of the motivation, ambition and leadership skills that ex-servicemen and women have to offer and the asset they bring to an organisation.'[34]

SOCIO-ECONOMIC STATUS

In the UK in particular, socio-economic status is gaining increasing recognition as a criteria for inclusion. Class-based societies such as UK and India have a particular history in terms of exclusion of certain groups based on social class, irrespective of ability. Now there is a moral as well as economic case that is being made for better inclusion of lower socio-economic groups in the job market.

In many cases this is based on ability. For example, a recent report highlighted that pupils educated at state school in the UK achieved higher grades at university than their privately educated peers.[35] In other cases it is less about ability and more about social cohesion, such as in very populous countries like India. However, in India there has recently been a backlash against the inclusion of lower castes at the perceived cost of opportunities for higher castes. Patel caste members have complained about perceived exclusion from government jobs in India's western Gujarat state. They have formed a protest movement led by Dinesh Patel, one of the five core members of the Patidar Anamat Aandolan Samiti.

EXPATRIATE WORKERS

Organisations operating globally have to decide whether to use local people or expatriates (expats). Clearly, this depends on geography. Historically many organisations have relied on expats as a key means of addressing international expansion requirements. Using international assignments was also seen as a key development vehicle for future leaders. However, these assignments are complex to organise and maintain, expensive to run and individuals are often difficult to re-integrate into the organisation after the completion of the assignment.

As a result, such organisations are now facing a dilemma as they recognise these difficulties but still want to use international mobility as a way to develop key global leadership skills. What are the options?

Take a more tactical and selective approach to mobility – for example, consider short-term assignments that avoid having to relocate any family members and ensure the person concerned returns to their previous role.

Consider regional mobility as opposed to global mobility.

Move international assignees to local terms and conditions.

Danny has personally witnessed many examples in Panasonic of Japanese expats who were, without doubt, capable from the point of view of company knowledge and functional skills, but failed when posted overseas to lead critical operations. As a result, local staff were demotivated and frustrated by the expats' inability to recognise the differences in culture between their home and host country. Regrettably the frustration led to a number of local staff leaving Panasonic.

In some cases it remains appropriate to send expats but two issues need to be resolved first:

Identify the roles they are best suited to fill.

Assess the expats before they are sent overseas to ensure they have the necessary leadership competencies to be successful in a different country/ culture. Further support could be both pre boards and on boarding as well as cultural training and mentoring.

Sending expats overseas often remains a homogeneous talent management strategy that has proven to be in many cases an expensive failure (the cost of the expat's salary/benefits and the cost of losing key talents). Far better to adopt an inclusive talent strategy in which an organisation also gives opportunities to local staff who speak the language, who have local experience and often have a network and contacts who can be useful to the organisation.

INTERNAL OR EXTERNAL PIPELINES

There is an ongoing debate about the merits and demerits of prioritising internal or external talent pipelines. These are well documented and are covered in many books and articles on talent management. The Conference Board together with the Chartered Management Institute published a 'CEO Challenge' report.[36] The results of interviews from 1,000 CEOs/presidents of organisations globally revealed the vast majority prioritised the creation of a strong internal talent pipeline rather than recruiting externally. However, in order to have a robust internal pipeline the following three factors were identified as critical steps:

Effective learning and development programmes

Improving employee engagement

Increasing efforts to retain key talents

On the one hand, to only focus on internal talent pipelines will result in continuing with the current staff who may be set in their ways and lack the diversity of opinions and experiences. On the other hand, to recruit externally is to deny opportunities to those who are already working for you and have demonstrated their commitment and potential to go to the next level.

There are many factors to take into account, such as to know which are the critical roles, identify the talent you have, clarify which level they are suitable for (executive, emerging talent or entry level talent), secure the involvement of the line manager and above all to understand the aspirations of those in the talent pipeline.

IT'S ABOUT CULTURE

The twelve aspects of diversity we have discussed play out in different ways. The key to making ITM work, however, is how it leverages them to positive effect as demonstrated in Figure 3.1. This is about culture. As Peter Drucker said, culture eats strategy for breakfast. However, assimilation can also kill difference and innovation, so it's important to achieve balance. A culture that is outgoing, welcoming and inclusive will leverage the above factors to better effect. The emphasis has to be on the individual, however unkind that may sound, because it is an individual responsibility to adapt to a common

Figure 3.1 HTM and ITM approaches to global diversity.

Diversity	HTM	ITM
Language	English (or equivalent)	English (or equivalent) and local language
Age	Inter-generational conflict	Learning from each other and avoiding stereotyping
Gender/gender ID	Focus on single variable gender	Focus on women with gender one aspect of their identity
Flexible working	Flexible working as a female issue	Flexible working for both genders
Ethnicity	Compliance based	Ethnicity one factor
Religion	Prohibited or monopolised and seen in conflict with LGBT	Multi-faith permitted
LGBT	Prohibited or seen in conflict with religion	Inclusive culture allows LGBT individuals to come out
Disability	Medical model	Social and medical model
Veterans	Charitable	Unique skill sets to offer
Socio-economic	Charitable	Moral as well as different skill sets to offer
Expatriates	Expatriates dominate	Expatriates and locals

world. But the organisation can also help the individual, for its own interest. Both individual and organisation working together stands the best chance of creating an inclusive culture.

WHY DO MOST ORGANISATIONS STRUGGLE?

At Panasonic, the global talent team was aware of global trends but struggled to implement a global talent strategy due to a number of reasons – difficulty to get buy-in from all relevant people, some parts of the business did not have or did not want to spend the necessary budget, different levels of maturity of the business in different regions, varying levels of expertise of human resources in the regions, and poor communication in some parts of the organisation despite being provided with all the information.

From an inclusive talent perspective there are a number of themes as to why many organisations find it so difficult to implement a global strategy:

Their talent process does not align with the overall business strategy.

There is not enough support from top management so there is no sense of priority from other members of management.

The HR function does not have the expertise or credibility. There is often too much focus on those identified as being high potential, resulting in more people being demotivated as they are not on the list.

The succession plans do not reflect the diversity in the business.

Career conversations are not held on a regular basis so as to understand the aspirations of the employee.

There will often be objections in some parts of the organisation as they are yet to see the benefits they will accrue by adopting a global inclusive strategy as opposed to one they have developed for their local business.

In our experience all these points can be addressed by implementing an inclusive and systematic talent management strategy that addresses the business needs. We will discuss this in Part Two, including how to gain the support and involvement of your CEO.

In many successful organisations it is not the culture to simply send a directive from the corporate centre instructing the organisation to follow the new talent policy. However, by listening to their concerns and where appropriate make an adjustment you will gain their support as they feel they have been consulted and you have addressed the points they made. The Japanese call this process *nemawashi*, and while it can prolong the decision-making process, it often creates more enduring, sustainable change.

INCLUSION IS A MINDSET

EXAMPLES OF USING LOCAL DIVERSITY

The Egg McMuffin was not invented by McDonald's corporate research and development team but by a single franchise owner in California who experimented with various breakfast items. At that time (1972) they only served lunch and dinner, and from the creative spirit of one individual McDonald's could globally launch a new offering that led to significant new business. By welcoming the diversity of ideas coming from all levels of staff, McDonald's benefited from a major new revenue stream.

Sue Chambers, VP Operations at Goodlife, a Canadian fitness centre group, explained that in one of their clubs on the west coast of Canada (which has a high Asian population) Goodlife employed an Asian sales person who could speak the language of many people living in that community. They also led the translation of marketing materials and contracts into the appropriate languages. When they opened a club where there was a large Indian population with Punjabi as the most common language, Sue said, 'Even though the manager of the club was not Indian they ensured that their staff reflected the local population's ethnicity. Membership increased above our expectations.'

At Panasonic in Europe, as part of the induction process, new staff were given information and practical examples of working for a Japanese company and aspects of the culture. They may well have had a Japanese boss and it was useful for the newcomers to have some insights into issues such as the decision-making process.

In all these examples each of the organisations benefited both financially and because their staff felt empowered to make decisions or be listened to by their organisation.

HOW AN INCLUSIVE STRATEGY HELPED HITACHI RAIL TO SUCCEED

Hitachi Rail has strategically gone out to market to acquire people with both the right skills and experience and also the ability to work in a Japanese culture. Hitachi has taken a bold decision to locate its HQ for its global rail business outside Japan but Alistair Dormer, CEO, and many of his team regularly travel to Japan to discuss business issues and gain approval for their expansion plans.

Hitachi then decided to develop their business in India. Initially ten Japanese expats were sent from Japan to study the business opportunities and develop relationships with key Indian decision makers. When Alistair visited India and met the ten expats he soon realised that this was not the right strategy as they did not know the business in India and faced difficulties in communicating with the appropriate officials.

One of the first decisions he made was to hire a local team headed up by an experienced Indian manager who knew the Indian rail sector and who personally knew who to talk to in order to win business. The Japanese expats mostly returned to Japan, and within a short period of time Hitachi started to gain a foothold in a large and growing market. Alistair told us: 'Rail deals are very political and you need local talent to secure and build the business.'

AN INCLUSIVE APPROACH AT OXFAM

Sarah Ireland, Head of Organisational Effectiveness at Oxfam, has worked there for 13 years in a number of different regions. During that time, Oxfam shifted its policy from simply sending expats to overseas projects/emergencies to a greater emphasis on recruiting local staff. Between 2002 and 2005 there were 250 staff working for Oxfam in Afghanistan, including 100 from overseas. However, after three years there were only five from overseas. It was recognised that local staff not only could communicate in the local languages but had a greater grasp of the culture and the overall complexity of the political situation.

The benefits of taking this strategy for Oxfam were that they saved money by not sending so many expats to Afghanistan and also improved the motivation of their Afghan staff by giving an opportunity to their colleagues.

Oxfam have decided to shift their International HQ from the UK to Nairobi, as their ambition is to be more globally balanced. This is the international equivalent of London 2012 shifting its interview room from a skyscraper in central London to the community centre in east London. In both cases, the organisation is moving towards the talent, rather than the other way round.

INCLUSION IS GLOBAL

Einstein said that everybody is a genius, but if you judge a fish on its ability to climb a tree, it will live its whole life believing it is stupid. Talent is everywhere in an organisation, not just residing in those selected as part of a high-potential scheme. We mentioned this theme in Chapter 1 when we talked about maximising the potential of a multi-generational, multi-cultural, cross-organisational, inclusive workforce (Talent 4.0). The challenge is for organisations to create a context where all talent can flourish and to recognise that talent exists in all geographies and at all levels of the organisation.

Instead of organisations being isolated, internally facing constructs, they are now interdependent parts of a global system. The boundary between what is 'internal' and what is 'external' will blur further. Employees and contractors are now interchangeable. The contract between individual and organisation will change dramatically. An ecosystem of co-dependence has emerged.

In Chapter 1 we discussed risk, resilience and productivity with examples from Chilean fish farms, Lehman Brothers and *On the Origin of Species*. In Chapter 2 we looked back at how a segregated mindset had evolved. In this chapter we have analysed megatrends and locally rooted global diversity. The future belongs to those who understand these – and then proceed to use diversity to mitigate risk, strengthen resilience and enhance productivity.

KEY TAKEAWAYS

1 We are facing three demographic megatrends – rising population in Africa and Asia, ageing populations in the West and parts of Asia and declining birth rates in several advanced economies, to below replacement levels in several instances. HTM is ill equipped to deal with this.

2 We are in the midst of a technological revolution that is replacing professional labour, creating information overload and leading to subsequent filtering. Inclusion is vitally important in countering bias and segregation in the generation of knowledge.

3 Diversity is geographically rooted at regional as well as organisational scales. Rather than ignore this, or simply transfer expats around an internal mobility system, ITM proposes leveraging and sharing best practice, which makes better use of resources and reduces costs.

4 There are significant regional variations in attitudes towards diversity, especially LGBT and gender issues, and how to cope with a multi-generational workforce. HTM policies tend to downplay these diversity traits and so fail to capitalise on increased productivity and innovation that could otherwise result.

5 Global ITM is hard due to bias and trust issues at the individual level, as well as regulatory and mobility issues at the regional level. But, as the examples of Hitachi and Oxfam detailed in this chapter demonstrate, it can be done.

NOTES

1   PWC's Megatrends, Demographic and Social Changes (2015/16).

2   *Guardian* (10 July 2014) Urban population boom poses massive challenges for Africa and Asia, *Guardian*, www.theguardian.com/global-development/2014/jul/10/urban-population-growth-africa-asia-united-nations

3   National Science Board, 2012.

4   The 2002 United Nations report *World Population Ageing: 1950–2050* provides startling evidence that HR management needs to take urgent steps when considering their strategic workforce plan (SWP).

5   Susskind, R and Susskind, D (2015) *The Future of the Professions*, Oxford University Press.

6   Bruno is a data scientist in the Innovation labs at the World Bank. His primary responsibilities are to lead the work on Big Data initiatives.

7   Interview with Bruno, Madin Saleh, Saudi Arabia, February 2016. Ochlocracy is the rule of government by mob or a mass of people, or the intimidation of legitimate authorities. As a pejorative for majoritarianism, it is akin to the

Latin phrase *mobile vulgus* meaning 'the fickle crowd', from which the English term 'mob' was originally derived in the 1680s. Ochlocracy ('rule of the general populace') is democracy ('rule of the people') spoiled by demagoguery, 'tyranny of the majority' and the rule of passion over reason, just as oligarchy ('rule of a few') is aristocracy ('rule of the best') spoiled by corruption, and tyranny is monarchy spoiled by lack of virtue. Ochlocracy is synonymous in meaning and usage to the modern, informal term 'mobocracy', which emerged from a much more recent colloquial etymology.

8 Bishop, B (2004) *The Big Sort: Why the clustering of like-minded America is tearing us apart,* Houghton Mifflin.

9 www.teachfirst.org.uk

10 Wilcocks, L and Lacity, M (2009) *The Practice of Outsourcing*, Palgrave Macmillan.

11 Bisson *et al* (2010) *Global Forces: An introduction, McKinsey Quarterly Review.*

12 Castellano, WG (2013) *Practices for Engaging the 21st Century Workforce: Challenges of talent management in a changing workplace*, Pearson FT Press.

13 Lane, K and Pollner, F (2008) How to address China's talent shortage, *McKinsey Quarterly Review*.

14 Farrell, D and Grant, J (2005) China's looming talent shortage, *McKinsey Quarterly Review*.

15 Mercer (2014) *Diversity and Inclusion: An Asia Pacific perspective*, Mercer, www.mercer.com/content/dam/mercer/attachments/asia-pacific/asia/Mercer_Diversity_and_Inclusion_An_Asia_Pacific_Perspective_ExecutiveSummary_10661D-HC.pdf

16 Society for Human Resource Management (2009) *Global Diversity and Inclusion: Perceptions, practices and attitudes*, SHRM, http://graphics.eiu.com/upload/eb/DiversityandInclusion.pdf

17 https://en.wikipedia.org

18 http://fairlanguages.com/what-are-the-top-5-world-languages-in-2050/

19 http://fairlanguages.com/what-are-the-top-5-world-languages-in-2050/

20 Verotti Farah, AG (2013) The value of a second language in Brazil, *The Brazil Business*, 13 May, http://thebrazilbusiness.com/article/the-value-of-a-second-language-in-brazil

21 Deloitte (2015) *Mind the Gaps: The 2015 Deloitte Millennial Survey*, Deloitte, www2.deloitte.com/content/dam/Deloitte/global/Documents/About-Deloitte/gx-wef-2015-millennial-survey-executivesummary.pdf

22 Evolving talent strategy to match the new workforce reality. PwC, University of Southern California and London Business School announced results of a two-year global generational study.

23 Hunt, V., Layton, D and Prince, S (January 2015) Why diversity matters, www.mckinsey.com/business-functions/organization/our-insights/why-diversity-matters

24 Yi, A (July 2011) *Mind the Gap: Half of Asia's Boards have no women, a risky position for governance and growth*, Korn Ferry.

25 *The Times*, 12 February 2016, p. 25.

26 World Economic Forum (2014) *The Global Gender Gap Report*, World Economic Forum.

27 Translates as 'raven's mother', meaning a bird that has flown the nest and by implication abrogated responsibility for its offspring.

28 www.pewresearch.org/fact-tank/2013/12/20/the-link-between-parental-leave-and-the-gender-pay-gap/

29 Charles Radcliffe, OHCHR video.

30 Tradition and religion have been used in the past to justify some savage practices including slavery, child marriage, denial of property and inheritance rights to women and female genital mutilation. Sexual orientation has not yet been used to justify anything like this. That's why opposition to it requires strong statements as espoused by the former British Defence Minister Sir Gerald Howarth. Regarding the UK Government's plans for equal marriage, he said there were plenty of people 'in the aggressive homosexual community who see this as but a stepping stone to something even further'. In the absence of facts, people resort to hypothesising about what they fear might happen.

31 See previous footnote.

32 See www.hrc.org and in conversation with Steve Humerickhouse, February 2016.

33 ILGA league table, International Lesbian, Gay, Bisexual, Trans and Intersex Association.

34 Deloitte Press Release (13 February 2014) Deloitte celebrates first year of military support.

35 Grove, J (28 March 2014) State pupils on same grades as private counterparts get better degrees, *Times Higher Education Supplement*.

36 Mitchell, C, Ray, RL and Van Ark, B (2013) *CEO Challenge 2013*, Conference Board, www.conference-board.org/retrievefile.cfm?filename=TCB_R-1523-13-RR_CEO-Challenge-2013-Report1.pdf&type=subsite

4

INCLUSIVE TALENT MANAGEMENT

In the first two chapters we showed how HTM falls short and the historical and personal reasons why a segregated mindset prevails. In Chapter 3 we looked to the future and came to the conclusion that HTM is unprepared to handle it. If we acknowledge we prefer sameness, but understand we need difference, then the only way to bridge our cognitive dissonance is through leadership. This is the essence of ITM.

We'll start with a few counterfactuals, a reminder of the consequences of HTM, before laying out the conceptual framework for ITM and the five-point business case for adopting ITM in your organisation.

CORPORATE DODOS

For over a century, Kodak was synonymous with photography. People would even refer to 'Kodak moments'. In 2012 the Eastman Kodak Company declared itself bankrupt. What went wrong?

In the 1980s Kodak owned about 80 per cent of the consumer film products market. They established a competitive intelligence department. Mary-Frances Winters, fresh out of a Kodak-sponsored executive masters of business administration programme, was charged with gathering competitive intelligence on Fuji. According to Mary-Frances, 'As early as the late seventies, Kodak showed that it was myopic in its thinking. They did not think that Fuji or any other company could compete with the Goliath Kodak.'[1]

Before the days of the internet, Mary-Frances analysed Fuji over nine months, using legal means, and discovered that Fuji planned to expand to the US market, even building plants in the US. When she took this information to the executive team, they thought her findings were totally inaccurate and that consumers, especially in the US, would always be loyal to Kodak. One executive actually said, 'I am sure that there will never be green boxes on the K-Mart shelves.'

Fuji became a formidable competitor to Kodak when film was still the primary means of capturing pictures. Winters describes the Kodak environment as one where new ideas were not only rejected but those who veered too far from groupthink were actually punished. Her boss told her that after her presentation on Fuji some of the executives wanted her to be fired for bringing such 'rubbish' to them. Winters left the company two years later to start her own business, which continues today.

In 2007 Nokia was the world's dominant mobile phone maker and enjoyed over 50 per cent market share. In 2013 it was bought by Microsoft for one-fifth of its previous market capitalisation as it hung on to a paltry 3 per cent market share. What went wrong?

In the early 1990s Nokia offloaded all its 'non-core' activities to focus solely on telecoms. This was at the same time as companies such as BT were starting to diversify out of telecoms to enter new markets. Nokia excelled at hardware but downplayed software. Apple, for example, appreciated the need for both and indeed encouraged multi-disciplinary teams, to stunning effect. Even today, Google places conscious emphasis on investing in sectors that do not appear currently lucrative, and gives its employees 20 per cent experimentation time, as a conscious risk mitigation strategy to be able to back the next big idea. Nokia put all its eggs in the hardware basket.

Swissair was a Swiss icon. It was synonymous with all that was reputable about Switzerland – safety, reliability and high standards. For most of its 71 years it was known as the 'flying bank' in view of its financial stability. In 2002 Swissair was declared bankrupt and the Swiss icon died. It was replaced by Swiss, a new airline and bought by German rival Lufthansa in 2005. What went wrong?

In the 1990s, facing varied commercial pressures, not least Switzerland's extremely limited internal market and exclusion from the EU, Philippe Bruggisser the Chief Operating Officer from 1996 pursued the 'Hunter strategy' designed by the consulting firm McKinsey. This was based on an aggressive acquisition strategy. Hubris had indeed come before the fall. The report into the collapse of the company highlighted the lack of board oversight of executive decision-making, particularly in relation to this over-expansion and its inability to meet its financial commitments. In scenes reminiscent of Lehman Brothers during the lead up to the 2008 financial crisis, challenges to the strategy were not welcomed, until it was too late.

In the examples of Kodak, Nokia and Swissair we see the consequences of largely homogeneous, mostly male teams insufficiently checked by different people with different points of view. These counterfactuals lead us to the simple business case for ITM, detailed in Figure 4.1. In the case of Lehman Brothers, the person who advocated a diversified strategy was actually fired in March 2005. Usually, intolerance of difference takes more subtle forms. In many instances it can be an unconscious refusal to allow different people into 'the club'. ITM advocates attracting diverse talent into the club, in order to increase the club's resilience, productivity and decrease its risk exposure.

Figure 4.1 The three-point business case for ITM

Talent management approach	Risk	Resilience	Productivity
HTM	Increases	Lowers	Can increase short run Can lower medium–long run
ITM	Lowers	Increases	Can increase medium–long run, dependent on inclusive leadership

ITM CONCEPTUAL FRAMEWORK

We have previously discussed the cognitive dissonance that arises from people acting differently to their stated intent. Figure 4.2 demonstrates that the principal way to overcome the traditional view of talent is through leadership. This is what the organisation (talent buyer) should do if it wants to engage in ITM.

Figure 4.2 ITM conceptual framework (organisation)

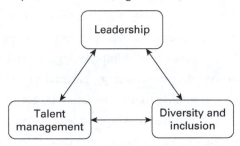

The talent buyer (the organisation) can increase its talent supply through adopting inclusive leadership. Instead of viewing diversity and talent as diametrically opposed, through making an effort to understand different candidates and adapt to different styles the organisation can actually increase its resource base and collective intelligence.

Similarly, the talent supplier (the individual candidate) can increase its value to the organisation through consciously choosing to highlight its different capabilities. Our advice for the candidate, especially those from underrepresented groups, is represented in Figure 4.3. Too often, career

Figure 4.3 ITM conceptual framework (individual)

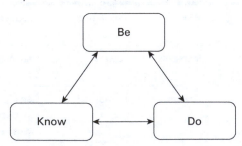

advice in the form of books, peer advice or counsel is to blend in. In the same way, organisations obsess over 'fit' candidates 'fitting in'. This decreases the value of diversity.

First, a candidate needs to 'be' themselves. This can sound trite but staying true to one's own values is a core ethical responsibility as well as a foundation for a happy and productive working experience. It is a candidate's own reference point in decision-making and their source of unique value to the organisation.

'Know' is about the skill set you own. In the London Olympics we replaced 'experience' with 'skills' as we were more interested in the talents a candidate brought to the table in terms of their own career and life, than if they had 'done' the job before. And 'do' is about a person's capacity to act, in line with being themselves and deploying their knowledge.

ITM is about celebrating difference rather than diminishing it. It is a very different approach to first ask ourselves how we can adapt as leaders before demanding that others change to fit our way of interpreting the world. Leadership means asking ourselves how we can absorb the extra work and adaption required in order to allow others to bring their whole selves to work. That's the only way to efficiently (as well as morally) get the best out of people.

ITM AS SHARED VALUE

Figure 4.4 Creating shared value

System	Ecosystem	Financial system	Human resources
Benefits of diversity	Different grasses in plots	Canadian banks during 2008 crisis	Board gender diversity and financial performance
Risks of homogeneity	Chilean fish farms	Lehman Brothers	Kodak, Nokia, Swissair

Inclusive talent management is therefore a call to action. This is not a business case for Diversity 101 or even Diversity 2.0. They can be found all over the internet and you can be the judge of how compelling they are. Figure 4.4 is a summary of what we have learned so far.

Figure 4.5 Approaches to shared value

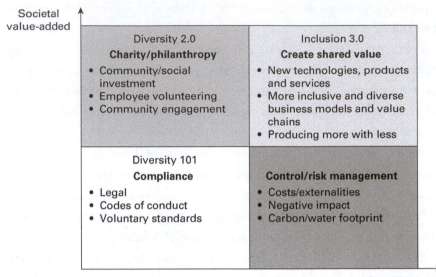

In Figure 4.5[2] we can see how the diversity paradigms play out in terms of creating shared value.[3] Michael Porter of Harvard Business School says that shared value 'involves creating economic value in a way that also creates value for society by addressing its needs and challenges'[4] Shared value is value that is created by organisations for themselves (profit, return on investment, shareholder value and so forth) as well as value for wider society (such as growth, social structure and new environmental solutions). This in turn benefits the organisation, creating a positive feedback loop.

Diversity 101 would sit in the bottom left quadrant. It is based on compliance and codes of conduct. It would create the least amount of shareholder value (which is expected and not a problem for many proponents) but it also adds minimal social value. Diversity 2.0 is an improvement on this situation and can be found in the top left quadrant, involving community investment, employee volunteering and other forms of charitable endeavour. However, it does not add any significant shareholder value, predominantly because it is comprised of a series of net cost initiatives. Only inclusive talent management, Inclusion 3.0, can credibly sit in the upper right quadrant, with a systemic, value-adding approach benefiting both the organisation and wider society. That's why real inclusion is an imperative – for business and for society.

What now follows is the business case for effective, inclusive ITM programmes. We have tried to take a more systemic perspective and offer five arguments based on customers, employees, growth, mathematics and ethics.

THE CASE FOR ITM

1 CUSTOMER GROWTH AND RETENTION

As we witnessed in Chapter 3, the world outside the organisation is changing faster than the world within the organisation. Without radically reflecting that world, the organisation will fail to connect with its customers, may lose market share and die.

The best example of this is the Olympic movement. The baby boomers who watched Seb Coe win Gold in the 1980 and 1984 Games were still watching him and the Olympics in Beijing in 2008 – but the new generation was not.[5] The Olympics fan base was ageing. The younger, more diverse, more global generation, empowered by technology, was not engaged. The most recognised brand in the world was slowly dying. It was in this context that London offered to reconnect the Olympic movement with a new, diverse customer base. That's why, 'in a world of many distractions', London offered to inspire young people to choose sport.[6] The movement chose diversity and inclusion, perhaps without even realising it.

Many current organisations are completely unprepared for the next few years. China will soon be the largest English speaking country in the world. The top quarter of India's population as measured by IQ is greater in number than the entire population of the United States.[7] Facebook has a billion users, is available in seventy languages and would be the third biggest country behind India and China. There are 31 billion searches on Google every month, up from 2.7 billion in 2006.[8] The idea that existing marketing departments full of relatively homogeneous staff can handle this new reality is not plausible.

In a very real sense, therefore, organisations are struggling to catch up with the world around them. Antonio Simoes, Chief Executive of HSBC in the UK, says that his ongoing challenge is to 'mirror our customers and reflect their needs and aspirations'.[9] As a retail bank with the widest possible range of customers and the most diverse marketing campaign of any major financial institution, Antonio has identified that 'our challenge is to keep pace with our customers' constantly changing needs'. The external factors within which

HSBC is operating are dynamic – the challenge is to instil them in the internal dynamics too. To open up and bring them inside the tent. To add value to HSBC by embedding some of that external, infinite diversity in the internal infrastructure where decisions relating to customers are actually made. At the moment, in many organisations, those decisions are being made in a relative vacuum.

The Greek philosopher Heraclitus forewarned us that 'Change is the only constant.'[10] Indeed, right now the pace of economic and technological change is unprecedented. Commentators have labelled current times 'punctuated equilibrium'.[11] In this phase of transition, from homogeneous cultures to heterogeneous ones, from local communities to global ones, from neoclassical economics to complex systems, many organisations are increasingly looking like dinosaurs shortly before they started to die off. Complex system analysis shows us the effects of demographic change, changing consumer tastes and globalisation. How many managers understand diversity as a tool to help build organisation resilience and capability to deal with this new reality?

If you spend five minutes online and watch the video 'Did you know?' on YouTube[12] you may start to question your current organisation. We would go further and suggest that the very idea homogeneous and comparatively static organisations can keep up with rapidly changing consumer tastes, market developments and methods of interaction is frankly laughable. Of course it varies from industry to industry and place to place. We are not talking here about an organisation such as traditional furniture carving business whose very core mission is to maintain 'traditions' often in the face of change. Or an antiques dealer whose value may actually increase in the face of change and people's dislike of it. We are talking here about the majority of organisations who are being outpaced by their customers in the same way teachers are being outpaced by the children in their classroom.

To reach a market audience of 50 million took radio 38 years. To reach the same audience took television 13 years, the internet four years, the iPod three years and Facebook a mere two years.[13] How does traditional market segmentation data work in this new exponential reality? How does an organisation know how different communities view them in real time via social media? How can its traditional recruitment practices run by people educated in a different era possibly keep up with developments that threaten the very survival of the business?

L'Oréal had a rude awakening to this new reality. The world's largest cosmetics and beauty company, it faced a 2005 Supreme Court of California ruling relating to Jack Wiswall, then general manager for designer fragrances. He allegedly told a colleague to fire a dark-skinned sales associate despite the associate's good performance, pointing to a 'sexy' blonde-haired woman and said 'God damn it, get me one that looks like that.'[14] Wiswall retired as President of the luxury products division of L'Oréal USA at the end of 2006. L'Oréal were also prosecuted, along with their recruitment partner (Adecco) a few years ago after a ten-year legal battle over recruiting '*Bleu Blanc Rouge*' – or French people who looked 'French'.[15] In July 2007 the Garnier division and an external employment agency were fined €30,000 for recruitment practices that intentionally excluded non-white women from promoting its shampoo, Fructis Style.[16]

We are not suggesting a token 'employ black person, serve black person' mentality, but we are suggesting that a homogeneous workforce is less prepared, or able, to deal with diverse markets than a diverse workforce. We are suggesting that Jack Wiswall may have been challenged more if he was surrounded by diversity. Homogeneous teams are simply not having the internal conversations that a more reflective, heterogeneous team would do. A diverse workforce can fast forward relationship building with new markets and it can solidify an organisation's citizenship in more communities than might otherwise be the case. It can be a cost effective way of building collective organisational intelligence.

An article in the *Financial Times* highlighted the case of Italy and its stalling growth. Entitled 'Italy's clubby system needs fresh blood', and acknowledging its potential ageism on the one hand, it goes on to say, 'Power networks spanning Telecom Italia, Mediobanca, Pirelli... and RCS Mediagroup... are running out of steam and need new ideas to survive in the face of globalisation and decline.'[17] It suggests that part of the cause of failure is the cross-shareholdings structure that conferred 'clubby power' on some of Italy's largest financial institutions and companies. The change needed takes the form of younger men (and even women) reaching the boardrooms of Italy's organisations, such as Generali, the insurance company. Here, the new Chief Executive Mario Greco, 53, has started to reduce its cross-shareholdings. Shares in the insurer, Europe's third largest by premiums, have 'ticked up by a third'. But Italy is still the country of septuagenarian politician Silvio

Berlusconi, imprisoned for sex with a minor,[18] and octogenarian chairman Giovanni Bazoli of Intesa Sanpaolo, Italy's largest retail bank in terms of assets. In April 2013 he was confirmed chairman for another four years.

2 EMPLOYER BRAND AND REPUTATION

In February 2015 Steve spoke with a class of Harvard undergraduates who were about to graduate. They were seeking career advice. His supposition going into the meeting was that he would offer some thoughts from his career and answer their concerns about the 'real world'. The reality was they were much more in touch with aspects of the real world than the teacher. They had tracked various companies on social media – through their 'official' sites as well as through others such as glassdoor.com to ascertain whether an organisation was telling the truth. They were up to date on how various minority groups viewed the different organisations and what they said about working there. Having experienced diversity during the college years, they are loath to now give it up. The new reality is that many graduates will actively seek 'diverse' organisations because they associate them with creativity, stimulation and fun. They are therefore initiating a virtuous circle of talent and diversity, which firms need to tap into if they want to hire them.

Klaus Schwab, founder of the World Economic Forum, has spoken of the move from capitalism to 'talentism'.[19] Demographic shifts mean that the best talent doesn't necessarily look like it used to – if an organisation is not appealing to diversity then it will lose out. The talent pool is increasingly international and increasingly diverse. The Corporate Leadership Council has undertaken research on the employee value proposition (EVP) and found that with a strong EVP companies can avoid paying a premium to attract the right talent. When most of the new entrants into labour markets in North America and Europe are minorities, the EVP needs to be diverse. Millennials, for example, wants 40 days' holiday per year. Generation X is more concerned with medical coverage. And since recruitment happens overwhelmingly online now, through Linkedin, apps and tagging, it's personal. Since people are infinitely diverse, diversity is in the ascendancy now, irrespective of whether recruiters are switched on, like it or get it.

As well as the personalisation of recruitment, the same dynamics apply to retention. Employees want an 'effective ecosystem'.[20] As well as safety and security, people want to participate in a fulfilling career, to do 'something more than the individual'.[21] In this sense, real inclusion becomes critical in terms of employee engagement. If we are seeking to recruit and retain the best talent, we need to appeal to the individual (infinite) diversity characteristics of each employee. Through adopting real inclusion policies LOCOG achieved employee engagement scores among minority groups that exceeded the average for all employees (which were already very high). This was captured in the regular YourSay staff survey and based on twenty diagnostic questions broken down by diversity monitoring. The fact that employees who identified with a minority group and who 'traditionally' would score less on equivalent surveys scored higher on this one strongly suggests LOCOG was effective in capturing discretionary effort.

Real inclusion is good for employee recruitment and retention. Consider the market for talent, which is in flux as never before; the top ten in-demand jobs in 2015 did not even exist in 2005.[22] The US Department of Labor estimates that the average current student will have 10–14 jobs by the time they are 38 years old. One in four current workers has been with their employer for less than one year.[23] In this mobile market staid organisations will not be able to attract or retain the right talent. Ten years ago, top banks, law firms or government agencies had to compete amongst themselves for the best and the brightest, as they perceived them. Today, the best talent is empowered by technology and information to enter different sectors (technology being the obvious one), to be more discerning in their choices, or to start up their own business. Why would a talented young person choose a discriminating, or even just homogeneous, environment when they have all these other options to choose from where they can be themselves?

As the *Economist* noted in 2006, many in human resources (HR) are unclear about the definition of talent, but it is clear that in increasingly global, increasingly flexible labour markets, diversity is emerging as a key differentiator in attracting such talent.[24] The recruiter Ann Marie Dixon Barrow has evaluated new research based on evolutionary ecosystems that suggests that diversity is essential for future success.[25] If evolution is the result of two forces – variation (diversity) and selection – then diversity (or choice) is a prerequisite of growth. Without choice, the best cannot be selected and therefore growth (amplification) is limited. We are in a time of 'punctuation',[26] when the world is changing rapidly and survival depends on being able to adapt. Variation, selection and adaptation are critical to success.

One of the insights in Laura Liswood's book *The Loudest Duck* is that many corporations seek to build a 'Noah's Ark' of diversity, with two of every kind represented to check all the boxes.[27] Savvy jobseekers see through that now. Whereas Diversity 101 or 2.0 programmes may recruit said 'couples', if they are the only ones in the Ark they may well feel isolated, non-included and leave. Real inclusion is about throwing open the doors beyond token recruitment efforts, or segregated 'initiatives' to systematise the recruitment machine. Only then will a minority have more chance of finding they are not the only one in the house and the tipping point is reached sooner and more comprehensively. Real inclusion is not only a transparent way to recruit diversity; it is also a risk-mitigating way to retain people. Real inclusion can help attract, retain and motivate employees effectively as well as ensuring that all talent pools are aware of the organisation and no talent self selects out, without the organisation even knowing.

3 PRODUCTIVITY AND GROWTH

The immortal line from Bill Clinton's 1992 Presidential campaign, 'It's the Economy, stupid', is as true today as it was then. But in the new digital, information and knowledge economy, human capital replaces natural resources as the basis for growth.[28] Technology is replacing lower-skilled jobs. The threat to growth comes from a shortage of high-skilled talent – and from people being able to be themselves and operate to their true potential. In a situation of resource scarcity it is vital that we maximise the productivity of the resource we do have – our people. Diversity 101 and 2.0 programmes are predominantly 'initiatives' that have a time and financial opportunity cost to growth. However, Inclusion 3.0 programmes instead focus on removing barriers to growth.

Barriers to enhanced quality economic growth and productivity are not just inflexible labour markets and taxes; they are also subconscious bias, implicit associations and sexist and homophobic attitudes that are deeply inefficient, as well as distasteful. In order to compete, an organisation needs everyone working to his or her individual optimum. Gay people kept in the closet, women suffering from glass ceilings and disabled people facing inaccessible environments are all inefficient barriers to more productive employees. In fact, the combined effect of these micro inequities is estimated to cost $64 billion per year in the US alone.[29] That amount represents the annual estimated cost of losing and replacing more than two million American workers who leave their jobs each year due to unfairness and discrimination.

Most of us would accept growth as essential to improving global human welfare. As Porter and Kramer assert in a paper,[30] 'Capitalism is an unparalleled vehicle for meeting human needs.' The 1987 Brundtland Commission report *Our Common Future* defined growth in terms of sustainable development, 'development that meets the needs of the present without compromising the ability of future generations to meet their own needs'.[31] At the 2005 World Summit it was acknowledged that 'quality growth' requires the reconciliation of complex social and economic demands as well as environmental limitations; the oft quoted 'three pillars' of sustainability.

However, after several decades of relative consensus on these definitions, 'the capitalist system is (in fact) under siege'.[32] Stakeholders are unhappy with the way many firms are pursuing growth and people do not believe that growth is improving their quality of life. This is in part because existing definitions of growth fail to sufficiently account for our most precious resource of all – people. Rather than people being the problem, how can we better utilise our human resources to ensure more quality growth?

Business people the world over focus on gaining value from the margin. The proportionately higher returns that come from engaging a new market, a new product, a new insight compared with existing ones. If this is true for markets, why is it not true for people? In increasingly competitive markets, value comes from the margin, from difference – a new way of enlarging the pie for everyone, therefore, is by reaching out to include more people in the pie in the first place.

We need to leverage people's differences in order to extract their marginal value. Therefore a real inclusion strategy, rather than being an 'add-on' or something we think about in terms of corporate social responsibility, should actually be core to a firm/government/economy if that said organisation wants to maximise its human and growth potential.

One example of this would be how we (don't) include disabled people. Most disabled people's talents are under-utilised. For example, because they can't commute to work or the office is inaccessible. Or it may be a less tangible reason, such as lacking self-confidence after years of struggling to defy the stereotype of disabled people in non-disabled people's eyes. There is a cost to failing to unlock the potential of millions of people who could otherwise bring substantial discretionary effort into the workplace. Disabled people with PhDs remain at home because public transport is inaccessible. The wasted potential is infinitely more than the investment required to bring that talent into the fold through a taxi or homework solution. There are easy technological solutions around this for employers committed to inclusion.

Another example would be how we treat lesbian and gay staff. If people feel able to be themselves, they are far more likely to deploy discretionary effort and work harder.[33] One of the reasons thousands of global gay professionals choose to work in London or New York, for example, is because they have equality legislation to protect them and open cultures to allow them to be themselves. This costs the respective cities nothing, but results in significant added income and resource. When gay people remain in the closet they are 10 per cent less productive than when they feel able to be themselves.[34] One recent seminar advocated a 30 per cent productivity increase for LGBT people who could be 'out at work'.[35] Yet 41 per cent of American LGBT workers remain closeted in the office.[36] The amount of energy wasted concealing their identity and making excuses about what they did at the weekend is at the expense of focusing fully on the job.

Understanding and valuing gender diversity when recruiting new staff has been recognised by many organisations as a business imperative. Gender intelligence understands and appreciates the characteristics that distinguish men and women, including attitudinal and behavioural traits that allow organisations to leverage the natural talents that both genders can bring to the table. Organisations that practise gender diversity secure and retain the better talent are able to make better strategic decisions and produce more relevant products and services that more accurately mirror their customers – all leading to superior business results.

Eiko Shinotsuka of the National Personnel Authority of Japan said that the 'insufficient utilisation of women as human resources, particularly in their intellectual resources' was a factor in Japan's slow growth.[37] More women attend college in Latin America than men.[38] This is not, however, reflected in the talent deployment across Latin American organisations. Sixty-eight per cent of the graduates from major art schools worldwide in 2012 were women – yet of the top pieces of art sold worldwide, none were by women.[39] Women received 45 per cent of the PhDs in science in Europe in 2006 yet occupy only 18 per cent of senior research positions.[40] Fortune 500 companies in the top quartile for female board representation outperform those in the lowest quartile by at least 53 per cent return on equity.[41] Colombia Business School and University of Maryland studied the S&P Indexed firms over 15 years and found a gender dividend of 1.6 per cent or $35 million on average.[42] Joe Keefe, Chief Executive of PAX World Mutual Funds, now insists on gender parity at all levels of his organisation from the top team down.

If the above examples of gender, sexual orientation and disability were replicated on a larger scale, unblocking barriers to quality growth such as racism and xenophobia, think of the efficiencies that could result. People perform better when they can be themselves. The problem is, in most organisations people are not able to be themselves. 'Company culture' often thwarts individual personality and, with it, the discretionary effort each individual could otherwise contribute. Even at Facebook, there is an obsession with 'fit' – if HR people continue to search for people who 'fit' with the existing culture, then real inclusion will never be realised. Engagement, discretionary effort and innovation are a feature of people's informal relationships and feelings. They do not come from diversity training. Instead of unfairness and discrimination we can engage people's discretionary effort, marginal productivity (and innovation) through releasing them to be themselves. Indeed, the MD of HireRight, Steve Girdler, talks about the need to 'kill corporate culture, not individual personality'.[43]

Of course, for many HR professionals, this is a big shift in approach from trying to integrate people into an established culture. This approach is not easy, and there is a tension between assimilation and allowing unique spirits to blossom. The art is to find the middle ground so that neither is lost. Yet in many ways, diversity is already present in the organisation – it is simply being inefficiently utilised. The discretionary effort each (diverse) person is capable of, capturing individual marginal productivity, is not being tapped into. By removing barriers such as tolerance of sexist language in meetings, fixed working schedules, alcohol only Friday drinks, steps instead of ramps, and then by marketing that fact to the entire talent pool, stakeholder community and customer base, a great return is possible. Diversity 101 may have brought two each of Noah's Ark into the organisation, but through the methods it has deployed it has created new barriers to their inclusion.

It is a simple, yet important, insight that rather than by constructing a whole host of new initiatives to 'build' a diversity and inclusion programme, we should focus on what barriers we can remove to the potential already present. There are barriers to employee productivity such as sexism and homophobia, and there are other kinds of barriers to suppliers including well-intentioned but overly bureaucratic 'equalities' interventions such as 'equality impact assessments' or sloppy and repetitive monitoring when bidding for contracts and tenders. ITM advocates their removal.

4 CREATIVITY, INNOVATION AND BETTER DECISION MAKING

Chas Bountra is a Professor of Translational Medicine at the Nuffield Department of Clinical Medicine, University of Oxford. At the Rejuvenation Biotechnology Conference San Francisco in August 2015 he highlighted the dangers of homogeneous people pursuing the same strategies. Of the top 10 global pharmaceutical companies, nine publish their pipelines so we can analyse what drugs are in development. Of the 168 molecules being developed to combat cancer, 124 were overlapping between different companies – they are all working on the same ideas, and in secret. Chas concluded that 'this is massively wasteful, unethical and bad for patient outcomes'.

A more inclusive approach involving different people and strategies was needed – transparency, not secrecy; collaboration, not competition; efficiency not wastage; long run not short run. This was not simply about including people, it was about stimulating better innovation. Currently there is a market failure – most pharmaceutical companies have now pulled out of psychiatry and brain research, deeming it too difficult.[44] Instead, they could be crowd sourcing science, pooling resources – creating an ecosystem that can more efficiently and quickly translate science into patient outcomes. Chas' own team at Oxford focuses research on the 'novel stuff' that no one else is researching.

Scott Page, at the University of Michigan, has proven how diversity can trump ability in group decision-making processes. In a nutshell, diversity reduces the average error in decisions. Scott developed the Diversity prediction theorem, whereby:

$$\text{Crowd error} = \text{average error} - \text{diversity}$$

Or, 'our collective ability is equal parts individual ability and collective difference'.[45] In other words, mathematics shows us that the more variation in the pool, the better the selective process. This is key to reducing 'groupthink', the tendency of homogeneous groups to aggressively agree with each other and create a positive feedback loop that may in fact be based on shaky, irrational foundations.

We are all a function of our background and experiences to date. Talent and background carry more or less equal weight in predictive capability and therefore more variation in the current population will lead to a more robust future population in the face of change. As Darwin identified a century ago – if we select from difference, we adapt and innovate and we can subsequently not only survive, we can even thrive. It is intuitively logical that the more diverse the team, the more likely its predictive capability in the face of uncertainty. It seems obvious, yet many organisations still tend to recruit from the 'best' universities, ending up with a highly concentrated pool of highly capable people all with similar skill sets. So if we hire 'brilliant' people from three 'top' universities they may all excel at skills A, B and C. But without other people who did not go to the 'top' universities, who may excel at skills D, E and F, the group lose out on an additional skill set, perspective and challenge to their prior assumptions.

There is a growing and authoritative body of literature on the benefits of diverse teams to decision-making and commercial success. McKinsey's ongoing study profiling gender diversity at board and senior level and demonstrating the correlation to financial performance is authoritative.[46] A Work Foundation report in 2006, *Rising to the Challenge of Diversity*, demonstrated how diversity can lead to lowered groupthink and better ideas.[47] Research from Tufts University demonstrated how diverse groups perform better than homogeneous groups using the example of juries and the legal process. They deployed 200 participants in 29 mock juries. They found that mixed panels of white and black people performed better than only white people or only black people.[48] Real inclusion is about creating 'constructive conflict' where 'diversity in teams creates a positive environment in which ideas synergistically resolve into higher-level outcomes than would be achievable in more homogeneous teams'.[49]

The organisation cannot see its blind spots, and cannot understand what it fails to include. In order to meet the demands of rapidly evolving customers, organisations need to encourage a few of the outliers to come inside the tent and educate their existing 'experts'. We can think of these people as 'tempered radicals'[50] – creative and brilliant, yet 'tempered' in order to be able to interact productively with colleagues inside the tent rather than cause unproductive disharmony. However, 'company culture' deters them. Think about this for a moment. In an effort to be 'inclusive' of 'diversity' we create a company culture that actually repels the very diversity we are in need of.

So how does it play out with these tempered radicals? Well, look at Wikipedia. Wikipedia is the ultimate example of what can happen when you encourage diversity and crowd source from diverse sources – you can build an encyclopaedia.[51] Imagine if organisations adopted a similar approach to Wikipedia's: organisational dynamic encyclopaedias capturing the ultimate marginal returns from outside the organisation. We need to nurture difference, and look after those tempered radicals. Unfortunately, as discussed earlier, most company culture does the exact opposite.

In an environment of real inclusion there is greater potential for internal crowd sourcing of ideas, challenging of ideas and refining ideas in real time. Procter & Gamble's 'Connect and develop' tool increased R&D productivity by 60 per cent.[52] LOCOG's internal, online communication tool *The Knowledge* saved Steve hours of research time by finding people with answers in real time. As we learned from *The Wisdom of Crowds*[53] it is logical that individual life experience to date and bias will limit the ideas any one individual can come up with alone, but diversity improves collective intelligence. Irrespective of IQ to some degree, individual errors will be mitigated by a diverse portfolio, just like with stocks and shares. And, unlike a suite of homogeneous Oxbridge economists, they are unlikely to all make the same error – those decisions can be catastrophic as we witnessed with Swissair, Nokia and Kodak. So having diverse teams can improve the quality of decision making at all organisational levels, reduce groupthink and allow assumptions to be challenged more effectively. Heterogeneous teams are, on average, better than homogeneous teams on creative and complex problems.[54] They increase the number of perspectives, provide better understanding of customer needs and flex management approaches.[55]

However, diversity needs to be managed, in order to avert its negatives, especially unproductive group conflict. Inclusive leadership is required. Diversity and conflict management tools range from the simple Myers Briggs indicator, to the Thomas-Kilmann conflict mode instrument, to six-hat thinking.[56] These all equip teams with tools to manage difference. Even getting peoples names right would be a start.[57]

In 2013 a supercomputer was built that exceeded the computational ability of the human brain.[58] Based on mathematical models, it might be an alternative to our biased minds – and a key aid to improving the decision-making capabilities of (male) boards. We would suggest until this computer becomes widespread, we invest in diversity in the meantime.

5 ETHICS

There is a moral imperative to reach out and include diverse talent in order to ensure inclusivity, efficiency and optimum productivity in a time of increasingly fast paced economic, technological and demographic change.

In the United States, the richest 1 per cent of the population now holds 40 per cent of the nation's wealth while 80 per cent of Americans share only 7 per cent of the country's wealth.[59] Forty per cent of Americans hold a negligible proportion. The widening gulf between 'haves' and 'have-nots', and the overburdened middle class, are destabilising economic as well as social forces.

There is a moral case for action. Inequality is increasing, not just economically to disparate individuals, but socially to whole groups in our societies. This trend is worrying, not least because large chunks of our societies are being left behind, rather like a melting iceberg. On a global scale this has implications for migration and immigration, health programmes, aid and development, geopolitics and war. On a national scale it has implications for social security, infrastructure development, crime and disease. Even at the organisational level, this has implications for recruitment, retention, suppliers, customers and product development.

The gulf between the top and the bottom is now at unprecedented levels. While companies fight for the 'top talent' and salaries go through the roof, some of those deemed 'unemployable' at the bottom are featured in a British television series, *Benefits Street*. Owen Jones described in his book *Chavs* in 2012 how the establishment had demonised the poorest into that one grouping, 'Chavs', in order to minimise their own need to take remedial action.[60]

The fact that life chances are to a large degree determined by where you are born, not your intrinsic worth, is a subject worthy of ethical consideration. The fact that some people were born into privilege and have been able to maintain that social status throughout their life with minimal effort, whereas some people, with equal intrinsic worth as a fellow human being, have remained in the comparative gutter is an issue of pressing ethical concern. One in four children in the UK now grows up in poverty.[61]

Joseph Stiglitz said: 'With inequality at its highest level since before the Depression, a robust recovery will be difficult in the short term, and the American dream – a good life in exchange for hard work – is slowly dying.'[62] Rising inequality and slow or negative growth are in fact intertwined. The *Economist* magazine ran a special feature in its October 2012 edition detailing how inequality is a serious threat facing the United States[63] Stiglitz offers four reasons for this – the middle class not spending, the middle class being 'hollowed out' and not investing in future capability such as education, declining tax receipts, and increasing boom and bust, extremities of the economic cycle.

Ethics has an emotional dimension too. To be clear, emotion has intrinsic worth: to have compassion, to care and to be human. But in addition, emotion is not just an end in itself; emotion is also a business case because through emotion we can reach the parts of our consciousness that a qualitative or commercial argument alone cannot. Advertising uses emotion every day in order to sell us stuff. Stories, rather than numbers, are sometimes far more effective at raising consciousness, providing inspiration and contributing to action.

Consider the graduation speech of a friend of Steve's, Brooke Ellison. She was hit by a car on her way home from high school aged eleven, was paralysed from the neck down and is the first quadriplegic person to graduate from Harvard. She said, 'It is only by way of the work that others do that my paralysis becomes not the totality of my existence, but only a part.'[64] She went on to remind the assembled class of 2004 that we are all paralysed to various degrees: 'There is paralysis of the spirit, which leaves some discouraged in the face of obstacles before them and powerless to make the necessary changes in their lives. There is paralysis of the mind, which leaves some ignorant to new ways of understanding people and the nature of their conditions. And there is paralysis of the heart, manifested in fear or uncertainty, which keeps some stagnant despite all that needs to be done.'

We encourage contemplation on that point. Brooke went on to say, 'the possibilities that await are only significant to the extent that we can view them as collective, and not individual opportunities... just like we are unable to move without the assistance of others, the world cannot move forward without our cooperation.' We are all paralysed to some extent, and by thinking about real inclusion we can begin to cure those paralyses. As Brooke concluded, 'For the spirit there is the potential for hope, for the mind there is understanding, and for the heart there is love.'

FUTURE-PROOF YOUR ORGANISATION FOR THE WORLD TO COME

There will always be a million other priorities that, in many minds, will always come before diversity and inclusion work. In the same way that economic planning is not as 'sexy' as disaster relief, or how action on climate change seems intangible compared with saving an endangered species this year, diversity and inclusion seems abstract in comparison with live organisational and personnel issues right here, today. The reactive impulse triumphs over the pre-emptive intention, even though the latter may in fact be more courageous, more creative and more useful. Yet we ignore the importance and relevance of inclusion at our own future cost. Inclusive organisations are, by definition, future-proofing themselves for the diverse world that is emerging around us.

This book is designed to equip the practitioner with the tools, evidence and the inspiration to bring about real inclusion in their workforce. That is what our increasingly diverse world needs its organisations to now do. When there is no or minimal cost to systematising inclusion, or even cost savings to be gained, then the main barrier to implementation becomes attitude. Whereas additional 101 or 2.0 initiatives require a degree of tolerance, embedding inclusion in existing systems becomes an intellectual and very practical operational challenge. The organisation is one part of life we can control to great personal and societal benefit. It is an area where with leadership you can make a significant contribution to the greater good. With arguments such as those advanced above, the choice to act upon our better instincts comes down in the final analysis to courage and willingness to make a difference.

Sir Tim Berners-Lee, inventor of the World Wide Web, said: 'We need diversity of thought in the world to face the new challenges.'[65] The framing of the challenge is of crucial importance. It will determine how it is perceived by the organisation, as well as suggest the motivation of the practitioner. Assuming we are proposing intelligent, contextualised Inclusion 3.0 work, that adds value to the organisation, the question before us is not therefore why should we engage in such work, but rather why wouldn't we?

In an article in *Forbes* magazine, 'Fostering innovation through a diverse workforce' they interviewed 321 executives with direct responsibility for their D&I programmes.[66] These were large organisations from the USA, Asia Pacific and Europe, the Middle East and Africa. The research concluded that for global organisations to be successful they need to be innovate and creative and this would only be achieved by having a diverse and inclusive workforce. So the real question for us to address in the remainder of this book is, if the case for ITM is so strong, why don't more of us just do it? The answer makes for uncomfortable reading, as the main barrier to achieving ITM may well be you.

KEY TAKEAWAYS

1   There is a simple three-point business case for ITM based on risk, resilience and productivity. The counterfactuals and first four chapters of this book constitute the evidence base.

2   ITM requires the organisation to proactively lead on inclusion and overcome a segregated mindset of talent and diversity. The candidate needs to bring their whole self to the table.

3 There are five compelling reasons for organisations to engage with ITM programmes based on customer relevance, employee attraction, removing barriers to growth, better decision making and ethics. The first four reasons have substantial empirical evidence behind them to make a case for (at minimum) correlation, and the fifth reason will resonate to differing degrees among individuals.

4 Diversity is a reality. Inclusion is a choice. Inclusive leadership is required to help us acknowledge the reality and then frame the conversation in such a way that people have genuine choice and can choose to act.

5 ITM is a way to overcome the limitations of HTM, as well as better acknowledge history and bias. It allows us to better overcome cognitive dissonance and actually add value to the organisation.

NOTES

1 Mary-Frances Winters is President and Founder of the Winters Group and prior to its foundation in 1984 she was affirmative action officer and senior market analyst at Eastman Kodak company, where she worked for 11 years.

2 Jane Nelson, Senior Fellow and Director of Corporate Social Responsibility Initiative, Mossavar-Rahmani Center for Business and Government, kindly shared this diagram with me following a conversation in her office at Harvard in April 2013. She is author of many books and articles on this subject, the latest of which is *Corporate Responsibility Coalitions: The past, present and future of alliances for sustainable capitalism* by David Grayson and Jane Nelson (2013).

3 Adapted from Nelson, J (1998) *Building Competitiveness and Communities: How world class companies are creating shareholder value and societal value,* IBLF in collaboration with the World Bank and UNDP; and Nelson, J (2000) *The Business of Peace: The private sector as a partner in conflict prevention and resolution,* International Alert, Council on Economic Priorities and IBLF.

4 Porter, M and Kramer, M (2011) Creating shared value, *Harvard Business Review,* http://hbr.org/2011/01/the-big-idea-creating-shared-value

5 Five generations are in the workforce: Traditional (born before 1946); baby boomers (born 1946–64); Generation X (born 1965–76); Millennials (born 1977–97); Gen Z (born after 1997).

6 Seb Coe speech, Singapore, 6 July 2005.

7 www.youtube.com/watch?v=YmwwrGV_aiE Karl Fisch, a Colorado teacher, produced this superb video for his high school class. There have since been several updates – and rip-offs.

8 Sullivan, D (2015) Google Hits the Billion monthly unique visits mark, Search Engine Land, 6 January, http://searchengineland.com/google-1-trillion-searches-per-year-212940

9 Conversation with author, Cambridge MA, April 2013.

10 http://en.wikiquote.org/wiki/Heraclitus

11 Stephen Jay Gould, https://en.wikipedia.org/wiki/Punctuated_equilibrium

12 www.youtube.com/watch?v=YmwwrGV_aiE

13 www.youtube.com/watch?v=C1LiJuUGpyY

14 http://en.wikipedia.org/wiki/L'Oréal#Advertising

15 *The Guardian* (7 July 2007) You're worth it – if white. L'Oréal guilty of racism

16 Conversation with Steve Girdler, 16 July 2013.

17 *Financial Times*, www.ft.com/intl/cms/s/0/7ef79b48-adaf-11e2-a2c7-00144feabdc0.html#axzz2ZyAImxDI

18 Sky News (2013) Bunga Bunga trial: Silvio Berlusconi guilty, http://news.sky.com/story/1107593/bunga-bunga-trial-silvio-berlusconi-guilty

19 Klaus Schwab, conversation in Nai Pyi Taw, June 2013 in response to question from Lucian Tarnowski.

20 Brown, J (2013) Future 2020 workplace workshop at Workplace Forum on Inclusion Minneapolis, 11 April 2013.

21 Brown, J (2013) Future 2020 workplace workshop at Workplace Forum on Inclusion Minneapolis, 11 April 2013.

22 www.youtube.com/watch?v=C1LiJuUGpyY

23 www.youtube.com/watch?v=C1LiJuUGpyY

24 *The Economist* (5 October 2006) The Search for Talent.

25 Ann-Marie Dixon-Barrow has over 20 years' experience delivering effective, practical, diverse solutions. This has involved developing innovative programmes to assist diverse professionals to obtain senior roles.

26 The world is changing rapidly and survival depends on being able to adapt.

27 Liswood, L (2009) *The Loudest Duck*, Wiley.

28 Pellegrino, G, D'Amto, S and Welsberg, A (2011) *The Gender Dividend: Making the burning case for investing in women,* Deloitte.

29 Burns, C (March 2012) *The Costly Business of Discrimination*, Centre for American Progress.

30 Porter, ME and Kramer, MR (2011) Creating shared value, *Harvard Business Review*, January–February.

31 Hinrichsen, D (1987) *Our Common Future: The Brundtland Report explained*, Earthscan Publications.

32 Porter, ME and Kramer, MR (2011) Creating shared value, *Harvard Business Review*, January–February.

33 Snyder, K (2003) *Lavender Road to Success: The career guide for the gay community*, Ten Speed Press.

34 Boulton, L (2013) Gay Advocates await Fortune 500's Jason Collins, *Financial Advisor*, 14 May.

35 Goldman Sachs presentation at The Conference Board, NYC, 26 June 2013.

36 Center for Talent Innovation (2013) The power of out 2.0: LGBT in the workplace, NYC.

37 Pellegrino, G, D'Amato, S and Weisberg, A (2011) *The Gender Dividend: Making the case for investing in women*, Deloitte.

38 Pages, C and Priras, C (2010) *The Gender Dividend: Capitalizing on women's work*, Inter American Development Bank.

39 Drue Katakoa, Fellow YGL, conversation in Myanmar June 2013.

40 Hagel, J, Seeley Broan, J and Davidson, L (2009) *Measuring the Forces of Long Term Change: The 2009 shift index*, Deloitte Development.

41 Joy, L and Carter, NM (2007) *Women's Representation on Corporate Boards*, Catalyst.

42 Ross, D (2010) Some research on the business case for diversity and the attitudes of male executives, Sanford C. Bernstein and Co. Center for Leadership and Ethics at Colombia Business School Symposium on DIversity at the Top, 10 December 2010, Deloitte.

43 Conversation with the author.

44 www.theguardian.com/science/2011/jun/13/research-brain-disorders-under-threat

45 Page, SE (2008) *The Difference: How the power of diversity creates better groups, firms, schools and societies*, Princeton University Press.

46 Hunt, V, Layton, D and Prince, S (2015) Why diversity matters, *McKinsey*, January.

47 Jane, A (2006) *Rising to the Challenge of Diversity*, The Work Foundation.

48 *Science Daily* (2006) Racial diversity improves group decision making in unexpected ways – according to Tufts University, *Science Daily*, 10 April.

49 Trompenaars, F and Hampden Tierner, C (2012) *Riding the Waves of Innovation*, McGraw Hill, pp. 74–75.

50 Marie Danziger in conversation with co-author Steve Frost in Cambridge, MA in March 2013.

51 http://bits.blogs.nytimes.com/2009/03/30/microsoft-encarta-dies-after-long-battle-with-wikipedia/

52 Martinez, M (16 March 2012) London Vanguard seminar.

53 Surowiecki, J (2005) *The Wisdom of Crowds: Why the many are smarter than the few,* Random House.

54 Trompenaars, F (2007) *Riding the Whirlwind*, The Infinite Ideas Company, p. 77.

55 Trompenaars, F (2007) *Riding the Whirlwind*, The Infinite Ideas Company.

56 Prause, D and Mujtaba, BG (2015) Conflict management practices for diverse workplaces, *Journal of Business Studies Quarterly*, **6** (3).

57 http://laughingsquid.com/bad-with-names-a-comic-about-forgetting-peoples-names-by-doghouse-diaries/

58 www.telegraph.co.uk/news/science/9886455/Mind-of-its-own-building-a-human-brain.html

59 Archer, D (2013) Could America's wealth gap lead to a revolt? *Forbes/Leadership*, 4 September.

60 Jones, O (2012) *Chavs*, Verso Books.

61 www.cpag.org.uk/child-poverty-facts-and-figures

62 Stiglitz , J (2013) The price of inequality, *New York Times*, http://opinionator.blogs.nytimes.com/2013/01/19/inequality-is-holding-back-the-recovery/

63 *The Economist* (2012) The United States: The rich and the rest, *The Economist*, 13 October.

64 Brooke Ellison class day speech, Harvard Kennedy School, May 2004.

65 http://thinkexist.com/quotes/tim_berners-lee/

66 *Forbes* (2011) Global diversity and inclusion: Fostering Innovation through a diverse workforce, *Forbes/Insights*, July.

PART TWO

HOW TO MEET THE CHALLENGE

Now we show how ITM works in practice. We identify a number of key stages in the talent management cycle and describe how you can create a more diverse and inclusive workforce by intervening in the right place at the right time. These recommendations are backed up with practical examples from organisations we interviewed.

In 2015 58 per cent of UK organisations had a formal diversity strategy.[1] However, many of these organisations are stuck in Diversity 101 or 2.0 approaches and could learn a lot from the subsequent pages. In addition, there is still a significant difference between public and private sector (87 per cent versus 47 per cent). This is an example of where the private sector can learn lessons from the public sector, which has been more proactive.

To the disappointment of the alpha executive, we can confirm there is no silver bullet available. Instead, there are millions of little arrows that can all help point your organisation in a more inclusive direction. The good news is they fall into two buckets, systems and leadership.

SYSTEMS

These are process changes, often small and on their own not revolutionary – but collectively they can change the world. We call them nudges. As we learned in Chapter 2, nudges are practical interventions designed to alter our frame of decision making.[2] For example, if retailers discount larger quantities of goods we are more likely to buy in bulk. The great thing about nudges is that they affect our unconscious decision making by changing our decision-making environment. They don't rely on 'training'.

We think we are objective when making decisions, but this is an illusion, because we always rely on our cumulative experiences to date, which are unique to ourselves and are therefore, by definition, biased. We rely on heuristics, such as stereotypes, rather than the facts – the facts are often hidden underneath the veneer we put on things to act as a cognitive short cut.

It's very hard to change people, much easier to change the environment within which they make decisions. In a Harvard Kennedy School study[3] a more diverse recruitment resulted when candidates were presented in groups, rather than relying on traditional 1–1 interviews. The group effect decreases the effect of individual unconscious bias, meaning that when women were judged 1–1 (by male or female interviewers) they were judged with a strong gender stereotype. When they were judged alongside men, 'factual' things in past performance dominated. The 'nudge' increased the objectivity of the process and produced a more merit-based (and diverse) result. Changing the environment, the frame of reference within which we make decisions, can lead to greater diversity.

In Chapter 5 we challenge current recruitment methodologies used by many organisations. In several cases, our interviews prompted them to question their own internal processes when they discovered they were relying on HTM processes for recruiting staff.

Chapter 6 examines better ways to develop staff by taking an inclusive approach. We explore the decision-making process in the assessment of people, and consider how that determines who achieves promotion and features in succession plans. We outline how important it is that development aligns with career plans and people are assessed using a transparent, fair and objective process that does not inadvertently discriminate.

Chapter 7 concentrates on retention, and demonstrates how ITM can better keep diverse talent. Organisations now need to provide multiple career paths for their people. We identify ten reasons people leave their organisations and suggest practical steps to improve retention.

LEADERSHIP

The second bucket of arrows concerns leadership. At core, it is about taking personal responsibility for becoming more conscious of the unconscious decisions we take every day, and reconciling personal interest with collective good. This, in turn, can also be in our own self-interest, and builds on what we learnt in Part One about zero sum games and enlarging pies.

Chapter 8 analyses inclusive leadership actions top down from the CEO and key directors, outlining the crucial responsibility they have in promoting and embedding an inclusive talent strategy. Our interviews with a number of CEOs reveal their motivation for championing diversity within their business and how their own personal history influenced their perspective. We share insights on how their active involvement has made a difference.

As leadership can be exercised at any level, we also discuss leadership bottom up. It is perhaps the most important chapter of the book because it concerns what the reader (that's you) can personally do and that doesn't need the permission, resources, or even time of anyone else.

Systems (nudges, tackling the unconscious) as well as leadership (consciously taking personal responsibility for inclusion) are both required in order to embed ITM. Figure 5.1 summarises this and as the pages that follow will demonstrate, it can be done.

Figure 5.0 How to manage talent inclusively

Systemic Unconscious (nudges)			Leadership Conscious (behaviour)		
Recruitment	Promotion	Retention	Understand	Lead	Deliver
Chapter 5	Chapter 6	Chapter 7	Chapter 8		

NOTES

1   The CIPD/Hays Resourcing and Talent Planning Report (2015).

2   For example, Thaler and Sunstein have developed a theory of nudges.

3   Bohnet, I., van Geen, A. and Bazerman, M. (n.d.) When Performance Dominates Gender Bias: Joint vs separate evaluation, Harvard Kennedy School.

5

ITM IN RECRUITMENT – FINDING DIVERSE TALENT

Recruiting people is like a love affair. There has to be attraction on both sides. Just as in love, we are irrational, yet we try and appear rational and frequently give verbose justifications for our sometimes questionable decisions.

In an HTM world, the recruiter (let's say the man) has historically had more power than the candidate (let's say the woman). We are being purposely very hetero-normative here, as it's HTM after all. However, things have changed. Now there is more balance in the relationship (phew) and increasingly the candidate has more information, and more options, than ever before.

Just as in love, there are problems. In one sense, the whole process of recruitment is a process of discrimination. We reject those we find unattractive, who we don't want to associate with, people that will lower our brand or status. We then have to justify why we reject them (but we've developed a whole suite of HR tools to do that).

Figure 5.1 How to recruit inclusively

Demand tool	How to increase demand for diverse talent
Purposeful planning – who do we want?	
1	Create strategic workforce plan and redesign jobs
2	Mobilise data and set targets
3	Change selection criteria and job descriptions
In the moment measures – nudges and leadership	
4	Reduce bias through awareness and nudges
5	Demand a balanced slate for all shortlists
6	Use mixed panels for interviews
7	Hire teams, not just individuals
8	Apportion accountability for decision making
Time efficient ways to go even further	
9	Use technology and algorithms
10	Consciously take risks to widen your portfolio
Supply tool	**How to increase the supply of diverse talent**
Proactive marketing – create the new norm	
1	Make your employee value proposition inclusive
2	Purposefully widen the talent pool
3	Target under-represented groups
Establish concrete talent pathways	
4	Establish a guaranteed interview scheme
5	Set up a returners programme
6	Make use of apprenticeships
7	Establish recruitment action plans with partners
Manage your stakeholders transparently and assertively	
8	Benchmark your recruiters and push them hard
9	Take advantage of government incentives
10	Communicate and set the norm

More than ever, an organisation's recruitment efforts need to be intrinsically linked to the organisation's goals and strategy. For example, if innovation is a key organisational goal, then this needs to be explicitly called out in the recruitment process. Recruitment, and especially 'diversity', can no longer be simply a 'department'. Every recruiter, indeed every employee, should be responsible for diverse hiring rather than having separate 'diversity recruiters'. HR professionals and leaders need to focus not only on the business priorities of today, but predict the skills, capabilities and mind set needed within their teams that will allow them to stay competitive over time.

We can begin the love affair from the supply side (the supply of talent) and we can look at it from the demand side (employer demand for candidates). This is shown in Figure 5.1, which will be our roadmap for this chapter. We start with demand; after all, people have to want and believe in diversity, because these expectations shape behaviours that determine outcomes.[1] If you want diversity, you have to convince people you are serious about it, because otherwise they won't even listen, let alone apply.

HOW TO INCREASE DEMAND FOR DIVERSE TALENT

PURPOSEFUL PLANNING – WHO DO WE WANT?

1 CREATE STRATEGIC WORKFORCE PLAN (SWP) AND REDESIGN JOBS

This is a prerequisite for inclusive recruitment. It is about putting a great deal of forethought into which people/capability you purposefully and deliberately want to develop. Professor Nick Kemsley, at Henley Business School, defines it as 'identifying the people and organisational capability needs of, and risks to, the business strategy... translating them to the workforce, and putting in place plans to deliver what's needed, when it's needed'. In other words, having a people plan for the next three years, rather than responding to panicked calls from line managers to 'find someone' in the next three months.

It's surprising more organisations don't have an SWP since they have the equivalent for other business functions, such as operational planning. An airline wouldn't launch a new route without analysing the competitors. A manufacturer wouldn't launch a new product without forecasting demand and supply capability. Yet HR professionals are accustomed to demands to *fill a vacancy*.

If it's about *plugging a specific hole*, prescribed with a narrow view and exclusive by nature, then it's a tactical approach. Understanding the busy and quiet periods, adjusting the numbers of staff, looking at shift patterns and rostering are important to maximise the effective use of existing resources or a numerical forecast of future resources. But it's very short term and operational. They are focusing on the question 'How much of what we already have do we need in the future'? This is more 'operational workforce planning'.

This question fails to ask 'what will we need that we do not currently have, and what do we have now but will not need in the future?' This may be partly due to the emergence of new technology, different customer requirements and the pace of change. But just as often it is simply a logical and necessary interpretation of the business strategy.

An SWP should:

1 Expand time – have at least a 1–3 year time horizon, as opposed to being lost in the operational here and now. This offers more opportunity to find better talent and develop the processes and environment to develop and engage it, rather than take the first candidate we find that 'fits'.

2 Expand space – by working across the whole organisation, we are not beholden to particular departments or individuals. It then allows us to see beyond silos and challenge vested interests and identify organisational level talent solutions.

3 Achieve economies of scale – we can save money, not only by looking for efficiencies in advance (eg bundling hires, bringing forward or delaying hiring according to market need) but also by reducing attrition through rushed, bad hires.

4 Manage strategic risk – we get to identify people risks to strategic execution sufficiently in advance to do something about them and hopefully steal a competitive advantage.

Taking a longer-term view, seeing the organisation as a whole and thinking of scale enables managers to fish in a larger talent pool, naturally opening up the opportunity to attract and select a more diverse range of people.

An SWP also offers the opportunity for micro-improvements, such as job redesign, to future-proof opportunities and appeal to diverse new talent. Rather than shoehorn flexible working practices into a 20th-century business model, use the SWP as an opportunity to redesign jobs in terms of hours, location, job description and agility. Look at the tasks, responsibilities and required skills (not necessarily experiences) and remove dud criteria that may unjustifiably favour certain people (see Section 3 below).

We discussed the future of jobs in Chapter 3. Alison Maitland emphasises the need to change mindsets around the notion of flexible working so it becomes a 'right for all' and not just a 'privilege for the few'.[2] She points out that where employees have real flexibility to select their work patterns around their other personal commitments they still achieve their agreed objectives. This applies to both men and women, and many organisations having introduced flexible systems have also improved the retention of their key talents.

The key point is that an SWP moves recruitment from being reactive to proactive. Make your SWP an inherent part of the business planning cycle, and regularly evaluate it to ensure that your workforce continues to fulfil your strategic objectives.

National Grid

National Grid is responsible for the transmission and distribution of electricity and gas across the UK and has significant holdings in the USA. Currently the bulk of their 24,000 workforce is aged 40–55, predominantly male, and they face a projected shortfall of skilled engineers in the next decade.

Consequently they are actively seeking to attract younger, preferably female, engineers into their workforce. National Grid recognised that where they had mixed teams, they could see more varied thought processes, different conversations and ultimately better-quality decisions. To be able to recruit the type of people they need to achieve their strategic targets their SWP needs to be focused on what a future engineer looks like, not a current one.

They already undertake scenario planning by identifying future sources of talent, attrition rates and upcoming retirements. The organisation is already running a number of talent pipeline programmes, from free learning resources for teachers, to open days and work experience placements. They are actively participating in initiatives between business, government and education to promote career opportunities in their sector.[3]

Avanade

Pamela Maynard is Area President of Europe for Avanade, a provider of digital services. Under her leadership, Avanade has made female recruitment in a traditionally male IT sector a strategic imperative and a key part of its SWP.

In its formative years, the organisation tended to recruit like-minded people. This led to an exclusive culture that initially served them well (as we learned in Part One, homogeneous teams can perform better than diverse teams in the short term). However, in order to grow the business they needed to respond to the requests of their customers. A new mindset was needed that included an emphasis on greater diversity in thinking and the importance of engaging differently with clients. Pamela said,

> In 2011 our focus was on technology, we had 150 men and me. Now we need to grow sustainably. In order to do this we need to change the culture of the business from one that values speed of development, decisiveness and competitiveness in the market place to one that values collaboration and partnerships. Consequently we recognised the urgency to shift the gender balance.

2 MOBILISE DATA AND SET TARGETS

Most organisations claim they want a diverse workforce but have no idea if they are achieving this because they don't measure it. If we value something, we measure it. It would be nonsensical for an organisation to have no data on profit and loss, or a transport organisation to have no data on load factors, or a supermarket to be unsure what goods to stock relative to the composition of the local community. If we agree with the business case in Chapter 4, then we need to be able to measure business performance in the area of diversity and inclusion. Otherwise, how can we say what good looks like, or whether we are getting better or worse?

Good people assume they are fair and hire the 'best' people because they 'treat everyone the same'. However, we know that our systems are biased, our own decision making is biased and if we treat different people 'the same' we end up with unequal results. At minimum, targets show us what good looks like in the absence of our biases messing things up. People often assume that creating targets is some kind of Stalinist intervention in an otherwise perfectly functioning labour market. In fact, data-informed targets are an intelligent and efficient way to correct market failure.

Integrating diversity data in management information is akin to integrating the SWP in annual business planning. It can add significant value as it provokes profound questions, at the right moments, about how an organisation manages its talent.

Most organisations have a breakdown by gender but few have statistics on age, ethnicity, disability and sexual orientation. In order to achieve a statistically high enough sample size you need to conduct an opt-out methodology rather than an opt-in methodology.[4] Data can be collected via staff surveys, engagement surveys or more comprehensively at on-time-sheets boarding, induction or at key moments such as supply of time sheets and banking details.

KPMG

As a professional services firm with a quantitative bias, KPMG was particularly susceptible to the problem of smart people who believed strongly in their own objectivity. The recruitment data for the last three years suggested that the firm was becoming more homogeneous and less diverse, year on year. Good people were hiring in their own image. Projecting forward three years, if this trend continued the firm would have fewer women and ethnic minorities at senior levels unless they took immediate action. When the market and the client base were becoming more diverse, this trend in the opposite direction was unsustainable from a commercial perspective.

KPMG projected the trend it wanted to see, based on the talent that was actually available in the market place and internally at lower levels. Based on proportionality[5] the firm derived targets of what a fully efficient talent market looked like. As Vice Chair Mel Richards said, 'It was a proud moment when KPMG became the first professional services organisation to voluntarily publish such detailed targets, beyond gender, in 2014. It was important for us to establish a benchmark against which we can constantly measure progress and adapt our approach accordingly. I believe organisations should be transparent and collaborative about not just their success but also their challenges on this journey.'

Simmons & Simmons

In 2005 Simmons & Simmons became the first international law firm to measure and publish its diversity data online. It continues to do so[6] and this transparency encourages faster progress than some of its competitors. In 2014/15, 30 per cent of its internal partner promotions were women and the board is now made up of 50 per cent female representation of elected members.

Staffordshire Police

In 2005 sexual orientation monitoring was still taboo, especially in the police service. When Staffordshire Police surveyed their people and asked them to declare their diversity details it showed that only 1 per cent of people identified as lesbian or gay, considerably less than the actual LGBT population. In other words, people didn't feel safe to declare.

They repeated the survey annually and made great efforts at cultural change within the force. Simply asking the questions and giving people the opportunity to declare showed that the Force was serious about making change. Every year, the LGBT declaration rate increased by about 1 per cent and by 2010 a total of 6 per cent of staff identified as LGBT. In five years, Staffordshire Police had changed the culture of the organisation from one where LGBT people stayed in the closet, to one where they could be out. This benefited not just the individuals involved, but all staff, who commented on the improved atmosphere resulting from people being able to be themselves.

3 CHANGE SELECTION CRITERIA AND JOB DESCRIPTIONS

After the Gulf of Mexico disaster, BP included 'assertive' as a new value in a decent attempt to encourage people to speak up and challenge decisions. However, when a white man is assertive he is usually acting within his norm and generally rewarded. When a woman or minority is assertive they may be perceived as acting outside their norm ('bossy') and be penalised. 'Assertive' is in this sense non-inclusive and could be changed in job descriptions and interview scripts.

Figure 5.2 Inclusive selection

Candidate	Sally	Ben	Mo
Stated criteria			
English language skills	4/5	4/5	3/5
Technical expertise	4/5	4/5	5/5
Fit	3/5	4/5	2/5
Subtotal	11/15	12/15	10/15
Scored criteria			
Perceived IQ	4/5	5/5	4/5
Accent	5/5	4/5	3/5
Likeability	4/5	5/5	3/5
Subtotal	13/15	14/15	10/15
Needed criteria			
Gaming ability	3/5	2/5	5/5
Social media skills	3/5	3/5	5/5
Tech savvy	3/5	2/5	4/5
Subtotal	9/15	7/15	14/15
Hiring decision			
HTM total	24/30	26/30	20/30
ITM total	33/45	33/45	34/45

Many organisations still have questionable criteria that they seek in candidates. They reward those who fit and penalise those who don't. Here's a more inclusive way to select.

In a simplified example (Figure 5.2) we rank three candidates by stated criteria (English language skills, technical expertise and 'fit'). Ben comes out top with 12, then Sally with 11 then Mo with 10.

Let's look at the unconscious selection criteria that are really driving the decision-making. The stated criteria are accentuated by unconscious bias. Ben increases his lead due largely to likeability and the associated perception that he is smarter. Mo falls behind because of his accent and the perception that this makes him less intelligent (and less likeable).

Only when we rigorously look at what is really needed in this job (and what's not in the current job description) do we refine our decision making. In fact, the organisation is going through a turbulent period of change and what's really needed are tech-savvy gamers who can help re-launch the firm's brand. Mo scores top on this but these criteria are not part of the selection process because the line manager or HR business partner has overlooked them. When they are included, you can see how Mo nudges ahead of both Sally and Ben.

ITM is concerned with enlarging the toolbox at an organisation's disposal and increasing the diversity of tools on offer to help solve the challenges the organisation faces. Instead of hiring more brilliant (but similar) people, we are actively looking for difference. This is not out of charity, but comes from a pressing need to diversify the toolbox to solve challenges we currently lack the skill set for. The old ways aren't working any more, and 'more Bens' isn't necessarily the answer.

O2

O2 is a UK mobile communications provider. Ann Pickering, HR Director, told us how a visit to a college in East London persuaded her to take a fresh look at their recruitment processes. She was so impressed by the people she met who, due to financial or cultural constraints, chose to live at home despite the fact they could have attended a Russell Group university. Henceforth O2 ignored which university applicants had attended.

On returning to the office, Ann instructed her HR team that future interviews would take place without interviewers having a CV. Instead they would focus on the three factors they felt best impacted success in roles at O2 – judgement, drive and influence. The online process no longer asks for details such as university or gender, in order to minimise unconscious bias.

As a result, the recruiters had access to a significantly bigger pool of talent and decision makers were no longer influenced by a candidate's educational background, freeing them up to focus on the critical success factors.

Penguin Random House

This publisher decided to use Tumblr (social media) to recruit people for their marketing function. This entry level programme targeted people who had an aspiration to work in marketing and may never had considered a career in publishing (which is very homogeneous as an industry).

The programme was designed to assess creativity, as opposed to experience, and was open to everyone including school leavers (aged 16–19), university graduates and those already working.

No CVs were requested and instead they evaluated applicants against seven criteria key to a career in marketing (curiosity, passion for our purpose, ideas and the ability to make them happen, digitally minded, social media savvy, persuasive and adaptable). They received more than 800 applications.

The results? Significantly more diversity in their new starters; a cake business owner and mother of one, a Canadian history graduate, a sixth-form student and a former software sales executive are now on an 18-month programme that includes orientation and two six-month placements in two of Penguin's publishing divisions.[7]

Neil Morrison, Group HR Director stated, 'We are passionate about this new programme because we wanted to hear new voices, see different perspectives and find fresh ways to tell our stories so as to complement the wealth of talent we already have.'

Tate Gallery

Vilma Nikolaidou, Head of Organisational Development at the Tate Gallery, said that they changed the selection criteria for their internships. Internships were previously unpaid and, as a consequence, mostly attracted people from privileged backgrounds. There was also no agreed process so opportunities were not advertised openly and transparently. Vilma told us, 'We changed what was an exclusive system as we wanted to attract a more diverse range of interns and provide more structured learning opportunities.'

In 2011 the Tate changed its policy on internships and introduced payment of the London and National Living Wage for interns. Clear learning objectives had to be established. The selection process came under the control of Human Resources and the opportunities were advertised on the Tate website, circulated to community partners and those on their outreach programmes. As a result they had significantly more applicants from diverse backgrounds and the diversity profile of the interns has changed. When selecting interns the Tate has also focused on longer-term potential, moving away from their previous practice of looking at people's educational background and readiness for the role.

IN THE MOMENT MEASURES – NUDGES AND LEADERSHIP

4 REDUCE BIAS THROUGH AWARENESS AND NUDGES

Unconscious bias (see Chapter 2) is omnipresent in organisations and likely to be more prevalent at times of stress and change (or when recruitment is done in a hurry). It occurs when we use the unconscious 98 per cent of our brain to make decisions rather than our conscious brain. It is impossible to eradicate unconscious bias because *a*) we are not conscious of it and *b*) it fulfils a need – without stereotypes and other cognitive shortcuts we would never get through the day.

First of all, we actually have to acknowledge we are biased. Whether we acknowledge this or not is a choice. We can then decrease bias in two ways – through conscious leadership (self-awareness) and through unconscious system adjustments (nudges). In the first instance, unconscious bias training typically includes tests to illustrate a person's prejudices. It's important to point out that this is an observation, not an accusation – we all have bias whether we like it or not. A good way to become aware of bias is through an Implicit Association Test.[8] These were first introduced in the late 1990s by Anthony Greenwald and Mahzarin Banaji. Essentially, they measure the association between objects, such as 'man' and 'car', or 'woman' and 'housework', and in so doing measure an individual's implicit association (as a measure of bias). More than 14 million tests have been completed since it was introduced in 1998 and so you have a robust bell curve to place yourself upon.

A systemic approach can make use of designed interventions to change decision-making at the point decisions are made. 'Nudges' are practical interventions designed to mitigate bias by gently pushing a recruiter in the direction of inclusive behaviour often without them even realising it. One example is selecting in groups rather than one by one. Another is framing or anchoring questions that lead to an issue being perceived in a different way. Take the response of females to a typical interview question: 'Are you open to an international assignment?' The result is very different if the question is re-phrased as: 'Would you be open to consider an international assignment at some point in the future?' Twenty-five per cent of women were more likely to answer positively in the second framing.[9]

UK Civil Service

In October 2015 the UK Government announced that the Civil Service would begin to process applications on a 'name-blind' basis where only the skills and not the names of applicants are considered. This followed a study commissioned in 2009 that demonstrated racial bias in recruitment, based on differing response rates to identical CVs that happened to have different names indicating racial and cultural background.[10] White-sounding names are currently twice as likely to receive a call back from recruiters than people with ethnic minority sounding names.[11]

John Manzoni, Chief Executive of the Civil Service, said, 'I'm delighted to expand the Civil Service's use of name-blind applications – it's vital we take a lead on this, as I'm confident this important step will help us build an organisation that is even more talented, diverse and effective than it is today.' Organisations who have pledged to recruit on a name-blind basis employ more than 1.8 million people and these include the BBC, the NHS, KPMG, HSBC and Deloitte.

Google

Google has questioned its policy of emphasis on educational background and examination results. Lazlo Bock, SVP of People Operations, said:

> It's one of the flaws in how we assess people — we assume that if you went to Harvard, Stanford or MIT that you're smart. We assume that if you get good grades you will do well at work... There is no relationship between where you went to school and how you did 5, 10, 15 years into your career. So we stopped looking at it.[12]

Instead, Google uses work sample tests or general cognitive ability to minimise unconscious bias related to the impression given by what school you attended. All applicants are interviewed at least four times.

Facebook

Facebook has introduced open source online courses on unconscious bias, available to all via its website. Its founder Mark Zuckerberg stated: 'There are far too few women and ethnic minorities graduating with engineering degrees.'[13] He has repeatedly said that they need a more diverse workforce to create better products for the 1.4 billion people who use Facebook every month. Worldwide, 31 per cent of their workforce are female but only 15 per cent of them are employed as engineers. Only 2.7 per cent are black and only 4 per cent are Hispanic. Facebook is encouraging its recruiters to interview candidates that they may not have otherwise considered.

5 DEMAND A BALANCED SLATE FOR ALL SHORTLISTS

One of the reasons HTM prevails is because HR blames the line manager for not choosing diversity and the line manager blames HR for not supplying diversity. Instead of wallowing in this zero-sum game, simply demand diverse slates. If we value diversity then make it a requirement of what you want to see at interview. Many organisations now insist on at least one woman and one under-represented minority in a pool of candidates for every open position.[14]

National Football League (NFL)

The Rooney rule was introduced in 2003 in the US NFL. (The rule was named after Dan Rooney, owner of the NFL team Pittsburgh Steelers and the then chairman of the League's Diversity committee.) Because 65 per cent of NFL players are African-American but less than 10 per cent of coaches were, the rule required teams to place minorities on the interview slate for a new coach or general manager. In the decade 2002–12 the proportion of minority coaches increased from 10 per cent to 20 per cent. The Rooney rule has raised awareness of hiring head coaches from minorities and the next step is to highlight the case for the benefits it can bring to the teams and their performance.

6 USE MIXED PANELS FOR INTERVIEWS

A partner in a professional services firm admitted privately how he had hired an average male partner. When asked why, he responded: 'The guy had been through so many rounds, met so many people, and it had all been going on so long.' Upon further enquiry, it turns out that the male candidate was originally referred to the firm by a friend in the firm, upon his redundancy from another job. It was a case of the old boy network, a mate helping out a mate. He had indeed been though so many rounds but all the rounds had been 1–1 interviews with other male partners. None of them had thought he was brilliant but all of them had thought he was a nice chap. So rather than make a decision they kept referring him on and on and on, hoping that the next interviewer would make a decision.

Instead, a formal process of mixed panel members (mixed in terms of gender but also in terms of department or function) could have probably eliminated this man earlier on in the process, saving vast amounts of time and money all round. Goldman Sachs, Lloyds Bank and KPMG now insist on at least one female executive in any panel when interviewing prospective candidates for senior level recruitment.

Mixed panels can bring transparency and cognitive rigour to selection. To maximise their effectiveness, have individual panel members come together only after they have individually reviewed the candidates. This will decrease the risk of groupthink and increase insights from different perspectives. Google have introduced a rule that managers cannot interview for their own team.

Leeds University

Leeds University clearly define that for every promotion interview at certain levels there has to be a chair, faculty representative, HR professional and an independent party (who has no direct involvement in the role and who can bring a different perspective). In addition it is stated that there should be no single-sex panels.

7 HIRE TEAMS, NOT JUST INDIVIDUALS

If you take your five-year-old child to the supermarket (never a good idea) they will choose their favourite chocolate bar at the pester-power aisle before checkout. They may scream and shout until they get it, rather like a partner in a professional services firm with their preferred candidate.

If you were to explain to the child that we were not returning to the supermarket for three months and they had to choose enough chocolate bars to last the time, they would choose a selection of different chocolate bars. That's because we put more emphasis on diversity in group selection, or over time. Indeed at the supermarket we discount bulk packs of similar chocolate bars ('family packs') and mark up 'selection boxes' of different sweets. We pay a premium for diversity, because we value it more.

If we apply this analogy to the recruitment process, we should hire in groups as opposed to a 1–1 basis, to reduce unconscious bias.

Following the usual 1–1 style there is every likelihood that the candidates will be partly judged on dud criteria, like attractiveness. And on a 1–1 basis we select candidates individually, unaware of the bigger picture that we keep recruiting similar people. But if they are interviewed at the same time then the evaluation is more likely to be based on their skills and performance – and even if the interviewers are highly sceptical of the business case for diversity they are still unlikely to put through five of the same people – they will prefer a selection box to a family pack. So if you are observing 10 people at an assessment and you have to select five, the five are more likely to be diverse than if you interviewed 10 people 1–1.

LOCOG

It became the new norm at the London 2012 Olympics and Paralympics to hold group interviews. This was initially introduced to speed up the recruitment process and save time and money, as we needed to hire lots of people in a short space of time. However, it became an effective inclusion methodology. The effect of having multiple interviewers (mixed panels) recruiting from a group of diverse candidates (balanced slates) made them more likely to choose a selection of different people rather than a group of similar people.

8 APPORTION ACCOUNTABILITY FOR DECISION MAKING

The example of the partners in a professional services firm passing the decision making buck for hiring an average candidate is what happens in the absence of accountability. Former Barclays Chief Executive Bob Diamond said, 'The evidence of culture is how people behave when no-one is watching.'[15] Indeed, people behave very differently when their decisions are transparent. People expect to be held accountable for profit and loss, so if we value diversity why not hold them to the same standard and make them accountable for the diversity of their recruitment?

LOCOG

At LOCOG, directors and heads of departments were held accountable for their diversity hiring decisions. The recruitment was broken down every month by a range of diversity strands (gender, ethnicity, disability, sexual orientation, local and previously unemployed) as well as by department, and included in the standard management information circulated to all directors. There were no quotas, but the data was tabulated in a league table by performance, so, for example, those departments that had hired most disabled people were top and those that had hired the fewest were at the bottom. To build upon Bob Diamond's observation, people did not want to be at the bottom of the league table and indeed won kudos from colleagues and the CEO for being at the top of the league table. LOCOG created a market in diversity as a public good.

TIME-EFFICIENT WAYS TO GO EVEN FURTHER

9 USE TECHNOLOGY AND ALGORITHMS

Improving the quality of HR forecasting helps organisations be proactive in planning future resources. It also facilitates projecting what percentage of staff will develop into more senior roles and what percentage will need to be recruited. By analysing current workforce data you can determine the competencies necessary to be successful in your organisation and help managers question whether they are the right competencies.

An article in the *New York Times*, 'Can an algorithm hire better than a human?'[16] emphasised the importance of having good data. It challenges our traditional way of recruiting by suggesting that software has the potential to automate and ultimately improve hiring of employees. Of all HR practices recruiting may seem the least likely process to automate. The opportunity to converse with applicants and check whether they 'are a good fit' for your organisation has traditionally been the norm. However, in some organisations this is beginning to change.

Gild

Gild, a Silicon Valley start-up, utilises information from the employer together with publicly available data (say from LinkedIn) in order to find people whose skills match those that the organisation is looking for. The algorithm calculates both whether those identified may be looking for a new role and when could be a good time to contact them, based on where they are in their career. They have identified a more diverse range of candidates than their clients normally do. Also, more women have been put forward for technology roles as well as people from a wider span of ages, educational and socio-economic backgrounds.

Another start-up organisation uses algorithms to analyse the language used in job adverts and they have identified 25,000 phrases that indicate gender bias. Words like top-tier, aggressive and mission critical attract more men. Words like partnerships and passion for learning attract more women.

Firefly Freedom

Deloitte and Standard Life are now using an online and mobile game called Firefly Freedom in their graduate recruitment. Designed by a UK organisation, Arctic Shores, it assesses innovation, creativity and problem-solving abilities of the applicants and takes about 20–30 minutes to complete. The challenges in the game reveal the personality traits and natural preferences of the player.

Rob Fryer, Head of Student Recruitment at Deloitte, said: 'Our intention is to find highly innovative people from less privileged backgrounds who otherwise may have been missed through our traditional recruitment processes.'[17] Deloitte, which recruits around 1,500 graduates and school leavers annually, introduced the game in October 2015 as part of the process to take on 200 young people for their business apprenticeship programme.

Robert Newry, Managing Director and co-founder of Arctic Shores, shared with us the story of a woman who performed very well in the game for one of their clients but had a disastrous result in a separate numerical test. Normally she would have automatically been rejected but the client put her forward to the next part of the selection process as she had demonstrated many of the key characteristics they were looking for.

10 CONSCIOUSLY TAKE RISKS TO WIDEN YOUR PORTFOLIO

The very nature of recruitment can be biased towards conservative, seemingly more risk averse candidates. However, what is risk in this context? Kodak,

Nokia and Lehman Brothers all thought they were 'playing safe' by preferring internal, more conventional candidates. Risk is relative.

Breaking the norm could be more accurately described as brave rather than risky. Hiring someone of a different gender, age group, nationality or ethnic background may stand out more but it doesn't necessarily mean it's more risky. People with the confidence to challenge the status quo may be more able to make necessary changes and challenge current thinking.

Virgin Money

As a challenger bank Virgin Money had a 'quest for better banking' and briefed agency TMP Worldwide on a search for a Head of Innovation. The problem is that brilliant entrepreneurs don't go 'looking for a job', and they think that banking is boring. Simon Wright, Managing Partner at TMP Worldwide, told us: 'We needed a big idea that would get people's attention and show that Virgin money was a creative place to work.' So they invited the press to a secret location and gave them a 'totally immersive assessment experience' before the candidates would experience it.

It consisted of six challenges and involved 22 actors. No preparation was required and they were testing the six skills of lateral thinking, resilience, enterprise, leadership, creativity and curiosity. For example, in one exercise the candidates had to talk their way backstage at a concert. Getting past the bouncer tested resilience. In another, they met an entire football team at half time that was 3–0 down with two injured players. Giving them the half-time pep talk measured leadership.

The journalists loved it and wrote about it, achieving a media reach of 30 million. Virgin Money interviewed ten people and hired Dhiraj Mukherjee, co-founder of Shazam. Dhiraj said, 'This was the most fun I'd had in ages.' When we asked Simon about cost, he said that it cost a fraction of a traditional headhunting exercise while significantly raising the profile of Virgin Money as a destination employer.

Contextual recruitment

Another 'risk' is the perception of 'lowering standards'. However, if a student has gained a B grade when other students in their school gained an average E grade, that may say a lot more about them than the A grade candidate that was coached amongst a cohort of other A grade students their entire schooling. We call this contextual recruitment.

Deloitte now uses contextualised academic data to recruit school leavers and graduates. Deloitte's objective is to ensure that the recruiters are making informed decisions by considering the context by which academic achievements have been made, including their financial background and personal circumstances. They will be given a range of standardised data based on the above points.

The Big Four

The world's four largest professional services firms, KPMG, EY, PwC and Deloitte have all introduced innovative interview selection methods. They learned that always going to the same universities and selecting graduates from the same courses was inadvertently perpetuating a homogeneous talent base. This ultimately ended up with recruits from similar backgrounds with similar life experiences.

The Big Four have publicly questioned their traditional recruitment strategy of hiring graduates with finance-based degrees from top universities. KPMG, for example, has changed the universities and courses it targets. Now graduates are being sought from a wider variety of disciplines as IT, law, humanities, languages and engineering. In addition there is now a greater emphasis on 'softer skills' such as communication, influencing others and the ability to work cross-culturally. This step recognises that the expectations of their clients has changed from a focus on functional skills to developing relationships and being responsive to their needs. It also recognises an understanding within the organisation that more diverse teams provide stronger client solutions.

HOW TO INCREASE THE SUPPLY OF DIVERSE TALENT

If you want a more diverse and inclusive organisation, it's important to start with demand side actions. Otherwise, people fall into the crutch of relying exclusively on supply side measures and relieving themselves of any responsibility to change their own behaviour. Only when you are satisfied that there are significant internal behavioural changes under way can you credibly articulate your position in the market place, otherwise you will increase your supply followed by increasing your attrition as recruits leave soon after being hired. If your organisation is now ready to receive diversity, then read on.

PROACTIVE MARKETING – CREATE THE NEW NORM

1 MAKE YOUR EMPLOYEE VALUE PROPOSITION INCLUSIVE

The Olympic rings were a symbolic rallying cry for many baby boomers. They connected with unconscious thoughts of childhood heroes winning gold in Mexico City, Munich or Los Angeles. They were a brand people wanted to associate with, and definitely to work for. But the rings didn't initially mean much to Millennials in Tower Hamlets, east London.

East London was the heart of the London 2012 Olympics and the turn-around point for the Olympic employment brand. In order to connect the world's most recognised brand with a new diverse generation, changes had to be made. The core values of the brand remained (joy of effort; faster, higher, stronger; celebrating humanity), but the relevance of the brand changed dramatically.

Out went the exclusive feel of a gentleman's club and in came the digital-savvy, open, even brash new brand of London 2012. For one week in 2007 the new London logo was the world's top story – many eminent commentators and members of the status quo reviled it. But it worked with the intended new target audience and helped London 2012 secure the most diverse workforce of any Olympics ever.

An employer brand is better known as the employee value proposition (EVP), and given that recruiting new staff is a significant investment, it's important to make it as efficient and effective as possible. An EVP is the mix of characteristics, benefits and ways of working in an organisation. Sometimes it's referred to as the deal struck between an organisation and employee in return for their contribution and performance. Organisations come unstuck when their EVP doesn't speak to their (new) target audience.

Rio 2016 Olympics and Paralympics Organising Committee

The Rio de Janeiro Organising Committee learned many lessons from London 2012. Their HR Director Henrique Gonzalez told us, 'We learned many assertive actions from London and a few mistakes from FIFA in 2014.'

In the 2014 Rio FIFA World Cup, three EVP mistakes stand out in the news. One, two white presenters were chosen over black presenters in the city of Salvador where 80 per cent of the population is black. Two, when the children entered the stadium with the teams, only three out of 20 were black. Three, Adidas T-shirts were approved that had a negative portrayal of women in an environment with concerns about sexual trafficking. Henrique and the team have used the counterfactual of the World Cup and the positive case study of LOCOG to achieve success in their own EVP and attract some brilliant diverse talent to help stage the Rio Games.

Shell

Shell International is a global oil and gas company. It created a set of fifteen two-minute videos entitled 'Be yourself'. They are freely available online[18] and feature employees with disabilities or families with a disabled member sharing their stories and encouraging disclosure. The objective is to show why it's important to be yourself at work and the positive impact this can have.

Jornt van der Togt, EVP HR Strategy and Internal Communications, stated: 'This is all about helping people to perform better, about our leadership attributes of performance and authenticity, and about our core value of respect for people.'

Rank

Rank Entertainments is a British gambling and leisure company with operations in the UK, Belgium and Spain. It called its EVP initiative PRIDE (people, recruitment, inclusive, diverse and engaged). The company wanted to reflect the authenticity of working life as well as the EVP being a powerful attractor of talent. The organisation also recognised that it has a number of disparate businesses and diverse skillsets. A PRIDE team was established and they consulted 600 of their workforce of 8,700 staff to ask their opinions of what it was like to work for Rank. Within this number they took an inclusive approach by ensuring they received the opinions of all generations and took into account diverse views reflecting gender, ethnicity and other groups. The slogan 'Where everyone counts' was agreed upon and it is now embedded in all their HR activities.[19]

2 PURPOSEFULLY WIDEN THE TALENT POOL

Estelle Hollingsworth, Director of HR, Talent and Diversity and Inclusion at BAE Systems, recognised that they faced a challenge in recruiting a diverse workforce. In early 2015 she spoke at a seminar attended by Millennials and asked who would be interested to join BAE. No one raised their hand.

On returning to her office she discussed this issue with both her HR team and others in different functions and she quickly realised that they had to start fishing in different talent pools as they were in danger of becoming irrelevant to a new generation.

People who lose their job in their 50s will generally find it more difficult to find another job compared with a younger person. Research carried out by Anglia Ruskin University in the UK together with the magazine *People Management* showed that under 30s are 4.25 times more likely to get an interview and 73 per cent of over 50s think they have lost out on a job purely because of their age.[20] This talent pool has potential as millions of workers from the baby boomer generation are increasingly looking to retire later.

Most organisations we interviewed have adopted an open posting approach to internal vacancies. By promoting internal career sites and job openings, businesses have opened up the internal talent pool and supported a more inclusive approach to talent development at the same time as reducing the impact of implicit and unconscious bias in the long-listing process.

Reaching out

The LGBT careers event for MBA students now attracts the world's top recruiters. What was once a niche market for the minority of LGBT candidates that were out, is now a major source of new talent and a way of organisations expanding their talent pool. There are similar MBA career fairs for black talent, women, disabled students and so forth. In fact there is now such a plethora that organisations can pick and choose what to attend and invest in according to their own resource gaps based on their own data.

Mitie

Mitie, a British outsourcing group, partnered with Mosaic (HRH the Prince of Wales' mentoring charity) to provide workshops, mentoring and training programmes for ex-offenders that ultimately lead to a work placement with

Mitie. These activities are designed to help people improve their transferable skills and abilities in networking, presentation and communication. This builds upon an existing Mitie Foundation programme involving an eight-week job placement that has succeeded in getting more than 70 per cent of candidates into employment.

Ruby McGregor-Smith, Chief Executive of Mitie and trustee of the Mitie Foundation, said:

> The Mitie Foundation is dedicated to creating opportunities for people of all backgrounds to join the world of work, by raising aspirations and unlocking people's true potential. We are delighted to be able to support Mosaic's efforts to help those who wish to turn their back on previous criminal activity to get back into the workplace and make a positive contribution to society.[21]

3 TARGET UNDER-REPRESENTED GROUPS

There are several groups that are under-represented due to circumstance and connectivity rather than lack of merit or ability. A pool of talent that organisations often neglect is people with disabilities. In the USA only 20 per cent of the 54 million registered disabled people are working.

South West Trains (SWT)

This British rail operator actively targets disabled people. SWT partnered with the charity Mencap to provide employment opportunities at Waterloo station for people with learning disabilities. Recruits were helped to understand what was needed in the role and were partnered with an experienced employee who could guide them and act as a mentor. Possible barriers were overcome, for example a hand-written check sheet that was a problem for people with dyslexia was changed into a diagrammatic check sheet. At the end of an initial trial period six people were offered permanent roles. Kelly Barlow, HR Director of South West trains, said: 'We found we were tapping into this previously unused talent and what we were getting was great people who are enthusiastic and want the job.'[22]

SAP

SAP is a German multinational software company focused on business operating systems. In Germany it has targeted people with autism as part of its recruitment strategy. Research has indicated that those with a mild form of autism can often perform complex tasks that require high levels of concentration typically much better than the average population. They also exhibit an enhanced ability to find patterns and make connections. A spokesperson for SAP AG noted: 'SAP sees a potential competitive advantage to leverage the unique talents of people with autism, while also helping them to secure meaningful employment.'[23]

LOCOG

At the London Olympics and Paralympics over 2,000 disabled people were placed into Games time roles. One of the key elements for achieving this paradigm shift was that under the 2012 *Access Now* programme all disabled applicants were guaranteed an interview. They were still only offered a role based on merit, but the recruitment team had to ensure that the job descriptions were relevant, specific and did not act as a barrier to possible success. The fact they were guaranteed an interview gave hiring managers the opportunity to meet talented individuals who under other circumstances they would not have met.

Paul Deighton, CEO of the London Olympics and Paralympics, told us: 'The key to success in diversity and inclusion is practical implementation. For example, we hired so many disabled people it became part of the norm.'

Kimberly-Clark

Kimberly-Clark is a US multinational personal care corporation. In 2009 a total of 85 per cent of their customers, but only 17 per cent of its directors, were women.

They discovered two factors in particular affecting the career development of their female staff. First, women were more hesitant than men about putting themselves forward if they did not have all the relevant experience. For example, if there were 10 criteria that were listed as required for a role, women would not apply if they only had eight of them, while men would apply if they had five or more. Second, job descriptions tended to ask for certain experiences that favoured men.

Sue Dodsworth, Kimberly-Clark's Global Diversity Officer, asked all recruiters to focus more on transferable skills when writing job profiles.

Female top talent were given focused development plans indicating skills gaps and agreed career goals. All senior management and critical role openings had to have at least one 'diverse' candidate. And female top talent had high visibility with top management. Their Global Leadership Team took responsibility for increasing the representation of females in senior positions.

Sue told us that Kimberly-Clark wanted to:

> look, think and behave like the people who use our products, so as demographics change we are aiming to ensure that we are in line with what is happening in our consumer base. We now have yearly goals that we measure our progress on a quarterly basis and then present these results to our Board and respective businesses.

By the end of 2015 female directors had increased to 32 per cent and women in middle management roles increased from 29 per cent to 35 per cent.

ESTABLISH CONCRETE TALENT PATHWAYS

4 ESTABLISH A GUARANTEED INTERVIEW SCHEME (GIS)

Disabled candidates are understandably cynical about recruitment initiatives, because the initiatives appear to be very Diversity 101 or 2.0 focused and they smack of tokenism. One of the most effective ways to circumvent this cynicism and connect with untapped talent is to demonstrate intent through guaranteeing interviews to qualified disabled people.

It is perfectly legal, ethical and commercial to target whomever you want. If you want to give a guaranteed interview to any candidate with a disability that meets the selection criteria for your job then why not? You are not guaranteeing someone a job, just the opportunity to interview for a job. But because we know that luck plays an element in any job search why not eliminate the chance element for people who are more cynical and face more challenges than most?

In the UK, the Two Ticks symbol is awarded to organisations that meet specific criteria, such as awareness training to recruiters. The symbol can then be used in recruitment adverts to indicate that the employer welcomes applications from disabled people. The UK Government's programme has been embraced by 3,500 employers.

Lloyds Bank

This bank guarantees an interview to disabled people who meet the minimum requirements of the role. This then provides the opportunity to discuss directly their application and what they can offer to the bank. Part of the ongoing commitment from Lloyds is that they will also guarantee opportunities for career progression. They also run a four-day personal development programme for their disabled staff. During the programme they are encouraged to think about how their disability affects their attitude to life and not just work and how they project themselves to family, friends and colleagues. There is also a disabled employee network (Access) that allows them to share information and receive ongoing support.

5 SET UP A RETURNERS PROGRAMME

To attract talent back to work, for example parents of young children or people post career-leave, organisations will need to be flexible in such issues as working hours, job-share and time off. In many countries there is now legislation ensuring family friendly policies are introduced but this is about going beyond compliance to attract people who might not initially consider you.

Research carried out by the Workforce Institute at Kronos and Workplace Trends focused on the theme of returners who they referred to as 'boomerang employees'.[24] They surveyed over 1,800 HR professionals across the US and concluded that employee engagement should not end when staff leave their organisation. Why let that investment go to waste?

From those who responded, 76 per cent stated that they are willing to re-employ leavers. The data suggests that 46 per cent of Millennials, 33 per cent of Generation X and 29 per cent of baby boomers would consider returning to their previous organisation. An added bonus of attracting back ex-employees is the additional diversity gathered from their experience outside that they bring back inside the organisation. (For more information see shesback.co.uk)

Goldman Sachs

Goldman Sachs launched a returnship programme in 2008 in the Americas which proved so successful that it was introduced in some other regions a few years later. It is targeted at professionals who have been away from the workplace for two years or more and are now seeking to return. Those selected are paid for a 10-week programme and are given opportunities in a variety of divisions. It gives the participants the opportunity to explore new areas of expertise and learn new skills that assist them with returning to the workplace at the firm or elsewhere.

NHS

The NHS has been particularly creative in regions where it has had difficulty in recruiting nurses. In these regions it targeted people who were previously trained as nurses but then left to raise a family and never returned. To help them back into the profession the NHS has offered refresher courses that have successfully attracted back talent with enhanced life skills that are invaluable in nursing.

6 MAKE USE OF APPRENTICESHIPS

Germany is not famous for its diversity and inclusion programmes. However, it is the trailblazer when it comes to apprenticeship programmes. About 60 per cent of German workers train as apprentices, not just in manufacturing but also in IT, banking and hospitality. The dual approach of continuing your studies in parallel with on-the-job training attracts a wide range of people from many different backgrounds. This inclusive strategy allows many young people to realise their passion and many proceed into more senior roles as their career develops.

Volkswagen

In the USA, where less than 5 per cent of young people train as apprentices, car manufacturer Volkswagen targeted unskilled people when they opened a factory in Tennessee. This strategy was surprising, as GM and Chrysler had laid off workers in the same area and there was an experienced pool of workers available. However, Volkswagen felt it could train for the skills they required, and attitude was the most important differentiator in a workforce.

The fact that they had no relevant previous experience made them more open-minded, flexible and willing to commit to the training. The result was that VW hired a more diverse workforce than had it taken the more traditional route of recruiting experienced assembly workers.[25]

7 ESTABLISH RECRUITMENT ACTION PLANS WITH PARTNERS

We have discussed the ecosystem and the idea that an organisation no longer exists in a vacuum. This is never more so than in recruitment. Besides looking internally, besides employing agencies and head-hunters, think even harder and more creatively about who you can partner with to access talent sources that hitherto have been untapped by your recruitment function. There exists a whole infrastructure out there in the voluntary, quasi-governmental, charity as well as commercial sectors dedicated to connecting diverse talent to opportunity. It is literally waiting to be used.

LOCOG

The London Olympics and Paralympics partnered with over 150 local charities and organisations from Elevation Networks and the Stephen Lawrence Trust (targeting talented black youth) to the Gay Business Association to disabled charities. Instead of these organisations lobbying LOCOG to 'take people', the relationship was reversed and they were asked to partner with LOCOG to help find and supply people. Once these organisations were convinced that there was a genuine demand there for diverse talent, they were more willing to help ready diverse talent for opportunities knowing there was more likelihood of a job. As with the GIS, this is to a large extent about combating cynicism.

Royal Mail

Royal Mail is an organisation that has been through significant change. As it transitioned from the public to the private sector this created different challenges and expectations. Liza Strong, Head of Organisational Talent and Diversity, said, 'We had to do things differently in order to thrive in a competitive environment.' To achieve this Liza and her team introduced new innovative and creative features to their resourcing approach. Liza continued: 'It's been a priority to attract more women and people from diverse ethnic backgrounds to reflect our customer base and bring more diverse voices into the workplace.'

A specific step that they took was to change the information they gave to Job Centres and employment agencies. The image of many people, including the staff working in these places, was that heavy lifting was required in many of the Royal Mail roles, and inadvertently making the majority of roles more attractive to men. This excluded many women from applying for jobs. They changed their marketing materials, informally introduced the term 'postie' (trying to avoid using postman), emphasised that trollies were provided to posties (to avoid carrying heavy bags) and they used more balanced imagery in their adverts. In addition, they set gender targets and their agencies were told that they had to provide a gender-balanced list of applicants.

MANAGE YOUR STAKEHOLDERS TRANSPARENTLY AND ASSERTIVELY

8 BENCHMARK YOUR RECRUITERS AND PUSH THEM HARD

The average head-hunter or recruiter has 'time to hire' as their primary KPI. The quicker they hire someone, the faster they get paid and the better the ratio of effort and reward. Rather like an airline that only gets paid when its planes are in the air as opposed to being on the ground, the incentive is to speed up the turnaround time. This causes problems when it comes to diversity.

If you want to challenge the status quo then you need to change the incentives. Change your sourcing model to one where you really are the client rather than the passive recipient of what someone else defines as talent. Place your recruiters in a league table according to female hires (or black talent, or introverts, or whatever the gap in your SWP is) and alter the reward structure accordingly. Bring them together regularly and praise best practice, and regularly exit the bottom 10 per cent of agencies. This will change behaviour. In isolation it is crude and could lead to unfortunate behaviour as head-hunters literally go hunting for women and prioritise gender identity over skill sets. However, as part of a balanced approach, and as part of all the measures we are suggesting in this chapter, we know it is effective.

Avanade

Avanade checks its recruiters are adhering to the instructions given to them, that they ensure a slate of diverse candidates with at least one female in all roles above general manager. They are told why diversity and inclusion is important to Avanade and they are expected to consciously reflect inclusivity in all their actions on behalf of Avanade. Jessica Brookes, Director of Diversity and Inclusion for Avanade in Europe personally meets the recruiting company to emphasise their commitment to diversity and inclusion and why it is a business imperative. Avanade also educates its internal recruiters accordingly.

9 TAKE ADVANTAGE OF GOVERNMENT INCENTIVES

Even in an era of cutbacks and decreased government spending there remain a plethora of programmes and incentives that business can take advantage of. The guaranteed interview scheme has already been mentioned, but additionally in the UK there are government grants for organisations employing 50 or fewer staff to take on apprentices or a fixed sum to take on someone who has been out of work for six months or more.

In Australia incentives are offered to organisations offering work to those aged 50 plus, to employ disabled people and to offer opportunities to school leavers. In Spain national legislation states that organisations over a certain size must employ a proportion of employees who are disabled. Organisations who do not meet the regulations have to pay a penalty.

It's not just about being a passive recipient of government programmes. By positively engaging in them you can help to mould and shape them to better suit your business requirements.

10 COMMUNICATE AND SET THE NORM

If you've made it this far you now have a lot of material to work with and communicate. Communication has to be ongoing and pervasive. When Steve travelled to GECAS in Shannon, Ireland, he was surprised and impressed to find they had posted diversity messages on the back door of the stalls in the staff toilets! These messages advertising a diversity event were guaranteed to get read at least once in the day.

Communications need to be three-way between organisation, employees and potential employees (including alumni). That is the only way to constantly challenge and refresh the EVP and build credibility and relevance in the marketplace.

It's inauthentic to communicate an EVP that is undermined by the reviews your own people leave on social media sites such as glassdoor.com. There is no point trying to communicate how diverse you are as an organisation if the mug shots of your board and executive team are clearly all white men. This is about real, authentic, and to a large extent public communication. When LOCOG started to target black talent it had to be honest that the vast majority of its existing staff were white. By being honest and focusing on what we wanted to achieve, most black applicants welcomed that honesty and applied.

In this chapter we have identified a number of actions that are critical in achieving an inclusive recruitment strategy. These include aligning your people and business strategies, having data to influence your decisions on your future talent needs, taking a wider perspective of your talent requirements, avoiding bias in your recruitment decisions and having a flexible approach to your talent pipeline. We recommend you start with the demand side, follow our suggested sequencing, and manage the expectations of your stakeholders.

KEY TAKEAWAYS

1 Purposeful planning – who do we want and who are we missing? Redefine talent, be proactive in changing your selection criteria and be prepared to take risks.

2 Establish concrete talent pathways – fish in bigger, different pools. Identify and engage with internal staff, ex-employees and other external sources for talent.

3 Create 'in the moment' nudges – don't waste time trying to change people's world view, use data as a critical bedrock to know how you are doing as well as to be taken seriously.

4 Leadership – expand time to hire, overcome thinking in silos and be aware of your bias. Leaders becoming more self-aware is probably the best investment of time you can make in them.

5 Transparent and assertive management of stakeholders. Look in the mirror – do they want to join you? Reshape your EVP to reflect ecosystem intelligence and connectivity.

NOTES

1 For a fuller discussion: Thomas, DA and Ely, RJ (1996) Making differences matter: A new paradigm for managing diversity, *Harvard Business Review*, September/October.

2 The excellent book: Maitland, A and Thomson, P (2011) Future Work: How business can adapt and thrive in the new world of work, Palgrave Macmillan.

3 Warren, C (2015) We know what the future looks like, *Work Magazine*, CIPD, Spring.

4 An opt-out methodology can best be explained via an analogy. Take organ donation. In the UK it is voluntary and there is only a 13 per cent supply rate amongst the population. In Spain, the assumption is that organs would be donated on death and if you don't want to do this then you have to opt out. Their supply rate is 34 per cent. Consequently, an opt-out methodology, with appropriate ethical and legal safeguards, is the preferred route to gaining a statistically high enough sample size.

5 For a fuller discussion of proportionality see Chapters 6 and 7.

6 www.simmons-simmons.com/en/About-Us/Corporate-Responsibility/Inclusion-and-Diversity

7 www.thebookseller.com/news/prh-selects-winners-scheme-307414

8 www.implicit.harvard.edu

9 See distinct nudges described by Nielsen and Kepinski. An excellent description of nudges can be seen on You Tube: 'Nudge, the animation: helping people make better choices' (12 June 2013), designed by Rotman School of Management.

10 Maitland, A and Thompson, P (2011) *Future Work*, Palgrave Macmillan.

11 Crush, P (2015) Government backs 'name-blind' CV's to end discrimination, CIPD, 26 October, www.cipd.co.uk/pm/peoplemanagement/b/weblog/archive/2015/10/26/government-backs-name-blind-cvs-to-end-discrimination.aspx

12 www.linkedin.com/pulse/google-doesnt-really-care-anymore-where-you-went-school-fairchild

13 Seetharamen, D (2015) Facebook is testing the 'Rooney Rule' approach to hiring, *Wall St Journal*, 17 January.

14 Zarya, V (2015) Why is the Rooney rule suddenly Tech's answer to hiring more women?, Forbes, http://fortune.com/2015/08/10/rooney-rule-diversity-in-tech/

15 http://news.bbc.co.uk/today/hi/today/newsid_9630000/9630673.stm

16 Cain Miller, C (2015) Can algorithms hire better than a human? *New York Times*, 25 June, www.nytimes.com/2015/06/26/upshot/can-an-algorithm-hire-better-than-a-human.html?_r=0

17 Coughan, S (25 November 2015) Computer game for Deloitte job-hunters, BBC News.

18 http://businessdisabilityforum.org.uk/about-us/newsletter/archive/2014/march-2014/can-you-be-yourself-at-work-shell-promote-an-inclusive-work-environment/

19 Woods, D (12 December 2011) Rank Insider: interview with Sue Waldock, Group HRD of the Rank Group, *HR Magazine*.

20 Bingham, J (2015) How over 50s face secret discrimination in job applications, *The Telegraph*, 4 August.

21 www.mitie.com/news-centre/news/2014/mitie-and-mosaic-launch-a-new-ex-offender-programme-welcomed-by-the-justice-secretary-chris-grayling

22 (12 November 2015) We were missing talent because we weren't inclusive enough, *People Management Magazine*.

23 www.cio.com/article/3013221/careers-staffing/how-sap-is-hiring-autistic-adults-for-tech-jobs.html

24 Schwabel, D (1 September 2015) Candidates are now competing against Boomerang employees for jobs, *Forbes*.

25 www.talentmgt.com/articles/7333-manufacturing-talent-apprentices-wanted

6

ITM IN PROMOTIONS AND DEVELOPMENT – GROWING DIVERSE TALENT

If recruitment is the love affair, promotions and development are the relationship. Just as in love, people need proof points that the organisation is listening to them and taking their needs seriously, otherwise it might all be over.

After finding diverse talent, organisations need to implement a development strategy that creates constantly recurring opportunities for all employees. That's not being charitable, it's placing intelligent bets. Only by each individual performing to his or her potential will the collective performance of the organisation be maximised. Why have diversity if you're not going to use it?

Development is about nurturing the talent you have, it's a bottom-up approach to ITM. Promotions are more concrete – they are about actively managing talent upwards, a top-down approach to ITM. There comes a point in a career when opportunities are determined more by confidence than technical ability. But confidence is not always correlated with ability, and the problem for organisations is that too many development and promotion opportunities are determined by profile, familiarity and likeability, instead of genuine merit.

Just as with ITM in recruitment, ITM in development can be approached systematically from the demand and supply side as shown in Figure 6.1, our roadmap for this chapter. On the demand side, without consciously seeking to pull diversity through, there will be an employee credibility gap – people won't believe their career is going anywhere.

Figure 6.1 How to promote inclusively

Demand tool	Pull people up (demand)
Purposeful planning – who do we want?	
1	Inclusive succession planning
2	Align incentives
3	Scrap performance management as we know it
In the moment measures – nudges and leadership	
4	Proportionality
5	Improve decision making through bias training
6	Use cross-functional mixed panels for interviews
Insist on transparency and accountability	
7	Benchmark functional areas on their promotions
8	Consciously take risks to widen your portfolio
Supply tool	**Build capability (supply)**
Proactive marketing to create the new norm	
1	Strengths-based approach
2	Communicate and set the norm
3	Honest conversations
Establish concrete talent pathways	
4	Target under-represented groups
5	Set up rotations and secondments programme
Create the toolbox for personalisation	
6	Generic to individualised learning
7	Use technology and gamification

How we frame promotions is vital. Not everyone presents in the same way, or needs the same pull factors, but just because some need more persuasion than others does not mean they are less talented. Indeed, many introverts[1] may be more talented than the organisation is aware of, yet without proactive engagement on the part of the organisation that talent may languish or simply walk.

On the supply side, we can look to build capability to enhance talent where it exists. Learning and development (L&D) is undergoing a revolution, moving from focus on the elite and the homogeneous to personalisation and scalability. This stands a better chance of creating an agile organisation. As the economy changes ever faster, without building and nurturing diverse capability there may be no market-relevant talent left to promote.

PULL PEOPLE UP (DEMAND)

PURPOSEFUL PLANNING – WHO DO WE WANT?

1 INCLUSIVE SUCCESSION PLANNING

The first requirement is that succession planning actually takes place. We are constantly surprised at the lack of planning in many organisations. Second, that plan should feature diversity as a key criteria alongside other variables considered as part of the deliberation process. 'Success' is when the executive team looks at a promotion list, consciously recognises a lack of diversity, and deems it a failure.

It's important to start with, and refer back to, the SWP we discussed in the previous chapter. Who do you want to promote? Are we challenging that image or person sufficiently? Have we redesigned jobs based on relevant factors attuned to the needs of the future business? Or are we still promoting people we feel comfortable with?

New roles or promotion opportunities are an excellent form of development and a key question to ask is, Do I need to look externally to fill this role? By having a greater understanding of the talent already working in the organisation, you should be better placed to promote internal mobility, giving opportunities for all your staff to grow and develop. As a rule of thumb, 1) look down 2) think diversity 3) look outside if homogeneous inside.

KPMG

Iain Moffat is Head of National Markets at KPMG UK. In 2014 all of KPMG's regional chairmen were white and male and the talent pipeline was (unconsciously) largely male. Iain and Steve led a series of sessions involving all regional chairmen to map the three-year talent pipeline for the business.

They placed their initial candidates' names on a large whiteboard in red ink in groups one, two and three years away from promotion. Then they re-wrote names of under-represented groups in different-coloured ink. This suggested that these groups had been de-prioritised in the process to date. Candidate-by-candidate they discussed the business case and the reasons for each candidate's position, and slowly and surely these groups started to advance from three years out to two years out to 'promotion-ready'.

Iain led the process to point out the group's collective blindspots. None of them were maliciously sexist or consciously discriminatory. But all of them had been susceptible to the blindspots of 1–1 promotions, without the big picture view of group aggregation. They simply didn't know the broader candidate group as well as the men and this group hadn't put themselves forward as obviously as the men. This process resulted in more competition, more rigour in decision making and more diversity in promotions.

BAE Systems

Diversity and inclusion is integrated into BAE Systems' succession planning activities. Line managers use a 10-question tool to support the identification of high potentials with the aspiration, ability and performance focus to take on broader or more senior roles. A combination of this and the BAE Systems Leadership framework are used to align individuals to future leadership roles and inform appointments. One of the competencies in the BAE leadership framework is recognising and valuing diversity to be able to maximise the benefit of working in diverse teams. A combination of these factors has resulted in BAE having a more diverse pipeline.

2 ALIGN INCENTIVES

When we spoke to a random sample of graduate recruits who had been with an organisation between one and three years we asked them about their ambitions. Most of them said they were planning to leave because they looked up and didn't see anyone like them. Furthermore, they looked up and didn't respect what they saw. They didn't want to do what they felt was necessary in order to gain profile, familiarity and likeability with a system they felt was immune to their personalities and values.

On first reading, this is terrifying for organisations as it appears their talent management is doomed. On second reading, therein lies opportunity. Instead of panicking, allow the individuals concerned to be the change they seek and to set the new norm they want to follow. That is one sure-fire way of reconciling individual needs with organisational needs. It allows the individual who was previously complaining or unhappy to take responsibility for setting the new course. And it allows the organisation to benefit from free consultancy on how to remain agile in the face of change.

Think of your employee population as an informed customer segment – by swimming with the tide we can stay closer to the market. We can more efficiently reconcile individual and organisational needs so that there is a common purpose and diverse talent actually has opportunity. Without this foundation, there is little point in undertaking 'programmes' or 'initiatives' because they will have no credibility with your people and they will be swimming against the tide.

By definition, an organisation is at its most efficient when the collective sum of its people's individual productivity is being maximised. Yet many organisations treat individuals as factors of production, which by definition is an average approach that ignores the marginal benefits diverse individuals can offer. In turn, if an individual feels treated as a factor of production then they will behave like one, decreasing their marginal productivity and value even further.

A classic example of apparently different needs is allocating work to flexible workers. In one organisation flexible workers were unlikely to be allocated to certain projects 'because the client wouldn't like it'. When we spoke to the client they were actually happy to consider it because they liked the individual in question and they were reforming their own flexible work arrangements and were keen to learn. This work allocation situation is one example of challenging current decision making, but you can imagine hundreds more. It's less about compromise and more about actually enlarging the pie for all parties.

3 SCRAP PERFORMANCE MANAGEMENT AS WE KNOW IT

In the article 'Kill your performance ratings'[2] David Rock, Josh Davis and Beth Jones wrote: 'In the context of neuroscience research, most performance management practices turn out to damage the performance they are intended to improve. That's because they are based on a fundamental misunderstanding of human responses, as revealed in recurring patterns of mental activity.'

The ranking system can be counterproductive as it makes the recipient hostile, as if they are under attack. In addition, it assumes that we all grow and develop in the same way. People with a fixed mindset have the attitude that we are born with a certain intelligence or talent and there is little anyone can do about it. As a result, many employees do not make the effort to seek ways to develop their career and sadly performance management systems accentuate this by focusing on the negatives.

Managers often seek an easy life by avoiding difficult conversations about areas for improvement and the steps needed to address such issues. At Panasonic, for example, Japanese expats were usually uncomfortable giving feedback to their local staff in the annual appraisal process and often they had to be persuaded to carry them out. Too much time and effort is often spent on it without getting the expected benefits.

In many cases the manager prepares poorly and probably dislikes the fact they have to have a direct and often difficult conversation with their member of staff. In the majority of cases both the appraiser and the person being appraised are left frustrated and demotivated by the entire process. A survey by the Corporate Executive Board, a management research group, found that 95 per cent of managers are dissatisfied with their performance management systems, and 90 per cent of HR heads believe that they do not yield accurate information.[3]

Many HTM organisations adopt a paternalistic stance to managing their people. They are perceived to know best as to the needs and requirements of their staff better than their people do. In many cases leadership development programmes are exclusive to a small number of selected staff. These are sometimes called high potential or fast track programmes for those selected to be the cadre of future leaders. Often there is little explanation as to the reasons why they were selected to join the programme and in many cases there is no alignment with an agreed career plan. There is a danger that those not selected feel demotivated. Fairer selection for development programmes and in allocating work is important not only in themselves but because they initiate a catalytic effect on careers. How we select creates ripples that can turn into talent tsunamis – for good and for bad.

Organisations are taking a fresh look at their assessment techniques in order to more efficiently use their talent. This includes IQ tests, assessment centres, personality questionnaires and face-to-face promotion interviews. Many people designing the tests now exclude questions that could be misleading or even discriminate against a specific ethnic group.

Cognitive ability tests are widely used to support decisions on talent, and therefore it is important for human resource professionals to be aware of the issues associated with these measures. For many years it's been understood that measures of general mental ability can be biased and have a significant negative impact on the selection of black, Asian and minority ethnic (BAME) employees. More recently, studies have shown that these measures of cognitive ability can also unfairly discriminate against the older worker.[4]

Personality assessments are also widely used for selection and development and are known to highlight differences between white males, minorities and white females. Rothstein and Goffin[5] argued that those responsible for choosing and administering personality assessments within organisations might not understand the complexities and importance of using personality tests appropriately.

Accenture

Accenture's revised annual review process was designed with four key elements in mind – it had to be strengths-based, personal with clear expectations on what is expected, offer real time feedback and be forward thinking. It is designed to be more engaging and motivating that would then lead to greater trust and collaboration. Its main focus is more about the individual, where they are today and is less procedural and formulaic. It is less about the process, more about the outcomes.

Microsoft

Microsoft scrapped its performance ratings and review process at the end of 2013. The process had been in existence for many years but after feedback from staff Microsoft realised that it was driving the wrong behaviours and outcomes and led to unproductive internal competition. Theresa McHenry, Microsoft's UK HR Director, said, 'It was having a negative impact on collaboration, risk-taking and innovation.'[6]

They replaced it with more regular 'connects' with the aim of creating a more agile system. She went on to say, 'It's now all about impact and making sure people know that it's not what they do, it's the impact they're having on others and how they are contributing to their own success, as well as their team, the business and the customer.'

IN THE MOMENT MEASURES – NUDGES AND LEADERSHIP

4 PROPORTIONALITY

Proportionality is the simple and hard to refute concept that promotion should be in proportion to the talent available. Let's say that in an organisation there were five grades, from A at the top to E at the bottom. Men and women were 50/50 at Grade E but this declined to only 20 per cent women at Grade A. If 30 per cent of the Grade B population is female, then we would expect 30 per cent of promotions to the Grade A above to be women. In this way, the Grade A 20 per cent female population would increase over time towards the 30 per cent incidence at the grade below.

This is a benchmark, the exact amount would obviously differ according to individual skill set, organisation/market conditions and so forth. But proportionality acts as a yardstick, a check and balance against bias.

To understand why this is so important, look at the data. Even though proportionality seems fair, most organisations have never met it and still bias certain groups (usually men and extroverts) over others. That's one reason why, over time, and at more senior levels, organisations become more homogeneous.

Referring to the data allows us to challenge subjective decision making. People will often use 'positive discrimination', or non-merit-based promotion, as an excuse to avoid promotion based on what's actually available. It's more likely that positive discrimination has occurred in the opposite direction, in the absence of proportionality.

The concept's simplicity allows it to be scalable across the entire organisation. It's a nudge that doesn't require much training. Its power lies in challenging previously held assumptions about the fairness of our promotion systems – now we have a check and balance to see if that perceived fairness is justified.

To be enacted, proportionality requires data to be mobilised. To be even more effective, that data should be used to set targets. To be the most effective those targets should be published so that transparency can be an added incentive to become more diverse.

KPMG

KPMG UK's audit function had few female partners in 2014. At the next level down 28 per cent of directors were female. Tony Cates, Head of Audit, implemented proportionality, so that in 2014 and 2015 promotions to the partnership were in line with the Director talent pool. This upward trajectory is accelerating as this process means greater visibility for existing female talent and the internal promotion process uses data as a check and balance on promotion decisions.

5 IMPROVE DECISION MAKING THROUGH BIAS TRAINING

Just as with recruitment processes, people responsible for making promotion decisions should have some bias awareness training. By being aware of in-groups and out-groups, and self and role, managers can become more sophisticated, more nuanced and less biased in the promotion decisions they make. For example, we have witnessed many nine-box grids that appear objectively derived but are full of bias. Often introverts and those in a manager's out-group sit furthest away from the promotion-ready box. The example of Iain Moffat walking his team through a succession plan with gender awareness shows how bias can be mitigated.

Unconscious bias training has now been introduced my more than 20% of large USA corporations (Google sent 13,000 staff on UB training in 2014) and the BBC sent many of its managers on a course in 2014. O2 has introduced training for all its leaders aptly named 'Bridge the gap'.

6 USE CROSS-FUNCTIONAL MIXED PANELS FOR INTERVIEWS

Again, as with recruitment panels, promotion panels should be mixed at least in terms of gender and department. The people on the panel should also demand mixed slates to interview. Nudges such as independently ranking candidates blind (to avoid name association bias) and then coming to a group afterwards (to avoid groupthink) can be helpful.

However, panels can be problematic for introverts or simply those who do not perform best under a falsely constructed setting. Consider alternatives to panels such as assessment centres, tests, on-job assessments and 360 degree feedback where appropriate. The challenge is how to vary the selection method to better suit the individual while having consistency and fairness to all candidates.

At one extreme is opportunity-led promotions, which probably wouldn't be in the SWP. These are ad hoc and arise unexpectedly. They tend to favour extroverts and well-networked people who have the 'inside track' and can quickly prepare and perform well. At the other extreme is the highly structured annual promotion round, which can allow introverts and others more time to prepare; however, it can disadvantage parents on paternity leave, because if they miss the annual round they may have to wait another year before having another promotion opportunity.

INSIST ON TRANSPARENCY AND ACCOUNTABILITY

7 BENCHMARK FUNCTIONAL AREAS ON THEIR PROMOTIONS

Just as recruitment diversity was benchmarked every month at LOCOG, functions can be benchmarked on their promotions. Apportioning accountability for decision making is a business efficiency imperative. Transparency is one of the best tools we have to challenge poor decision making and HTM. We know from experience that certain individuals would not have been promoted if the decision maker had to stand by their decision in a public forum.

We have designed several proposals for promotion committees for clients. These allow greater scrutiny of decision making and increase the efficiency, objectivity and accuracy of selection.

Objections to such transparent structures usually range from time commitment to other decision makers not knowing the person/business case. The response to the first challenge is the cost benefit of time investment versus the cost of a bad hire, especially at senior levels. The response to the second challenge is that if the candidate is good enough they should stand up to scrutiny by people who have the whole organisation's interests at heart.

Goldman Sachs

Goldman Sachs develops diverse talent across the firm in a number of ways, such as a sponsorship initiative that pairs high-potential diverse professionals at the vice president level with a partner sponsor to help raise their profile, promote visibility with senior leadership and advocate for their career progression. This culture of sponsorship results in greater engagement from managers, year over year increases in the number of diverse promotions, and a multiplier effect as participants who have been sponsored often go on to sponsor others.

8 CONSCIOUSLY TAKE RISKS TO WIDEN YOUR PORTFOLIO

Promoting people on the basis of familiarity, likeability or even favour is one of the worst things an organisation can do for its future capability. This is risky behaviour that organisations unconsciously take part in every day. Even worse, such candidates are justified as 'known' or 'safe'.

An organisation needs people who do not fit the mould, but who can still play ball. Debra Meyerson, author of the book *Tempered Radicals*,[7] discusses staff who are prepared to walk a tightrope between conforming and rebelling. Their differences stem from diverse traits such as race, gender, sexuality, values, beliefs or social perspectives. Organisations need people who are prepared to challenge, question norms and influence others in a positive way.

There is of course the moral imperative to give people a chance. As one of the main variables in career development is luck and opportunity, a little humility amongst those who have made it wouldn't go amiss.

Avanade

Jessica Brookes, Director of Diversity and Inclusion at Avanade Europe told us that taking risks on internal appointments is something that the organisation embraces as it supports internal mobility and injects fresh perspectives. Otherwise, there are too few examples of staff challenging decisions or policies as they have become accustomed to doing the same things in the same way. Jessica told us:

> I am an example of the organisation taking a risk as they appointed me in September 2015 as Director of Diversity and Inclusion for Europe from the role of Global Head of Communications. I was looking for a new challenge and despite not having a background in diversity and inclusion it was felt I had the right characteristics and behaviours to take on the role.

BUILD CAPABILITY (SUPPLY)

If people believe there is a credible tone emanating from your organisation and there is genuine demand for diversity, let's now look at how to increase capability and increase the supply of talent.

PROACTIVE MARKETING TO CREATE THE NEW NORM

1 STRENGTHS-BASED APPROACH

Playing to people's strengths is surprisingly counter-intuitive for many organisational cultures. Most organisations tend to focus on what a person did wrong, not what they do right and how we can leverage and scale it.

The use of psychometrics is increasing with tools that allow managers and staff to understand their unique talents and have a common language to discuss it. Without this common language, the approach can be too open to personal bias and may lead to misunderstandings. Paul Brewerton, Joint Managing Director of Strengths partnership, told us: 'We have found that the strengths approach provides a crucial part of the diversity and inclusion puzzle – this approach helps individual employees to understand their unique combination of strengths, talents, skills and experiences.'

When used in a talent/performance management context the employee's line manager has the opportunity to discuss with them the best way to leverage their strengths in the best interests of the individual and the organisation. The result is a more empowering, enabling conversation for the employee, where they feel valued, recognised and understood. This will then encourage them and mean they are more likely to deploy discretionary effort.

PhotoBox

The online photo service organisation engaged 50 managers in a series of leadership development workshops over a four-month period. The objectives of the modules were to improve people management skills, develop high-performing teams and support personal development and strengths building. To embed learning and recognise the value of diverse perspectives and unique strengths, peer coaching groups were set up, comprising a mix of delegates from different functions, who met on a regular basis.

Delegates were also required to work on a 'personal business project', an action-learning project designed to unlock ideas and strengths to improve leaders' contribution to the organisation's goals and vision. The programme culminated in a friendly 'Dragon's Den' that provided an opportunity for managers to present their business ideas and to share learning.

Several of the business ideas put forward by managers were adopted by the organisation, one leading to an estimated £250k financial saving. By focusing on individual strengths and developing solutions-based, inspirational leadership skills, PhotoBox has created a more positive and energising work culture. Of the managers attending the programme, over 90 per cent felt a high level of confidence that the programme would improve their effectiveness as a manager.

2 COMMUNICATE AND SET THE NORM

As we have discussed in prior chapters, norms exist in organisations. Marketing and communications can be used to change the norm. Chris Yates and Pooja Sachdev, authors of *Rewire*, argue that communications should be prioritised to influence and change people's mindsets so that they can recognise that diversity creates a more inclusive, effective and innovative environment. Basically, diversity and inclusion leaders should place their budget behind communication as the best way to shift the norm.[8]

A counterfactual is helpful to emphasise how important communications is in creating understanding. Steve had to deal with a failed promotion candidate who happened to be a white man. He was very upset and convinced he had 'lost out' to a woman because of positive discrimination. In fact he hadn't, he was just an average performer and she was exceptional. The fact he didn't realise that was not entirely his fault, it was more a failure of the organisation to communicate.

LOCOG

At LOCOG, the communications team embraced diversity and inclusion and ran it as a theme in all internal and external communications using the strapline 'Everyone's 2012'. This was then a theme picked up by external speakers at staff meetings, articles in staff newsletters and agenda items in meeting papers. By everyone (including the proverbial straight, white male) feeling part of the mission, people supported the inclusion work of the organisation. This helped to change the norm from a zero-sum game to enlarging the pie for everyone.

3 HONEST CONVERSATIONS

One way of reconciling organisational and individual needs and enhancing communication is to shift away from an exclusive, paternalistic and command and control culture to an employee-driven culture. When people are listened to, encouraged and equipped to drive their own career, they are more empowered, leading to a more agile and engaged workforce. This builds organisational capability. Constant conversations, as opposed to the ritual of an annual (dishonest) conversation, allow organisations to be more effective, agile and scalable.

Accenture is initiating a 'continuous feedback' culture and Expedia has created a 'passport to performance' system of regular 'check-ins' which they say is more coaching orientated. Because it happens in the here-and-now, continuous feedback is more likely to be honest and fair. At Gap, managers conduct monthly conversations in a new performance management process called 'Grow, Perform and Succeed'. By redesigning its performance management processes it has created a more positive environment in order to have more meaningful conversations.

There is evidence to suggest BAME people and other minorities are less likely to receive honest feedback from white managers, due to a complex combination of factors including fear of saying the wrong thing. Yvonne Coghill, Director, Workforce Race Equality Standard – Implementation, at the NHS, who is herself a black woman, explained that due to the experiences many have had living in white dominated societies, BAME employees are less likely to have confidence or feel comfortable talking about their experiences. In a programme with a majority of white people, they might be less likely to speak up and more hesitant to admit mistakes. On the whole in the UK, BAME people are less likely to come from privileged backgrounds and are less likely to be promoted into higher level positions. Simply knowing this can be helpful to having honest conversations with them and provides more context by which to explore what people can do.

Avanade

Avanade educates its managers to have honest conversations with their staff, including how to cover sensitive issues that may be linked to their background. One key aspect is using the information from 360 degree feedback to discuss directly with the member of staff the areas of improvement. During the conversation there will be a focus on their career path, and in particular the manager will raise the topic of possible next steps. According to Jessica Brookes, Head of Diversity and Inclusion for their European Region, they want to avoid an 'up and out' culture so an honest discussion could lead to them having a sideways move.

ESTABLISH CONCRETE TALENT PATHWAYS

4 TARGET UNDER-REPRESENTED GROUPS

Everyone has talent, but not everyone has opportunity. This is why we need tailored approaches. If you have ever wondered why minorities should be prioritised for training programmes, here is a synopsis of capability building programmes for you.

4.1 WOMEN

Many organisations concentrate on developing their female talent and too often try to change the women rather than leverage their diversity. Learning to be more assertive or better negotiators can be useful but ignores the systemic obstacles to women's leadership in their organisation policies, practices and culture.

Female capability programmes to increase the supply of talented women are no substitute for demand for female talent in the first place. But if they are not your sole solution to lack of gender diversity, and if there is serious commitment to gender balance, then programmes to build a sustainable female talent pipeline are a good idea. They are a focused way to ensure that your largest minority is being developed for future executive roles.

Programmes include coaching and mentoring, sponsorship and leadership development programmes aimed exclusively at women. Indeed we were told by several organisations that many of their women have the talent, experience and skill to progress into senior leadership roles but a lack of confidence, role models and balancing work/life priorities holds them back.

02

HR Director Ann Pickering told us: 'I firmly believe that sustainable diversity will only be achieved if we create a strong pipeline of female talent and our Women in Leadership programme is on the way to achieve this goal – developing the potential of talented and ambitious women, so that they're ready to take their rightful place in senior leadership roles.'

Ann confirmed that the majority of those women who have attended the programme have moved into new, broader roles and she felt confident that such moves might not have been achieved if the programme had not been in place.

Hitachi

Historically, Japanese organisations have struggled to actively promote gender diversity due to deeply rooted cultural beliefs of the role and responsibilities of men and women. While this way of thinking is changing in Japan, there is still a long way to go to achieve Western levels of gender diversity.

To combat this, Hitachi established a Women's Interactive Network in Europe. Stephen Pierce, Hitachi Europe's CHRO, told us that it provides learning opportunities, research, online connections, events, mentoring and ongoing support to women at all levels. Hitachi now measures ongoing progress in gender diversity at employee level, manager level and senior manager level through an annual survey.

At Hitachi in Japan two key performance indicators were implemented in 2013 to ensure as many female employees as possible are able to take up leadership roles and to participate in management decision making. Progress on the indicators is tracked through the Hitachi Group Women's Career Success Survey, which sets and tracks numerical targets.

Avanade

Avanade has implemented a number of development interventions specifically targeted at women. For example, it has a six-month leadership programme (Avanade Leadership Program for Women, or ALPW) aimed at women in manager and group manager positions. The programme is a mixture of internal and external modules with a particular focus on supporting leadership development. For those in more junior roles there is another six-month programme called Realize Your Potential. Recognising that building self-efficacy is key to female development, they have also introduced a women's executive mentoring programme, which connects 24 women with top executives. Avanade has benefited from an 85 per cent increase in the female leadership population between 2012 and 2016 and women now account for 20 per cent of the workforce.

4.2 BAME TALENT

BAME is a term that works in a Western white majority context. It refers to the largest minority group after women, but in comparison with the 'gender agenda' its profile and progress is languishing. There are, however, positive programmes that have delivered results.

NHS

People from a BAME background represent around 22 per cent of the NHS workforce. Without the 308,000 BAME staff the NHS would struggle to maintain the services to the general public. In 2002 the Royal College of Nursing published a groundbreaking report, *Getting on Against the Odds*.[9] It laid bare the fact that at the time only 12 of approximately 600 executive directors of nurses were from a BAME background.

The CEO of the NHS at that time, Sir Nigel Crisp, and the Minister of State, John Hutton, launched the Leadership Race Equality Action Plan (LREAP), of which the Breaking Through programme was a part. A budget of nearly £3 million was made available to create programmes to support staff from a BAME background.

In 2007 a selection process along the lines of its graduate recruitment process was introduced with online tests (verbal, numeracy and situational judgement) and an application form. If two out of the four were above the acceptable level the applicants were called back to attend a development/ assessment centre. This was over two days and included interviews, role-plays and group exercises. In 2007 there were 112 initial applications, 40 made it to attend the assessment centre stage and finally 12 were selected. Word of mouth recommendations and general positive feedback led to increased numbers, and in 2008 there were 21 successful participants and in 2009 some 24 were successful.

For these three years of the programme each participant left their role for 18 months and was placed into a higher-level position. They had classes, an international elective in India, an internal mentor, an external coach and a senior NHS executive as a sponsor. The scheme was widely supported within the NHS and funding was provided to backfill the role for the 18 months that the person was away.

Of the 57 programme participants in 2007–09 some 68 per cent gained promotion, and while a few took up opportunities overseas most have stayed within the NHS. In October 2015 the Next Generation Career Accelerator programme was introduced and targeted at BAME staff. It includes group work, coaching and a dedicated sponsor.

4.3 LGBT TALENT

Steve established the Stonewall Leadership programme in 2005. The whole rationale was to turn a perceived barrier into a personal resource and differentiator. A large part of this is framing. One of the reasons many LGBT people are not open about their sexuality is because the norm is straight and they may be persecuted or face discrimination. In a safe inclusive environment a person's sexual orientation can actually be a positive differentiator. People generally perform better when they can be themselves. More than 600 organisations now send their LGBT talent on Stonewall's programme, run in conjunction with leading business schools.

Having visible role models, especially those who we don't ordinarily see, is crucial to changing workplaces. The programme focuses on the idea that the most effective leaders are able to be themselves. It is a continuing professional development accredited and intensive two-day residential course, which offers a selected group of 36 professionals an opportunity to reflect on how their identity as an LGBT person impacts on their role as a leader in the workplace. They also have the opportunity to network and forge on-going relationships with other lesbian, gay, bi and trans professionals from the private, public and third sectors.

Individuals who participate in the Stonewall Leadership Programme have reported at the six-month reunion improved confidence, greater feelings of assertiveness and self-belief and clarity about personal career and development drivers. Additionally they have the motivation to become a visible and influential role model within the organisation.

Having LGBT leaders who are able to be themselves in the workplace provides an indication that others are encouraged to be themselves too. In addition to facilitating more LGBT promotions, alumni of the programme have inspired others to come out, encouraging diverse talent at senior levels.

4.4 DISABLED TALENT

Organisations that have adopted the Guaranteed Interview Scheme for recruitment should now consider extending it to promotion opportunities. The same logic would apply and it would encourage disabled talent to progress within the organisation. A corollary of this is to audit the promotion process for accessibility.

Kate Headley is an auditor of recruitment processes. She has introduced a number of initiatives such as online platforms, audits and a range of L&D services. Helen Cook is an expert on employing graduates with disabilities. She has held a 'disability café' to build confidence amongst disabled candidates. Kate Nash has also established a portfolio of successful open and in-house training courses for disabled employees. In October 2015 they launched an online platform called Purple Space to facilitate the sharing of best practice amongst organisations that want to drive culture change around the theme of disability. Storytelling has proved to be particularly effective. When those with disabilities share their experiences and successes at work it transforms perceptions. It often shifts some people who are sympathetic to a disabled colleague to someone that truly recognises the value they bring to the organisation.

4.5 DEVELOPING INTROVERTS

Establishing an inclusive talent strategy that gives development opportunities to all staff also needs to embrace the diversity of personalities. Those people who are more open, talkative and comfortable with self-promotion tend to excel in more traditional training settings, get noticed more readily and are often highlighted as high potentials. Introverts, on the other hand, internalise their thoughts and by the time they have had time to think others have often spoken up.[10]

People responsible for running development programmes need to understand such traits in order to leverage the potential of all participants. Simple changes can be made to learning programmes, for example taking care not to directly spotlight individuals, building in different methods of encouraging contributions, or providing advance notice of questions so people can be prepared with their answers. Once people feel more confident to express themselves their energy and passion can often be seen.

Proportionality is a great resource for introverts. The system can pull them up rather than them having to 'build profile' when it might be inauthentic for them to do so. Coaching is another resource that can disproportionately benefit introverts. For more on this see 'Role and self' in Chapter 8.

4.6 YOUR AGE IS LIKELY TO INFLUENCE HOW BEST YOU LEARN

Each generation will have different life experiences, views and attitudes that create a challenge for those responsible for the design of learning interventions. Baby boomers (born 1946–64) have traditionally valued classroom based training and asking them to switch to technology based training, more suited to Millennials (born 1977–97), could disengage them. Conversely, younger generations have always worked with a computer, mobile phone and search engines so are far more open to learning through digital technology.

This was confirmed by a Chartered Institute of Personnel and Development report, *Developing the Next Generation*,[11] which revealed that 53 per cent of HR professionals who responded to the 2015 Learning to Work Survey have experienced differences in how young people like to learn in comparison with other generations of staff.

As a result, the learning function will need to be much more flexible and adapt the content, style and methods of training delivery to accommodate a multi-generational workforce. They will need to reassess their leadership and high potential programmes and make them more inclusive to all generations in order to provide a steady flow of ready now talent for critical roles.

Implementing mentoring, reverse mentoring and coaching will both transfer knowledge and enhance understanding between the generations. Additionally, allowing the individual to self-select their preferred learning style will increase their engagement.

5 SET UP ROTATION AND SECONDMENT PROGRAMME

We have often heard the excuse 'She's not ready' or 'He doesn't have the experience'. How you allocate work is important in building credibility and promotion cases and challenging such assumptions. Rotating people in and out of the business is one way to fast track experience.

KPMG and AIG

The KPMG African Caribbean Network, Diversity and Inclusion Team and a number of supportive partners hosted a client dinner with AIG Insurance. One output of the dinner was the CEO of AIG agreeing then and there to mentor one of the BAME dinner guests. This was then scaled up into a full cross-organisation mentoring programme involving other financial clients and extended to government departments. Today, more than 100 BAME middle managers are rotating through various organisations picking up valuable experience and networks to help the next stage of their career.

CREATE THE TOOLBOX FOR PERSONALISATION

6 GENERIC TO INDIVIDUALISED LEARNING

Learning and development professionals need to be more aware than most of the changing world we live in and then respond and lead accordingly. People work in different locations and time zones, and the days when the majority of staff worked in the same office have, in the main, disappeared. Staff work flexible hours, can be home-based, on part-time contracts and many are considering portfolio careers. To address these changes our learning and development initiatives need to be agile, creative, keep pace and be more inclusive in nature, given the greater diversity of needs and working patterns.

It's time to customise L&D. People now approach their learning experiences in the way they approach their shopping experiences. Depending on their mood and objective they will sometimes buy items online but on other occasions they will prefer to go to the bricks-and-mortar shops, where they can seek the advice of others and touch the products.

Having recognised the needs of both the organisation and the individual concerned an individualised development plan can be created. This can more effectively tailor to a diverse range of learning styles and needs ranging from self-directed learning to content curation, just-in-time learning and social learning, discussed below.

During Danny's years working at Panasonic he was frequently involved in running global leadership programmes. They would be held in English, which immediately favoured those for whom it was their native language. Depending on the circumstances, simultaneous translation into other languages would be made available but this was rare. It was therefore necessary to speak slowly using simple words and frequently check the understanding of all the participants.

From a cultural perspective those originating from Asian countries tended to be much quieter and less responsive than those from Anglo-Saxon cultures. Certainly Japanese participants would rarely ask a question or express an opinion. This goes back to their school days where it was the norm not to question the teacher but simply accept what they say.

The tried and tested 70:20:10 concept of how staff learn is widely accepted and followed by many organisations. The ratio relates to learning on the job, learning by individual support (like coaching, mentoring and sponsorship) and learning by attending courses. This concept has given organisations the confidence to shift their focus to on-the-job learning, recognising that it is the most effective, reduces costs and is more inclusive as it opens up development opportunities to many more people. Peter Cheese, CEO of the Chartered Institute of Personnel and Development, argues that it's time to move away from initiatives to a learning culture: 'For many organisations learning interventions are still viewed as discrete projects that each require their own business case.'[12]

Research into how people learn, concentration spans and the best ways to transfer learning into the workplace have proliferated. Much has been written about bite-size learning, massive open online courses and blended learning. Today, 70 per cent of people turn to search engines such as Google to research and more of us are using You Tube to find out 'how to do' a particular action.

There is no doubt that easy access to learning materials has meant more and more people can benefit.

Those responsible for L&D in their organisations still need to assess the business need, the culture of the organisation and the target population before deciding on the best strategy. Just-in-time learning can support inclusion. By using bite-size training at the right moment in decision-making processes, behaviour can be nudged. For example, completing an IAT within 24 hours before interviewing candidates will help decrease interviewer unconscious bias.

The London School of Marketing has put a number of its lectures onto video, breaking lectures down into six-minute videos so that students can access them on their mobile devices. This is an example of mirroring and exploiting habits from our personal lives and transferring them into a work or study situation.

Bouygues

Emmanuelle Roderie, Learning and Development Professional at energy organisation Bouygues, explained how they ask all their staff to take five minutes at 5.00 pm each day to connect to an online learning programme of their choice. This '5@5' as it became known proved to be a popular way to learn something new and then share with others as appropriate.

Telus

The Canadian telecommunications organisation Telus employs around 40,000 people. In 2007 it had an HTM approach to developing staff with people selected to go on courses. Employee engagement was measured at 53 per cent. There was no culture of open leadership and customers scored it low when asked if they would recommend Telus to others.

In 2009 it developed a culture of learning based on three equal parts – formal, informal and social. One year later the Telus Leadership Philosophy was introduced where all staff were encouraged to use their own initiative and take ownership of their own development. This inclusive strategy was then embedded into other talent management activities. By 2013 Telus had 83 per cent engagement with employees and 73 per cent of customers saying that they were likely to recommend it to others.[12]

UK Foreign and Commonwealth Office

Despite being based in 270 locations globally and with more than 75 per cent of its 14,000 workforce employed locally, the main focus of development was targeted at a relatively small number of staff who were invited to join leadership programmes.

However, with the strong support of the then Foreign Secretary, William Hague, a Diplomatic Academy was established in February 2015 that offered programmes to all staff globally to enhance their diplomatic skills. It is mostly e-learning but includes videos and links to other resources.

The Foreign and Commonwealth Office (FCO) established self-facilitated learning groups, designed, written and delivered by internal staff. Besides being cost effective it allowed them to utilise the great experience and expertise that already existed within the FCO.

This is the first time an inclusive development programme has been introduced by the FCO. Jonathan Marshall, Head of Learning, told us: 'It is helping retention as our staff feel that they are being developed and we are investing in their career.'

A key success factor has been the identification in each location of a learning and development champion who promotes the programme and sometimes acts as a facilitator. This in itself has provided development opportunities for people in the FCO. One comment Jonathan received from a local Learning and Development champion was: 'We were nervous to begin with as we are not experienced facilitators or subject experts but we quickly realised that we had more knowledge and expertise than we realised.'

7 USE TECHNOLOGY AND GAMIFICATION

Finally, we can make use of technology and gamification like never before to engage talent in different ways. We can be more user-led (and therefore more efficient) than we have ever been. Gamification can support the targeting of a wider talent pool, as we saw with the Arctic Shores game was developed for Deloitte and Standard Chartered.

New technology, the rapid increase of social media, just-in-time learning and research into how best we learn have all had an enormous impact on the mindset of both employer and employee. One impact has been the reduction of traditional classroom training, which is usually expensive to run and hard to measure.

Digital learning can be both inclusive and exclusive. It is available to everyone but more comfortable for digital natives to use. Millennials who have grown up with social media and using digital technology are more likely to accept it as a methodology of learning. It does, though, put the choice of when and where to learn into the hands of the learner and as a result allows for greater flexibility.

The use of digital learning has expanded since the early years when e-learning was mainly used for health and safety and compliance training. The user experience was often poor, with boring, static programmes and products that would regularly break down. Such programmes would often be generic so that staff did not feel it was addressing the needs of their particular situation, nor did it necessarily reflect the values and culture of their organisation. Digital learning will continue to expand and grow. Already we see gamification, virtual reality and artificial intelligence being incorporated into learning programmes.

BP

BP actively uses digital technology in a self-orientated programme, targeted at newly recruited graduates. Using a prescribed format the graduates were asked to produce a 20 seconds video clip, for example how to find a mentor, that could be shared as user-generated learning content. This could then be posted on an internal site. They are developing others by sharing their experiences with other graduates.

ITM in promotion, top-down, is about pulling talent through. Development is principally concerned with creating an efficient labour market and building organisational capability and thus sustainability. Organisations need to make specific changes to their development interventions bottom-up in order to adopt an inclusive talent strategy. Doing so will help their staff to feel valued and appreciated as their individual needs and aspirations are taken into account. In turn, creating a greater sense of empowerment will help people to take more responsibility for their development, building a virtuous circle that enhances the diversity of approaches and practices within an organisation.

By recognising that their staff, depending on their age, gender and ethnic background will have differing preferences in the way they learn and using digital technology more creatively to deliver solutions that recognise these differences, talent professionals can have a huge impact. Challenging your organisation's underlying talent management philosophy and adjusting assessment processes will go a long way towards ensuring a level playing field in decision-making. In this way, we come closer to achieving a true meritocracy.

KEY TAKEAWAYS

1 Who do you want? Think about your inclusive succession plan, align incentives and scrap performance management as we know it.

2 Transparency is a better way to meritocracy. Implement proportionality, reduce bias in decision-making and increase accountability, publicly if possible.

3 Customise L&D, allow people to drive their own development. Adopt a strengths-based approach and allow honest conversations to take place.

4 Develop programmes for your diverse talents – establish concrete pathways.

5 Make use of technology and gamification. The personalisation of learning can increase its efficiency and impact.

NOTES

1 We don't mean people who are simply quiet, but introvert in its wider definition (how they take decisions, how they digest data etc).

2 Rock, D, Davis, J and Jones, B (2014) Kill your performance ratings, *Strategy+Business*, *PwC*, **76**, Autumn, www.strategy-business.com/article/00275?gko=c442b

3 Corporate Executive Board (2012) *Breaking Through Performance in the New Work Environment*, Corporate Executive Board.

4 Klein, R, Ones, D, Dilchert, D and Wiernik, B (2015) Cognitive predictors and age-based adverse impact among executives, PsycEXTRA Dataset

5 Rothstein, M and Goffin, R (2013) *The Oxford Handbook of Personnel Assessment and Selection*, Oxford University Press.

6 Mitchell, L (2014) Are annual appraisals losing impact? *HR Magazine*, 25 November, www.hrmagazine.co.uk/article-details/are-annual-appraisals-losing-impact

7 Meyerson, D (2003) *Tempered Radicals*, Harvard Business School Press.

8 Yates, C and Sachdev, P (2015) *Rewire*, Bloomsbury.

9 Royal College of Nursing (2002) *Getting on Against the Odds*, NHS Leadership Centre.

10 Cain, S (2013) *Quiet: The power of introverts in a world that can't stop talking*, Penguin.

11 CIPD (2015) *Developing the Next Generation*, CIPD, www.cipd.co.uk/binaries/developing-next-generation.pdf

12 Peter Cheese as expressed at the Learning and Development Show, Olympia, London, A new vision for L&D, 11 May 2016.

13 Kalman, F (2012) How Telus keeps learning plugged in, Chief Learning Officer, 18 June, www.clomedia.com/articles/how-telus-keeps-learning-plugged-in

7

ITM IN RETENTION - KEEPING DIVERSE TALENT

The cliché is that people don't leave organisations, they leave bosses. In fact, the evidence is pretty close to this – it suggests that people leave (and join) organisations above all else because of culture.

Men are more than twice as likely to get fired than women and young people are disproportionately unhappy about their boss's attitude.[1] Introverts and women are less likely to complain, will take longer to make a decision and are more likely to quietly leave. Poor performers are more likely to stay than high performers and this makes highly talented people even more likely to leave. Several CEOs have told us privately this is their worst nightmare.

Ronan Dunne, CEO of O2, told us that its turnover rate for senior management is about 2 per cent, much lower than the industry average, which is nearer 7 per cent. This can lead to stagnation if not carefully managed so the company monitors this carefully and at times actively supports people to move on.

Indeed it is not always desirable to retain everyone. ITM does not advocate tolerating poor performers. And a diverse workforce becomes more likely with a steady stream of (diverse) new staff who feel included and able to challenge the status quo. Turnover is not necessarily a bad thing. The sensitivity here is that employees are now not just employees – they are your customers, suppliers and brand ambassadors. We are operating in an ecosystem and we are just as dependent on employees as they are on us. When people leave you, make sure they do so on good terms.

The psychologist Frederick Hertzberg developed a two-factor theory, which focused on 'motivators' and 'hygiene factors', that correlate with 'culture' and 'technical' fixes – see Figure 7.1. Motivational or cultural factors would include elements such as respect for the line manager, sense of purpose and aligned values. Hygiene or technical factors would include pay, policies and benefits. Many organisations still place too great an emphasis on hygiene factors and rely on them to keep talent. This may be more likely in developing countries, but cultural factors are the major cause of dissatisfaction.

Figure 7.1 Cultural and technical factors in retention

Hertzberg Factor	Motivational (culture)	Hygiene (technical)
Aspect of leadership	Self	Role
Practical example	Social background	Job description

Culture is the critical variable. The problem is that we too often apply technical fixes to cultural problems, and then are surprised when they don't work. HTM may assume that remuneration is the key to retention, but in fact culture trumps even money.

Over 50 per cent of people leave because they are unhappy, not because they want a rise.[2] The top 10 reasons people give for leaving their job are: lack of advancement, lack of work/life balance, poor relationship with boss, conflict with colleagues, lack of organisation vision/purpose, lack of recognition/empathy or appreciation, lack of opportunity to use skills, lack of autonomy and independence, lack of fun and, finally, salary level.[3] Inclusion is key to each of these points, but this is rarely acknowledged. ITM is your retention strategy. We've broken it down in Figure 7.2, which forms the journey for this penultimate chapter.

Figure 7.2 How to retain diversity

Reason for leaving	ITM solutions
1 Lack of advancement	Inclusive succession planning Cross-organisation mobility Transparent promotion process Targets Mentoring and reciprocal mentoring Sponsorship
2 Work–life balance	Life balance Job redesign and flexible working
3 Boss	Inquiring about self Psychological contract Line management accountability
4 Colleagues	Inclusive environment Honesty and trust Employee resource groups
5 Lack of organisation vision	Authenticity Clear induction CSR Communications
6 Lack of recognition/empathy	Recognition and feedback Storytelling
7 Not using or learning skills	Self-directed learning
8 Insufficient autonomy	Ability to make an impact
9 Lack of fun	Bring your whole self to work
10 Remuneration	Fairness Transparency

1 ADVANCEMENT

The number one reason talented people leave organisations is because they think their career is not going anywhere. We spoke to junior auditors in a professional services firm who confided that their boss wanted them to keep doing what they were doing because he was dependent upon it. The boss perceived their career development as a threat to his part of the business.

Not everyone wants to be CEO, but most people want to think the route to the top is a fair one. And people want the flexibility to move laterally or even take a step back at certain life moments. This sense of fairness is very important and people leave when they sense unfairness.

INCLUSIVE SUCCESSION PLANNING

Inclusive succession planning ensures that diversity is an integral part of promotion processes. Organisations typically only include 13 per cent of skilled professionals and 38 per cent of mid-level managers in succession management programmes.[4] All your talents need to understand that their contribution is being valued. Assess the pipeline in terms of diversity, and use proportionality as discussed in Chapter 5. If your succession plan is less diverse than your organisation as a whole, then you may be heading in the wrong direction.

Royal Mail

At Royal Mail every executive has to complete a talent pack containing a succession plan, identifying critical roles and successors. From these lists the gender mix and age are closely monitored. Liza Strong, Head of Organisational Talent and Diversity at Royal Mail, told us that the current priority is to have a succession plan in place that reflects the diversity of their customer base. Liza said: 'We have embraced an organisation-wide culture change programme and diversity sits at the heart of that change.'

CROSS-ORGANISATION MOBILITY

Rather than being 'stuck' with their line manager and in their department, give employees a sense of belonging to the whole organisation. Connecting people to other parts of the organisation through resourcing, work allocation, informal gatherings, social activities and networking opportunities gives a sense of belonging to a more diverse community. At minimum, this gives the talented employee a glimpse of a world beyond their line manager.

Goldman Sachs

Goldman Sachs tries to foster a work environment that advances the leadership and management skills of women, educates managers and employees on inclusive behaviours and supports women through the maternity cycle by offering flexible work arrangements and onsite childcare.

By using targeted skills development programmes and sponsorship initiatives for women at various stages in their career, Goldman Sachs aims to increase the retention of female professionals and year-on-year promotion numbers. In 2015 the firm promoted 30 female managing directors, which was 27.5 per cent of the promotion class and an increase from 16 per cent in 2013.

TRANSPARENT PROMOTION PROCESS

A meritocracy requires that talented people can see a career path open to them. One of the most demotivating elements of organisational culture is a secretive promotion process. One of the best remedies for this is the proportionality and transparency approach outlined in the previous chapter. The example of KPMG going public with targets and using proportionality for all promotions shows how knowing that there are open checks and balances in the system gives people confidence that they have a fair shot at advancement. Targets in particular can spell out what an efficient and successful talent management strategy looks like and call out secretive and unfair practices.

As a guideline, many organisations will target two-thirds internal promotion (build) and one-third external hiring (buy). However, in reality almost 50 per cent of the organisations surveyed are more dependent on hiring externally than developing their own people. This can be positive or negative for diversity but it can be demotivating for internal talent seeking advancement.

Big Lottery

Big Lottery is a non-profit organisation responsible for distributing millions of pounds of the UK National Lottery money to community groups and charitable projects. Its promotion process was previously exclusive, as people were selected by their manager. To be more inclusive, projects that could lead to promotion were posted on social media (as the company's internal site was not well regarded). These detailed the skills and experience necessary and anyone could apply. In order to ensure as many people as possible were aware of this communication strategy a social network was established with 100 volunteers and they were each asked to share the information with

10 others. A thousand people became connected and this activity became known internally as the 'Big Connect'. A more diverse group of staff applied to lead projects, increasing their engagement, motivation and retention.

Universities

The UK university sector has recently made efforts to demystify the tenure process for new faculty. Guidelines and criteria have been made public and the evaluation process is now more transparent, for example number of papers published and in what calibre of journal. Tenure may not be guaranteed but at least candidates now have some idea what progress they are making. However, higher education still remains a sector with significant diversity challenges. A brilliant 25-year-old man who combines medical research and business acumen has been passed over for recognition in a British university, largely on account of his age. He has taken his talents to an American university. This brain drain is somewhat ironic for the university sector.

TARGETS

Many people instantly recoil at the idea of targets – for a fuller discussion see Chapter 5. However, those against proportionality-based targets are often average performers from the dominant group who have most to lose. Diversity is the enemy of mediocrity. As measures of a more free market, more transparent labour market, targets can offer hope to under-represented groups.

Many of the organisations we spoke to recognised the importance of setting targets linked to their diversity and inclusion policies. These have to be clearly communicated and reinforced by the leadership team. Targets are not an end in themselves, they are a means to an end, a measure of behaviour. It's behaviour that drives the numbers, not the other way round.

Unilever South Africa

Paddy Hull, Learning and Development Director for Unilever in Africa, shared with us the challenges it has been having in retaining its black talent. On examining its workforce demographics in the period 1994–2014 it found that, despite the fact that 80 per cent of their customers were black, only 14 per cent of their workforce were black and this figure had not increased. Although Unilever had introduced a number of initiatives, according to Paddy the company was 'better at buying black talent than building black talent'. Unilever recognised that in order to develop its business in South Africa it was imperative for the workforce to reflect the customer base.

In 2014 only one in six of its directors was black and so Unilever set out targets and a timetable for improving representation. Recognising that more black role models were needed to inspire others, for each of Unilever's targets a transparent roadmap was agreed with specific measures identified. A communication and engagement plan was established, involving special events, town hall meetings, Freedom Days and other activities. To evaluate the impact, a quarterly survey with five questions was sent out to all staff around the theme of inclusivity.

MENTORING AND RECIPROCAL MENTORING

Mentoring increases the possibility that staff will stay, by on average one-third.[5] It provides an opportunity, outside the confines of line management, to discuss career and developmental aspirations and how they align with the organisation's strategic plan.

Mentoring can help improve the development and progression of under-represented groups and extend career development opportunities to all staff rather than the select few. Dr Julie Haddock-Millar, Senior Lecturer in Human Resource Management at Middlesex University Business School, told us, 'In recent years, mentoring has become an essential ingredient in the success of diversity management in the workplace and in achieving societal change to support and value difference.'

The standard mentoring relationship has involved a younger employee or new starter taking advice and guidance from a more senior and mature colleague. This old model of mentorship is in some respects outdated and one-sided. Reverse mentoring has existed informally for many years and it was Jack Welch, retired CEO of General Electric, who was one of the first to recognise the benefits of having a young mentor help him understand the potential of the internet for the business.

Edelman and Burson-Marsteller

These communications companies have both introduced mentoring and reciprocal mentoring schemes in which executives mentor Millennials and in return they then mentor their elders in digital and social media. Edelman has named it a 'matchmaking process'[6] and Burson-Marsteller the *Being More* campaign.[7] This win–win situation has led to both parties learning valuable information and being able to see, at first hand, the value of having a diverse workforce. Having a different perspective from someone who has had a range of different experiences can lead to more creative and innovative ideas. Dan Baer, the 60-year-old Chairman and CEO of Burson-Marsteller, has a mentor half his age who he sees for an hour every month. He stated, 'A lot of this was to help those of us who didn't grow up in the digital and social media environment to better understand what was going on.'

SPONSORSHIP

If mentoring is advising, sponsorship is advocating. It is proactively managing the career of the person you're mentoring. In her book *Forget a Mentor, Find a Sponsor*[8] Sylvia Ann Hewlett explains that mentors advise and sponsors act. Putting it another way, if mentors help define the dream, sponsors are the dream-enablers.

Many organisations are recognising the need to be more proactive in supporting talented women and people from the BAME community. Creating pathways to sponsorship is important for all under-represented groups and people to increase the talent options available to an organisation.

In order for the benefits of sponsorship to be sustainable, it needs to be robust, have support from senior management, be available at different career transitions and feel safe (to be able to seek advice from someone who does not look like you and is not naturally in your 'in-group').

Research conducted by the Center for Talent Innovation in the USA[9] has shown that 68 per cent women with a sponsor are satisfied with their career advancement (the figure goes down to 57 per cent for those without a sponsor) and minority employees are 65 per cent more likely than their unsponsored colleagues to be satisfied with their advancement.

Deutsche Bank

The bank's Accomplished Top Leaders Advancement Strategy (ATLAS)[10] was established in 2009 with the goal of improving the gender balance at senior levels and increasing the number of women in the pool eligible for senior positions. It involves pairing women on the programme with a member of Deutsche Bank's Executive Committee (from a different line of business) who will act as their sponsor. This will involve them championing them to be considered for future top positions.

The women on the programme are also diverse in that they are from different ethnic groups, different functions and lines of business. The programme includes a number of assessments to help the participants and their sponsors to identify specific goals to focus on. The women then also act as mentors to other women at lower levels of the bank. Since the programme was launched in 2009, some 45 per cent of the women who have participated are now in more senior or expanded roles.

2 WORK–LIFE BALANCE

LIFE BALANCE

We have spoken much about Millennials' approach to work as part of life. Indeed people want more out of life than simply a 'career'. If the job is getting in the way of life then increasingly it is the job that will have to change rather than the other way round. Four principles, trialled at insurance company SwissRe,[11] are particularly helpful to consider:

One size does not fit all.

Work smarter not longer.

Focus on the team rather than the individual.

Create an atmosphere of trust, openness and transparency.

The application of these principles facilitated such topics as job-sharing and home working, creating a more flexible environment. Crucially, we need to move away from perceiving these principles as a cost on business, and see them instead as an investment in our people.

If work is to be a healthy, successful part of our life then it will compete with many other priorities, from relationships and family to sport and recreation. But the days of stop/start are largely over. Technology, the nature of work and connectivity in general mean that we now find new ways to achieve balance in our life. Good work should not compete with our life, but complement it.

Time and space are precious commodities. Do we always have to be physically in the office and do we really have to be connected 24/7? In Japan there still exists a culture in many organisations of working long hours. In more traditional organisations employees do not leave the office before their boss. In one case, a UK expat manager recognised his Japanese staff would not leave the office while he was still working. Even by telling them that it was OK for them to go home this practice was so deeply ingrained in the culture that they continued working. He then devised a new strategy—he would say good night at 7.00pm, leave the office and go to a local coffee shop. He would return to finish his work around twenty minutes later to find all his staff had left the office.

When a senior executive at Credit Suisse told a town hall meeting he was unable to answer any more questions as he had to attend his son's school play it set the tone. It sent a strong message that having a work–life balance is important to everyone, regardless of his or her level.

SAS

This software analytics company states in its mission statement that its employees do not have to choose between their work and their lives. A culture of trust permeates through the company, with the leadership team encouraging a work–life balance. Staff are trusted to manage their own time to achieve their agreed targets. Amenities on-site include hairdressers, swimming and other leisure facilities, and it is commonplace to see the top management team taking advantage of them. The Vice President of HR, Jean Mann, said: 'We know we hire smart people and we trust them to get the job done. In turn our employees are committed to perform.'[12]

JOB REDESIGN AND FLEXIBLE WORKING

Some organisations face a steep learning curve in this area. Value creation is now less dependent on time served and more on knowledge gained. And knowledge can be created and disseminated in any number of ways at various times and from various places. Offering flexible working is less doing employees a favour and more re-engineering the business model of the entire organisation to be more effective in the marketplace.

Job share is one example of job redesign. It allows two people to hold down one full-time job and carry out their job alongside family and other life commitments. Millennials in particular want to work in a flexible way that suits their lifestyle. Recent advances in technology have created the infrastructure to make it happen. Staff can be connected 24/7, have the possibility to work from home, and are simply translating their experiences using social media into a work situation.

KPMG's Flextra scheme allows employees to choose the suite of working styles that suits them, from purchasing more holiday to topping up gym memberships and health benefits. IBM has experienced some of the highest employee satisfaction scores since introducing its flexible working arrangements – its staff are more satisfied with their jobs and have a greater sense of accomplishment. Gary Kildare, Head of HR at Cisco, commented that its employee engagement survey shows that flexibility is one of the two top issues mentioned by staff. At Google, Matt Brittin, Head of Operations in the UK and Ireland, said: 'Our engineers work whatever hours they like, as long as they co-ordinate with colleagues and deliver what they have agreed.' He added that people are evaluated on results and not by how many hours they work.[13]

UK Foreign and Commonwealth Office

The FCO's Learning Academy team was designed around the talent in situ. It includes staff job sharing, working from home, working compressed hours, part-time, remote working in the UK, remote working internationally (someone moved to Barbados with her husband's posting and kept her job; another uses the local FCO office in Munich; and another is based in Canberra, Australia where some staff were recruited locally). That's all within a team of 20 staff!

3 THE ROLE OF THE BOSS IN RETAINING STAFF

Many of us spend more time with our boss than with our partner. While we have often put a great deal of thought into our choice of partner, often our bosses are not a choice.

Bosses generally get into trouble when they either micromanage (more common amongst female managers) or are absent (more common among male managers). In both cases, bosses could benefit by being more inclusive leaders and taking a genuine interest in the people that work for them.

INQUIRING ABOUT SELF, NOT JUST ROLE

Don't ask 'what do you do?' but 'who are you as a person?' Taking a basic interest in the individual being managed sounds simple but is so important. For a managed person to deploy discretionary effort you have to touch their inner self, not just their role. Only by knowing the person can you deploy a strengths-based coaching approach to determine what can be achieved by each member of the team, rather than taking a retrospective view of what they have done in the past. We will explore this in more detail in Chapter 8.

PSYCHOLOGICAL CONTRACT

Theodore Roosevelt said: 'People don't care how much you know until they know how much you care.' He was referring to why people stay with their organisation and the importance of the psychological contract. The CIPD define this as 'the perceptions of the two parties, employee and employer, of what their mutual obligations are towards each other'.[14] It must make people feel that their organisation and in particular their manager have a genuine interest in their development and investing in their future. Ultimately it will have more of a bearing on their likelihood to stay with the company than their visible contract.

Paul Deighton, LOCOG

Paul was Steve's CEO at LOCOG. In 2012 Steve's dad passed away unexpectedly just before the Games and Paul was incredibly supportive, in spite of organising the largest event in the world with just weeks left to run. After the Games were successful, headhunters and recruiters were in constant contact with LOCOG employees and a norm developed to 'take advantage of the moment'. Paul advised and reassured Steve to ignore this pressure and take some time off to grieve for his father. Paul told Steve that the relationships he had developed over the last decade would survive three months' absence. And indeed they did.

LINE MANAGEMENT ACCOUNTABILITY

People behave differently when their actions are public. Many organisations recognise the key role that managers play in the engagement and motivation of their staff, which will ultimately play a part in their retention.

Total 360-degree feedback can help, as can engagement surveys broken down by area of accountability. Ultimately this comes down to inclusive leadership and a manager's self-awareness, bias and mitigating actions. We'll discuss this in more depth in Chapter 8.

Bank of America

The bank puts questions about diversity and inclusiveness into its biannual employee engagement survey and compares the results for any team that gets at least seven responses against those of a normative group of companies. 'We've also built a diversity-and-inclusion index that tells us if people here feel they are treated fairly and to help us ensure that people of diverse backgrounds can succeed at Bank of America,' said Brian Moynihan, CEO. 'With this data, each team can have a dialogue to determine what we're doing well and what we can improve to make Bank of America a better place to work.'[15]

4 COLLEAGUES

Just as with bosses, we often spend more time with colleagues than family. As humans we have needs and being 'in role' for long periods of time will not fulfil those needs – in fact it may make our needs greater. So allowing individuals to be themselves rather than just play a role is vitally important for inclusion.

BUILDING AN INCLUSIVE ENVIRONMENT

There is only so much 'the organisation' can do. Ultimately the organisation is the collection of people within it. So ask what you can do to contribute to the culture you want to see. People want to feel that they are making a contribution in whatever job they are doing. It's important to all of us that our efforts are appreciated and to work in a culture of affirmation.

Red Hat

An example of an organisation that took steps to create an inclusive culture is the US multinational software company Red Hat. Its Chief People Officer De Lisa Alexander said, 'Meritocracy is a great driver of innovation, but if we want to get the best ideas, we need diversity of thought and an inclusive environment where everyone feels welcome to participate and offer different perspectives.'

Red Hat has made inclusion one of its global goals and added some questions to the annual employee engagement survey to measure it. These include: 'I have opportunities to work on assignments that are important to my career', 'Diverse perspectives are valued at Red Hat' and 'I feel comfortable speaking up at team meetings, even when my views differ from my co-workers'.[16] Earning respect and gaining influence at Red Hat then becomes more based on the work that you do, the ideas that you have and the efforts you make to contribute.

HONESTY AND TRUST

In the new ecosystem, your co-workers are also your customers. Looking after them as you would look after your customers is therefore strongly recommended. Establishing trust, proactively looking after their concerns and making them feel special are traits that apply to both your customers and your people. Honesty and trust don't just make for a more pleasant working environment, there are efficiency gains too because people then spend less time double-checking facts and more time doing the job.

LOCOG

The emotional engagement of staff and volunteers was a key factor in the retention strategy of the Organising Committee of the London Olympics and Paralympics in 2012. Paul Deighton, CEO, told us, 'Retaining talent is a big challenge but the more people feel valued and appreciated the more they are likely to stay.'

The retention rate for the permanent and temporary staff was very high with fewer than 100 full-time and temporary staff leaving their roles over five years and 96 per cent of the 70,000 volunteers completing their committed time.

All staff and volunteers shared a common vision, 'Everyone's 2012', they all shared a sense of purpose 'to inspire a generation' and they all recognised that they personally had a key role to play in order for the Games to be successful. Every person, from the chairman to the receptionist, was called a Games Maker. The goal for those working for the Games, in whatever capacity, was for them to feel a sense of inclusion.

EMPLOYEE RESOURCE GROUPS

If employees cannot truly be themselves in their immediate team then one source of help is an employee resource group (ERG) or network. This is an association of people with common interests, often diversity-based. For example, women's networks, LGBT associations and black caucuses. Often these networks go beyond immediate need and become proactive networks to win new business, advance careers through mentoring and sponsorship programmes and decrease attrition of particular groups.

To better include everyone, ally networks have emerged. For example, there are now LGBT and straight allies networks, the #HeforShe campaign as well as women's networks. These are often more successful because they appear not to have vested interests at heart.

Barclays

Barclays Bank has seven employee networks. The Cultural Awareness Network (CAN) and the Embrace multicultural network have reviewed recruitment processes to address factors disproportionately affecting BAME candidates and instigated strengths based interviewing and work placements for BAME students. They have implemented extensive mentoring for BAME applicants to help them prepare for the assessment processes and 'lifecycle' mentoring to prepare high-potential internal BAME candidates, including mentoring circles and speed networking.[17]

5 VISION

AUTHENTICITY

In an age of social media transparency people can see through annual report or graduate recruitment PR. If an organisation is inauthentic it risks motivating staff purely on hygiene factors and missing out on more valuable discretionary effort due to motivation through purpose. As organisation and personal boundaries blur, people will be more choosy about who they work 'for' or 'with' as it will impact their personal brand. Organisations that fail to understand this will not attract certain talent and may not gain the full commitment of the people it can.

CLEAR INDUCTION

Integrating new people quickly makes them feel welcome. Induction training, allocating a buddy and regular feedback sessions can all help. The challenge from an ITM perspective is to ensure that diverse talent sees and hears diversity in these initial impressions in order for them to believe that the culture is inclusive. If you don't explicitly call it out people will not assume inclusion.

Unilever South Africa

To make new starters feel engaged a new orientation programme was introduced with a Zulu word *sawubona* (meaning I see you) being used to symbolise the welcoming approach intended for new joiners. In addition mentoring, coaching and career conversations were all put in place and made available when appropriate. Once a month existing staff were encouraged to have lunch with someone they have never met before, in what was called a *sawubona connect*.

CSR AND RETENTION

Working in an environmentally friendly way can motivate people. An organisation's contribution in reducing its impact on issues like fuel efficiency and reduced carbon emissions can lower costs and increase engagement. At Oxfam and the NHS, staff recognise that they could probably earn more money in equivalent roles in the private sector. However, being responsible for looking after less privileged or sick people and those in need lead to a powerful sense of self-worth and satisfaction, both very strong factors in the desire to stay working in their respective organisations.

However some sectors will find it challenging to promote their CSR credentials. In the case of mining this awareness has prompted a campaign for them to be seen as partnering with the local community in which they work. Besides offering employment, they also prioritise locally based suppliers to be given the first option to provide goods and services.

Nokia

Nokia communicates to its employees the company's long-term goals in reducing carbon emissions to zero and that its flexi-base station product consumes 70 per cent less energy than previous models. This then helps its customers to reduce their costs and their carbon footprint. Nokia also encourages staff to volunteer and participate in activities to better the lives of those in their local communities.[18]

IMPORTANCE OF EFFECTIVE COMMUNICATIONS

Values need to be clearly communicated both by the organisation and by each leader. Employees want to know that their values are aligned with the company. The business philosophy of Panasonic, which included its mission, values and actions, was a key factor why Danny stayed with them for 21 years. Two-way communication is also key in any successful inclusive culture, and organisations should treat their employees the same as if they were their customers by listening to their views and suggestions.

LOCOG

Every six months staff were asked to complete a 20 question survey and the three statements that registered very positive comments were: 'The people I work with are committed to delivering a memorable Games', 'Working at London 2012 will enhance my future' and 'I am proud to say I work for London 2012'. In 2008 BAME and LGBT employees scored below average on these questions. By 2012 they scored above average, indicating that inclusion had been successful.

6 EMPATHY

Just as in a relationship, people want to feel listened to. Recognition does not have to be financial, it just has to acknowledge when someone has gone beyond the call of duty. A simple thank you is often sufficient. When people are never recognised, they stop trying.

In Laura Liswood's book *The Loudest Duck*[19] she tells the story of an elephant and a mouse being in the same room. Due to its size the elephant knows little about the mouse. On the other hand the mouse knows everything about the elephant. In an organisation those at the top will feel that they work in a meritocracy and feel they have worked their way up based on their ability. However, they may not recognise the advantages they had on their journey and the fact that others from a less privileged upbringing may not have had the same opportunities.

There is huge empathy deficit in many large corporations. The result is many companies do not create environments where great talent can thrive and flourish. We have tended to merely focus on specific contexts, short-term results and commercial returns. Those in management positions need to develop the empathy that allows them to appreciate what it might be like to come from a different background than the majority of people who work in the organisation.

RECOGNITION AND FEEDBACK

An empathic culture is particularly important for Millenials who are demanding a different kind of working experience: they are looking for connections; they want their voices – and their workplace requirements – to be heard. In most cases organisations are making slow progress in meeting diversity targets so it's becoming widely accepted that we need to recognise the wide range of social, biological, psychological and organisational factors that influence how we think and operate.

For empathy to become a core internal value, it must be prioritised and valued through the whole organisation, not just relegated to one department, which is usually the HR department. It has to start with the CEO demonstrating empathic behaviours and creating an empathic environment with a focus on improving internal culture.

Belinda Parmar developed an organisation called Lady Geek and works specifically on building empathy in organisations to retain diverse talent.

She says, 'The good news is that empathy can be demonstrated in the form of easy to implement nudges. Change small things and the bigger things can follow more quickly.'[20]

Unilever

At Unilever two-day inclusivity workshops were set up for everyone at manager level. In one of the exercises a 'race for life' was held, and, depending on how you respond to a number of questions, each participant either takes a step forward or a step back. The nature of the questions relate to your background and upbringing. The results showed that staff with an Indian or white background end up in general much further ahead than the black staff. 'This indicated to everyone,' Paddy Hull said, 'that we still don't have a level playing field when it comes to opportunities in South Africa.'

STORYTELLING

Demonstrating that your organisation actively welcomes diversity amongst its employees can be achieved by introducing a story-telling model, a powerful means of cascading information.

Royal Mail

A Royal Mail delivery director joined the company initially as a casual worker then joined their graduate scheme. She worked as an Executive Assistant and then after several other management moves she became Director of a branch, having three senior managers reporting to her. One of these managers was in his mid-fifties and had a reputation for being difficult and set in his ways. After a number of conversations and discussions he totally changed his attitude and is now a great advocate of her leadership and the company. She made changes, was not afraid to take risks, exited certain staff professionally and encouraged everyone to speak their mind. She says that she comes to work every day with 40 of her best friends, is hard-working but maintains a good work–life balance.

Showcasing these kinds of personal stories has helped the Royal Mail to promote opportunities for women in what has traditionally been a very male-dominated organisation.

7 USING AND LEARNING SKILLS

Before, the organisation was often the source of knowledge and learning. Now, through self-directed learning, people can educate themselves online, and information and knowledge is more widespread than ever before. The organisation is now in competition with people's own lives. A challenge is to turn that potential competition into collaboration and allow people to learn and grow at work as well as in the personal lives. If people do not gain net knowledge from their work then it begs the question, why bother turning up?

SELF-DIRECTED LEARNING

Organisations recognise the need to 'let go' and trust their employees to identify the most effective way for them to learn. The core performance and standards need to be established and agreed and then employees need to take ownership of their development. Access to technology is key, as is developing learning communities and understanding the ever-changing needs of the business.

Singapore Airlines

Singapore Airlines attributes its low attrition rate to its training initiatives targeted at Millennials. The company has identified the key element as being its self-directed learning strategy, which allows an employee to select the most appropriate module from a menu at any one moment. This could be language skills, management training or a range of soft skills.

8 AUTONOMY

ABILITY TO MAKE AN IMPACT

The biggest competitors for talented staff are not necessarily competitor firms, but self-employment. If an organisation is too controlling people may seek solace in running their own business or simply leave. The ability to make an impact is important, as is a clear understanding of what is expected right from the start of joining an organisation.

LOCOG Leadership Pledge

All staff were invited to sign a pledge launched by Archbishop Desmond Tutu. The pledge emphasises the priority given to diversity and inclusion and states: 'I am committed to deliver a memorable Games, with a lasting legacy that truly encompasses the world in a city; where each individual in

LOCOG takes personal responsibility for an inclusive approach that is fully integrated into every business decision.'

There was no obligation to sign the pledge and the fact that 96 per cent of full-time staff did sign demonstrated their individual commitment and buy-in to being part of an inclusive Games. Signing up became a conscious action, galvanising everyone to feel that they had a personal stake in contributing to achieve a common goal. The fact that most staff chose to put their signed copy of the pledge on their desks became a constant reminder to them of the LOCOG values (team, open, respect, inspire, distinct and deliver). It also became a framework for decision making.

NHS

In October 2015 NHS England and NHS Employers launched a pledge to employ more people with learning disabilities, which local NHS organisations are encouraged to sign up to. To be effective three steps were identified. First, a commitment to the Two Ticks accreditation, which we previously referred to. Second it is necessary to create an action plan that results in the employment of more people with disabilities. Finally, success stories are shared so other parts of the NHS will be able to learn from their work.

9 FUN

BRING YOUR WHOLE SELF TO WORK

Human beings like to have fun. If people have to dress in a particular way, speak in a particular way, act inauthentically, then the fun dries up. Allowing people to have fun, within an agreed framework, is a free way to allow people to be themselves inside rather than outside the organisation. The division of 'fun' in personal time and 'hard graft' in work time is a difficult one in a time when the work–life boundary is blurring. Allowing people to be their whole selves at work is a smart strategy to gain discretionary effort from happier employees.

Zappos

At Zappos, the online shoe retailer, fitting in to the company culture is seen as so important by the founder that new employees are offered $2,000 dollars to quit after the first week of the four-week induction if they decide that the job is not for them. Having fun is regarded as a key characteristic of its staff – if they enjoy their job as it will translate to their customers as well.

South West Airlines

The airline is famous for a culture of having happy and friendly staff. This is regularly commented on by its customers as a reason why they choose to fly with the company. Employees are encouraged to go the extra mile to make customers happy, empowering them to meet the vision. Anyone flying with South West is likely to encounter such behaviours, the flight attendants are more informally dressed and even though safety is of paramount importance they don't always stick to the standard scripted announcements that we usually get on other airlines.

10 REMUNERATION

There is a classic economic experiment where a sample of Harvard graduates are offered two choices. They could either take $100 and everyone else received $200, or they could receive $50 and everyone else received $25. Most people chose the option where they received the higher level than everyone else, even though it was a smaller absolute amount.

FAIRNESS

In other words, relativity and fairness matter, often more than absolute amount. To illustrate this point watch the Capuchin monkey fairness experiment on You Tube.[21] Two monkeys can see what each other receives from the laboratory technician in response to offering a rock. Every time one monkey offers a rock it is given a grape. The other one receives cucumber. In capuchin monkey land, grapes are more valuable commodities than cucumbers. Soon, one of them becomes very displeased when in return for the same effort (giving a rock) he receives only cucumber, whereas his neighbour (making the same effort) receives a grape.

Most people in the UK would think the Prime Minister's salary of £142,500 is more than fair, given his job. Most people would question some private sector salaries in the upper seven figures range when comparing like for like job descriptions.

TRANSPARENCY

From 2018 UK organisations in the private sector that employ more than 250 staff will be obliged to publish the pay gap between average male and female earnings.

There has, however, been little improvement in the gender pay gap in the UK for the last 10 years, and in December 2015 it was reported to be 9.4 per cent. There are many variations, depending on whether you work in the public or private sector, which industry and by age group. In the UK women are paid slightly more than men in the 22–29 age group but then from aged 40 onwards earn considerably less than men.

To date, five organisations in the UK have published figures on a voluntary basis. Tesco has simply announced a single percentage figure between male and female staff for each year on its website. PWC has also published a single figure inside its Transparency Report. Friends Life, in its Corporate Responsibility Report, gives more detail, showing a gender pay differential in ascending grade order, giving the average female pay relative to average male pay. The figures are then commented on, with insights as to possible reasons for variations from the previous year.

Genesis Housing Association

In the Openness and Transparency section on its website, Genesis publishes a range of data including workforce gender split and data on pay levels across different grades. It shows that there is little differential in the gender pay gap. Many people who may be interested in careers with Genesis have visited the website to look for diversity and inclusion information and can see that the awards it has received for its transparency has led to it building a reputation as an inclusive organisation.

Above lie the top ten reasons people leave organisations, coupled with practical interventions you can make to keep diverse talent. Of course, attrition is a natural part of organisational life and it is not always a bad thing. Underperformers and those not willing to embrace an inclusive culture may need to move on. But as we said with reference to exit interviews, you can never over-communicate and you can never intervene early enough. Finally, here are a couple of ways you can be pre-emptively inclusive.

PREDICTIVE ANALYTICS

Credit Suisse

Credit Suisse has a dedicated team who study variables that may potentially lead to a member of staff quitting. HR or the supervisor can then intervene pre-emptively to encourage them to stay, literally by holding a 'stay' interview, and can identify compensation, performance ratings, supervisory skills and time in role as key data points. They then contact the staff they have predicted as being restless and talk to them about possible new assignments or new challenges. Even if the person concerned is not interested, they are motivated by the fact that the company is showing concern about them and their future.

The reasons for leaving were different between the sexes. In the case of women it was more likely personal reasons whereas for men it was mainly for career advancement. Predictably, younger employees have higher voluntary attrition than older ones.

ALUMNI AS CLIENTS

In the new ecosystem where employees are also customers, it's important that people leave on as good terms as possible. McKinsey has based much of its growth as a business on exporting its people to client organisations, who in turn procure their services. Now KPMG has also established an 'office of career transition'.

Attrition is not necessarily a bad thing, but the way it is done can make all the difference. One simple check and balance is to conduct a proportionality assessment in reverse to check the diversity of exits.

People who are intellectually challenged, emotionally engaged, clearly valued, and appropriately rewarded rarely leave. Moreover, they perform at high levels and are your organisation's biggest asset, beyond the annual report clichéd statements.

The traditional way of thinking has been to expect your employees to be loyal and stay with you for many years. This was the norm from those of the baby-boomer generation. People from that era who work in HR and are responsible for recruitment would possibly not invite people to attend interviews where they had too many jobs on their CV and therefore there were doubts about their employability.

We have now moved from the corporate era to the ecosystem era. Employees are customers. They are your brand when they are with you and even more so when they leave. Ensure that good people are more likely to stay through appealing to self as well as role. And ensure that when people do leave they are your brand ambassadors.

We now live in a world where the majority of staff are Millennials; they are more likely to feel that moving companies is the right course of action, and they do not have the same degree of loyalty as previous generations. However, as we have described, there are many business benefits of being able to retain your talents and working in an inclusive culture will be a key factor in influencing their decision to stay or to go. The challenge to retain your talents will differ from region to region, between different generations and in different sectors. The approach to retaining the ones you want to keep must be personal.

KEY TAKEAWAYS

1 Diversity *is* engagement and being inclusive *is* a retention strategy. Treating people as diverse individuals is an efficient way to gain discretionary effort.

2 Treat employees as customers — they are increasingly spontaneous, virtually and hyper connected and are part of an ecosystem beyond just your organisation. Encourage people to bring their whole selves to work.

3 Fairness – ensure rigour and openness in promotions, mobility, succession planning, mentoring and sponsorship.

4 Don't underestimate the role of your executives and line managers in retaining your talents — they are the daily lived experience for most people and must recognise their responsibility in promoting ITM. Knowing someone's self is more powerful than knowing only their role.

5 Transparency and honesty – in an age of social media it is better to be honest about the good and the bad and try to improve, than to spin a lie that results in increased attrition.

NOTES

1　Winfrey, G (2014) Top 5 reasons employees quit, www.inc.com/graham-winfrey/5-reasons-employees-leave-their-jobs.html

2　HR Grapevine (2013) Top reasons people quit their job revealed, www.hrgrapevine.com/markets/hr/article/2013-11-29-top-reasons-people-quit-their-job-revealed

3　Winfrey, G (2014) Top 5 reasons employees quit, www.inc.com/graham-winfrey/5-reasons-employees-leave-their-jobs.html; Heathfield, SM (2015) Top 10 reasons why employees quit their job, http://humanresources.about.com/od/resigning-from-your-job/a/top-10-reasons-employees-quit-their-job.htm

4　Korn Ferry (2015) *Succession Matters: Part 2*, March, Korn Ferry.

5　Clutterbuck, D (2011) 'Mentoring and retention', *Report on Mentoring and Retention*, Clutterbuck Associates, emphasised the benefits of mentoring and its impact on retention. His research concluded that a mentoring programme which has been widely accepted and supported will be key in the retention of its staff.

6　Edelman Engage (3 January 2014) The benefits of reciprocal mentoring, www.edelman.com/post/the-benefits-of-reciprocal-mentoring/

7　Burson-Marseller (May 2010) Mentoring Millennials, https://hbr.org/2010/05/mentoring-millennials

8　Hewitt, SA (2013) *Forget a Mentor, Find a Sponsor*, HBR Press.

9　Center for Talent Innovation (26 September 2013) https://globenewswire.com/news-release/2013/09/26/576205/10050148/en/Center-for-Talent-Innovation-research-reveals-vast-majority-of-companies-are-losing-out-on-innovation.html

10　Women for Hire (2014) Women and Deutsche Bank: ATLAS Female Leadership Programme opens in London, http://womenforhire.com/advice/women-and-deutsche-bank-atlas-female-leadership-program-opens-in-london/

11　Schutte, S (2015) The top 10 UK employers for work:life balance – as ranked by employees, *Real Business*, 24 July.

12　Johnson, F (2014) These companies know how to treat employees right, *The Atlantic*, 9 December, www.theatlantic.com/business/archive/2014/12/these-companies-know-how-to-treat-employees-right/425868/

13　Brittin, M (27 October 2011) The end of work as we know it, Cass Business School.

14　CIPD (2010) *The Psychological Contract*, CIPD.

15 Groysberg, B and Connolly, K (September 2015) Great leaders who make the mix work, *HBR*.

16 5 tips for promoting an inclusive environment, 5 May 2015, Opensource.com, https://opensource.com/business/15/5/5-ways-promote-inclusive-environment

17 Business in the Community (2013) *Barclays Recruiting Diverse Talent Award*.

18 Nokia (2013) *People and Planet Report*, http://company.nokia.com/sites/default/files/download/nokia_people_planet_report_2013.pdf

19 Liswood, L (2009) *The Loudest Duck: Moving beyond diversity while embracing differences to achieve success*, Wiley.

20 Parmar, B (22 February) 8 ways to lead with empathy, World Economic Forum.

21 www.youtube.com/watch?v=-KSryJXDpZo

8

LEADERSHIP – HOW YOU CAN MAKE A DIFFERENCE

The Great Wall of China took centuries to build and stretches for 5,500 miles. However, its entire purpose was undermined in 1644 when the military general Wu Sangui opened the gates, allowing in northern enemies, ultimately leading to the fall of the Ming dynasty.

An organisation can have the best ITM system in the world, the most highly regarded diversity team in the industry, and all the systems and processes worthy of a world-class organisation. But they count for nothing if the CEO and senior figures in the organisation don't understand, lead and deliver inclusion.

Aristotle developed the three artistic proofs of leadership and persuasion: logos, pathos and ethos. These correspond with understanding, leading and delivery. Logos is an appeal to logic, and uses reason to generate buy-in. Pathos appeals to peoples' emotions and touches their own sense of self, in order to create followers. Ethos is an appeal to ethics, and relates to the character and credibility of the leader.

Understanding (logos) was covered in Part One of the book. We are all biased and can easily fall into HTM – indeed we may already be in it. It is important to have an historical sense of how we developed a segregated mindset – civil rights, evolution, the reasons we all believe we are objective even though we are quite the opposite. Similarly, we need to be aware of megatrends, where we are going and how fast things are changing. ITM is not something that 'just happens'. It happens as a consequence of conscious, inclusive leadership.[1]

What does leading inclusively (pathos) look like? Inclusive leadership is personal, sometimes messy and is about having the courage to make ourselves vulnerable. It is about adapting and absorbing risk so that people can bring their whole selves to work rather than remaining rigidly in their role. It's about being transparent, authentic and mobilising others. It's about appealing to heart as well as head.

Delivery (ethos) is dependent on behaviour – do as I do, not just as I say. In this chapter we analyse those behaviours that give the CEO and other leaders the best chance of making a difference. Holding people accountable, campaigning rather than dictating, being courageous to challenge norms and delegate without guarantees of return. We will look at some tangible examples of what inclusive leadership looks like in practice, everyday.

In 1970 Noel Burch came up with the conscious ladder of competence, seen in Figure 8.1. This provided a four-step framework of leadership moving from unconscious incompetence through to conscious and unconscious competence.

This is a useful framework for thinking about inclusive leadership. At first, we may not even know we are biased, we have the wrong intuition – we are unconsciously incompetent. Then, through discussion, perhaps through training and some implicit association tests, we become aware of our bias, we become consciously unskilled. This can be a low moment for executives as they are now aware of the problem but feel unable to solve it. We can then become consciously skilled by proactively trying to mitigate our bias through applied leadership, and if we are successful this may even become habitual, leading to unconscious skill. We'll go into what some of those skills look like later in the chapter, Figure 8.2 is our roadmap.

Figure 8.1 Hierarchy of competence

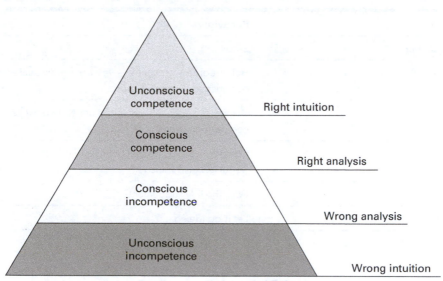

Figure 8.2 How to lead inclusively

Tool	Behaviour
Understand	*Logos*
1	Know your self
2	Talk to the person (self)
3	Flex your role to fit the person
4	Articulate inclusion
4.1	Redefine diversity and inclusion – skin in the game
4.2	Rediscover the business case – enlarging the pie
4.3	Re-frame the conversation – why wouldn't you?
Lead	*Pathos*
5	Adaptability – lead as well as manage
6	Transparency – challenge secrecy and build trust
7	Authenticity – speak from the heart
8	Mobilise the group – leadership is collective

Figure 8.2 *continued*

Tool	Behaviour
Deliver	*Ethos*
9	Hold people accountable – delivery is individual – conjunctive/disjunctive tasks
10	Campaign – Inspire people and generate positive competition over compliance
11	Courage – challenge bad norms and don't tolerate disguised discrimination
12	Walk the line (judgement)
13	Let it go (delegate)

UNDERSTAND (LOGOS)

Leaders gain credibility through knowledge. In terms of the business case for ITM, leaders could gain credibility through demonstrating that they understand diversity as a means to lower systemic risk, increase organisational resilience and enhance individual and team productivity. Employees see right through the CEO who proclaims their love of diversity while not understanding it. One reason Millennials are suspicious of Generation X and baby-boomer leaders is because they 'made it' under one set of rules and now they are preaching a different set of rules for the next generation.

We start with a contradiction that lies at the very heart of leadership and which must be resolved if we are to lead inclusively.

1 KNOW YOUR SELF

As professionals we claim to like diversity, but as human beings we still prefer sameness. This is essentially a confusion between self and role.

Self is who we are as human beings. As we defined at the start of the book, diversity is a mixture of DNA, social context and accumulated life experience to date. Who we have as close friends and colleagues (our 'in-group'), where we live and who we love, all come together to make us who we are as individuals. They reinforce our sense of self and give life meaning as well as define our own sense of place in the world.

Being aware of this is essential if you want to lead inclusively. If you are not aware of your own in-group then you can't consciously include people from your out-group.

Role is what we choose to do with our time on this planet. It could be a train driver, a photographer, a writer or a CEO. Within those professions we may have choice over how to fulfil our role. Admittedly, some people have more choice than others. Talking about 'choice' to a single parent struggling to juggle the kids and the day job may not be a welcome discussion. But assuming some agency, it could be to coast along and live for the pay cheque or it could be to charge ahead seeking the next promotion. It could be to look out for oneself or it could be to work as part of a team. It could be to remain within the comfort of our existing in-group or to reach out to the out-group. In this sense we can superficially embrace inclusion, or truly achieve real inclusion by consciously moving out of our comfort zone.

Our self is sacrosanct. Who we are as individuals is not up for debate. Diversity training that essentially attacks our self is inevitably doomed to failure. Not only that but it is ethically dubious as who has the right to tell others who they should be as humans? The diversity advocate wagging the finger looks suspiciously like the intransigent executive who lacks empathy and is concerned only with someone's job description.

There is no point in trying to change people's selves. Who people are is hard-wired. A one-hour training session on diversity cannot even hope to change minds in regard to self. Indeed, it may confirm and exacerbate existing biases. But without recognising our in-groups, without knowing our self, we cannot lead inclusively.

Karen Blackett

Karen's role is Chairwoman of media agency Mediacom. She is particularly aware of her self as a black woman in a predominantly white and male world. She said:

> I think there was always a competitive streak and that I had to push myself. That was the influence of my dad who always said 'You've got to be the best at everything and try twice as hard.' It was also due to my early athletic career and a focus on the value of sport in developing a competitive streak. I was always concerned with doing the very best at whatever I was doing, be it schoolwork or hobbies. So it's about the competitive part of my DNA, I suppose.

Dame Stephanie Shirley

In Chapter 1 we mentioned Dana Denis-Smith who had established Obelisk. A generation earlier Dame Stephanie Shirley was one of the first entrepreneurs who recognised that in the 1960s there were few opportunities for women, especially in the emerging technology sector. Her company Freelance Programmers mainly employed females and was built on providing flexible and rewarding jobs designing and writing software. In order to win in a male-dominated industry she referred to herself as Steve, thereby 'opening doors to business opportunities'. She had to change her policy of employing mainly women when equal opportunity legislation became law in the 1970s but by that time she had built the business to a turnover of $3 billion and when it floated it made 70 of its staff millionaires. Dame Shirley said: 'A lot of people go into business to make money but I went in with a mission for women.'[2]

2 TALK TO THE PERSON (SELF)

As we discussed in Chapter 2, we all have in-groups and out-groups. In addition, we can manage people according to their role (job description) and according to their self (personality). These concepts are summarised in Figures 8.3 and 8.4.

Figure 8.3 Role and self

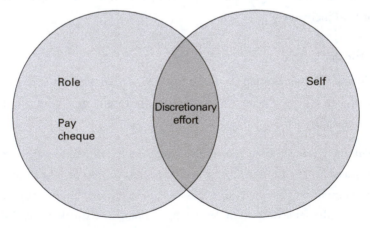

Figure 8.4 In-groups and out-groups

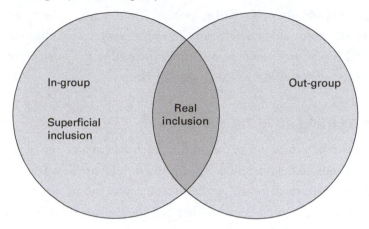

Note: For more on real and superficial inclusion see *The Inclusion Imperative*

There is genuine value in talking to the person as a human being rather than just in their role. If you talk to the self you can move the relationship from transactional to personal. This is more valuable and sustainable, and allows the possibility of garnering discretionary effort.

Sacha Romanovitch

Sacha's role is CEO of accountancy firm Grant Thornton. She was adopted by a Russian father and an English mother. She recalls her father suffering discrimination at work because he was a foreigner. Her great-aunt Monica worked for Coutts Bank. In the 1930s male managers were given a pint of beer at lunchtime but this benefit was not given to women. Great-aunt Monica was determined to find a way to ensure she also received the same perk. She went to see her doctor and managed to persuade him to prescribe her a glass of Guinness a day for medical reasons. Coutts relented and she enjoyed her lunchtime drink alongside her male colleagues.

This insight into Sacha's self helps explain how she plays her role. She takes the time to learn about individual personalities in her organisation, beyond their role. She consciously includes out-groups. For example, to encourage ideas and hear from the 'quiet voices', Sacha has introduced an online platform on which people are encouraged to share their views – almost 2,500 have done so. In addition, over 500 have attended in-depth three-day workshops to become 'advocates' working on the tipping point principle whereby they then had responsibility to engage others and bring them into the fold, and to date Grant Thornton has received approximately 500 'solid ideas' (one example was putting together the buying power of many of their SME clients to gain bigger discounts).

3 FLEX YOUR ROLE TO FIT THE PERSON

If you only talk to someone in their role, rather than as a person, you will be stuck in a transactional relationship as shown in Figure 8.3. This could be valuable to the extent of their pay cheque, but you will miss out on discretionary effort. In Figure 8.3 we see that pay cheque is within the context of role –if paid to do a job, a person remains in role to execute it. But in order to gain discretionary effort from the employee we have to allow them to be themselves. Furthermore, they may have to flex their self considerably to fit into the role you are prescribing, which would be inefficient. Far better for you to intentionally flex your role so that they have more chance of remaining in their self, being happier, more authentic and more productive.

Think about your role and what it is that you want to get done. It is not contradictory to be a white, straight man in one's being and yet advocate plurality in one's role. Indeed for the CEO or senior leaders of a modern organisation this tension (as opposed to contradiction) is an important one to hold. The tension is between your own self and role, their self and role and your in-groups and out-groups.

You might be the CEO, the HR director, the chief diversity officer, the executive champion, or a leader in any number of roles in your organisation or professional situation. How you can hold this tension will help you make your mark as an inclusive leader.

Making yourself vulnerable is one way to reach people's own selves and to include out-groups. In nine out of ten circumstances if you instigate vulnerability and sharing of your self, it will be reciprocated.

Don't think contradiction, think tension. And think how good you are at holding that tension. Know your self and hold it sacred. But nudge your role – take mini risks, learn and grow as a leader.

Peter Cheese

Peter's role is CEO of CIPD, the UK HR professional body. He believes that diversity encompasses multiple perspectives – where I work, what I do and how I work. He has therefore led an organisational change programme so that the organisation better practices what it preaches. Peter explained that by adapting the organisation to become more agile and responsive to professional member needs, members and employees can contribute more.

Alistair Dormer

Alistair's role is CEO of Hitachi Rail. He lost his father when he was young so he grew up in a one-parent family. He was third of four siblings and became the peacemaker of the family, helping resolve disputes. When he left naval college at 21 he joined a ship and had five more experienced staff working for him. He realised if he only used his rank to direct them, he would forego their experience. He therefore flexed his role and encouraged them to make their own decisions rather than look to him for instruction, as would be normal in the rank structure. Instead, he coached them to contribute based on their strengths and experience.

4 ARTICULATE INCLUSION

How you define and articulate inclusion will determine how it is received by colleagues. If colleagues perceive it as your agenda, or only in your interests, you are unlikely to get buy-in. But if you can redefine inclusion as having their own interests at heart too, show the simplicity of the business case and re-frame the conversation, you stand a better chance of people coming on board.

4.1 REDEFINE DIVERSITY AND INCLUSION – SKIN IN THE GAME

One of the most effective tools leaders use is to make inclusion clearly in the other person's interests also. In other words, we both have skin in the game. For example, the UN campaign #HeforShe is about male executives championing gender equality, rather than women championing gender equality alone. Gender equality is in men's interests, as having more women involved in decision making is more likely to help the organisation empathise with diverse clients, decrease groupthink and increase cognitive diversity in decision making. As most men still believe 'gender' is a 'female' issue this redefinition is important.

Ronan Dunne

Ronan's role is CEO of O2, the communications company. Ronan trained as a chartered accountant and early in his career he had two consecutive female bosses, a rare situation in the 1980s. He felt they were instrumental in fostering an inclusive working environment. Working in the City he noticed a difference immediately, including from an ethnic perspective. Despite being white and male, the most common profile of City workers at the time, he felt being Irish meant he did not fit 'the mould' of many others. He felt an outsider. At that time he was working for a French bank where it was particularly important that you went to a well-regarded university. Ronan wasn't French and didn't go to university. By bonding with other 'outsiders' he realised they could all benefit from greater inclusion in the predominantly French culture, including French people who didn't attend the 'correct' universities. He felt his female boss was instrumental in fostering a sense of belonging.

4.2 REDISCOVER THE BUSINESS CASE – ENLARGING THE PIE

A game Steve plays with his MBA students is to have an arm wrestle. He invites students to pair up with the person next to them. People frequently sit next to people they consider more likely to be in their in-group and not out-group so they feel may more able to go head to head with their neighbour. The goal is to score as many points as possible in 30 seconds. Players earn one point for each time the back of their opponent's hand touches the table. Usually 90 per cent of the class, predominantly male, scores 0–2 points. About 10 per cent of the class, predominantly women, has scored 30–40 points. How can that be?[3]

It is the responsibility of the inclusive leader to show how letting others win can allow the individual to win also. By not resisting, we can both score more points and enlarge the pie rather than be stuck in a zero-sum game. Advancement or winning is not only dependent on strength, it's a question of lowering the resistance of your would-be opponents. This can be achieved through teamwork, generosity or empathy rather than brute force. This example is directly applicable to the real world situation of promotions. Instead of allegations of positive discrimination, people realise that genuine meritocratic promotions are in everyone's interest.

Sacha Romanovitch

Sacha mentioned that having a diverse workforce creates business opportunities as 'cross -thinking creates better answers'. She told us:

> We have won business recently by ensuring that those pitching for the business come from different backgrounds. One of our management team trained as a surveyor and their approach based on their background convinced the prospective client that we had a breadth of experience that could best support their activities. Another example was when we won an account in the manufacturing sector. One of our team had worked in the steel business and the client could recognise that he understood their business and we won their account. Had we all had similar backgrounds we simply would not have won this business.

4.3 RE-FRAME THE CONVERSATION – WHY WOULDN'T YOU?

Any significant business decision should be subject to scrutiny and properly interrogated. However, the bar seems to be higher for diversity than for other issues. We have witnessed hiring decisions, investment decisions and marketing decisions made on 'gut instinct' whereas diversity frequently requires a Nobel economics prize business case in order to be taken seriously. We advocate avoiding that bear trap and instead of trying to prove why, pose the question why wouldn't you? If you really believe the business case of lowering systemic risk, increasing productivity and resilience then why wouldn't you engage in ITM?

LEAD (PATHOS)

With understanding comes credibility. Leadership then becomes about managing the gap between what we now understand and what our actions demonstrate we really value. This builds on what we learned about cognitive dissonance in Chapter 2. One way to bridge that intention/action gap is to be empathetic. Walking in someone else's shoes allows you to transgress the inconsistency in your own thoughts. Seeing the world through a different lens allows us to breach cognitive dissonance.

To understand your leadership lens, think about your commute to work. Do you drive? Cycle? Take the metro? Walk? Do you drop your children off at school, on the way? Whatever way you get to work affects the way you see the rest of the day.

If you change to another mode of transport, you will have a different day. For example, when a partner at a London law firm switched from having his driver collect him every morning at 6am to cycling twice a week he gained a genuinely different perspective on his work (as well as losing weight). He appreciated the perspective of the cyclist much more than he ever did and the importance of cars keeping their distance and avoiding the cyclist lines and marked zones at junctions. But he noticed much more than that. As he moved at a slower pace and there was no window shielding the noise and wind from his face he noticed shops that he had previously ignored. He noticed people's faces and learned to read pedestrians more. One day he even tried walking (he had his driver drop him off a mile from the office) and the differences were accentuated further. Was this extra time an opportunity cost on his working day? His conclusion was quite the opposite – it was an investment in curiosity and noticing things he had previously ignored. For him it became meditation and a genuinely different lens on the world.

The commuting analogy can be applied to any scenario where we decide to walk in someone else's shoes. Wayne Dyer, an American author, said, 'If you change the way you look at things, the things you look at change.'[4] It makes us more empathetic, but it is also in our own self-interest to understand the world from other people's perspective.

5 ADAPTABILITY – LEAD AS WELL AS MANAGE

Looking at the world through different lenses is a process of adaptation. Another is being globally minded, curious and culturally aware. An open

Figure 8.5 Technical versus adaptive work

Type of work	What's the work?	Who does the work?
Technical	Apply current know-how	Authorities
Adaptive	Learn new ways	The people with the challenge

Source: Adapted from Ron Heifitz and Marty Linsky (2002) *Leadership on the Line,* Harvard Business Press, 'Distinguishing technical from adaptive challenges'. See also Dean Williams (2005) *Real Leadership,* Berrett-Koehler

mind does not necessarily come naturally, it needs to be consciously practiced, the conscious competence we referred to at the start of the chapter. Adaptation does not necessarily come naturally either, but adapting to new circumstances as quickly as possible is critical to remaining relevant in changing markets. An approach that encapsulates this principle was advocated by Konosuke Matsushita, founder of Panasonic. He emphasised the importance of having an open mind – sunao in Japanese. This is the level of the human mind where it becomes free, transparent and able to think, and able to decide with minimal prejudice.It allows us to see things as they really are. Having a sunao mind and being flexible in approach can be the difference between engaging and alienating a diverse, multi-cultural workforce.[5]

Many people in positions of authority apply current know-how to try to solve new challenges, as shown in Figure 8.5. However, an adaptive approach can yield superior results. If you always do what you've always done, you will always get what you've always got. The more diversity in your toolbox, the more resources you have to solve new challenges. This can be disruptive as it can challenge existing hierarchies and power structures in organisations. It is dependent, therefore, on people with authority being humble enough to acknowledge that they don't have all the answers and perhaps allowing 'junior' people or 'external' people to lead on key projects.

LOCOG

For many at LOCOG, at least at the start, putting on the Games was a technical exercise. It was possibly the largest and most complex technical exercise imaginable. Delivering 26 simultaneous world championships over 134 venues, with a workforce of 200,000 and the entire world watching, followed by 20 more simultaneous world championships two weeks later for the Paralympic Games, was the ultimate technical challenge. The 2012 Olympic Games was comprised of 26 world championships (39 disciplines) across 34 venues, 8.8 million tickets, 10,490 athletes, 302 medal events, 21,000 media and broadcasters, 19 competition days, 2,961 technical officials, 204 National Olympic Committees, 5,770 team officials and 5,000 anti-doping samples. In order to cope with this challenge, people understandably resorted to technical know-how.

Past Games had endured real challenges, from venue readiness at Athens 2004, terrorism at Munich 1972 and Atlanta 1996 to boycotts at Moscow 1980 and Los Angeles 1984. Given this, it is perhaps understandable that many would have relied on what we already know and have learnt over the years. They would have proclaimed success as simply the successful staging of the event, as indeed happened in London in July, August and September 2012.

For others inside and outside the organisation, it was more than that. Technical excellence was a prerequisite to success, but not success in and of itself. Nine billion pounds and the chance of a lifetime constituted too great an input to only produce a technical output, no matter how impressive. We needed to change the system, we needed to engage in adaptive work. This latter group prevailed. 'Legacy' became the key word, and the mission of the organisation became 'to use the power of the Games to inspire change'.

6 TRANSPARENCY – CHALLENGE SECRECY AND BUILD TRUST

Secrecy is increasingly hard to justify and increasingly hard to maintain in the digital age. Rather than fight megatrends, build trust through being open. Trust is free and a very efficient way to manage people.

UK Sport launched the Equality standard for sport that benchmarked sporting federations and governing bodies on their diversity performance and published a league table online. Benchmarking is an alternative to quotas and more agile, market-led and transparent. Knowing that people could see their performance encouraged executives in sporting organisations to think about their leadership and behaviour. This contrasts with the secrecy surrounding FIFA. You can judge how things turned out.

Paul Deighton

Paul's role was CEO of London 2012. He said:

> In my role at Goldman Sachs and more recently as Minister in the previous
> coalition government I put the emphasis on getting the right talent in place
> and having a diverse culture. It was important to demonstrate to all LOCOG
> management how crucial diversity and inclusion were to our overall success so
> it was necessary to lead by example, by showing how important it was to me.
> Then it made it easier to state my expectations to all the team. The Executive
> Committee wanted to please and so the tone from the top was crucial.

Paul championed setting public targets and orientating the entire HR
process to meet them through recruitment, promotions and retention as well
as several pioneering 'nudges', such as group interviews.[6] The benefits of this
transparency included lower recruitment costs through bundled hires, use of
created talent pools and shortened time to hire. Procurement costs were
reduced through online procurement and increased competition achieved
through transparency and supplier outreach. Supplier diversity and innovation
was achieved in the torch design, user-led translation services, novel video
production, state of the art ceremonies production and bus transport services
from minority suppliers all over the UK.

Had targets not been set and success defined in 2008 there would have
been no plan, measurement or road map on how to get there. For example,
without explicit targets the majority of people who would have applied to
be Games Makers would have been middle- or upper-class people who
could have afforded the time off work, were prior networked and were not
reflective of the communities of East London where the majority of events
were held.

7 AUTHENTICITY – SPEAK FROM THE HEART

In 2014 Elisabeth Kelan produced a report *Winning Hearts and Minds*[7],
which reviewed how CEOs can advocate the case for gender equality.
It found that rather than giving a rehearsed (or even worse read) script on
the business case for gender equality, it was far more authentic, effective and
engaging for leaders to just talk.

Simon Collins

Simon's role is Chairman of KPMG UK. He talked about how he felt bad as his wife's career 'survived the birth of our first child. But not our second.' He talked about why gender equality was important to him personally. When KPMG launched its targets he gave an interview to the *Financial Times* and said, 'We are as equally prepared to fail as we are desperately hoping to succeed.' In KPMG's inclusion week in 2014 Steve chaired a panel called 'Manning up' that interviewed leading (alpha) men in the organisation. The first question he asked them was, 'Would you want your daughter to work here?'

From February to July 2014 Simon championed a process to co-create the firm's inaugural inclusive leadership strategy. This involved 500 employees co-drafting a strategy of the what, why and how in terms of KPMG becoming a more diverse and inclusive organisation. Colleagues were literally walked through a room in groups of 10–15 and invited to comment and edit the strategy in real time with Post-it notes and captured interviews. This appealed to self and their personal stake in a more inclusive environment.

Creating a personal connection to the inclusion agenda has produced quantitative results. Female graduate recruitment is steadily increasing from 36 per cent in 2014 towards 50 per cent in 2016. There is more diversity in promotions, for example audit female promotions to partnership were 50:50 in 2015.

Qualitative measures include more inclusive leadership from partners resulting in enhanced client conversations, more pitch wins, better work allocation to diverse talent, pull through of diverse talent through mentoring and sponsorship and genuine behaviour change, especially amongst the target audience of senior white men.

8 MOBILISE THE GROUP – LEADERSHIP IS COLLECTIVE

Leadership is collective. By consulting others, rather than imposing will, a group can be mobilised to better solve challenges. It also decreases the fear factor of challenging the prevailing norm alone as a single actor. Communicating that an inclusive talent strategy is a high-priority issue for them through social media, town hall meetings and internal communication tools is important. Whenever the CEO articulates her or his vision for the company, ensure that ITM is part of it.

DELIVER (ETHOS)

Nothing creates momentum like results. Tangible actions and proof points of inclusion will galvanise people. As Indra Nooyi, CEO of PepsiCo, said, 'It's not just about the money, it's how you make the money.'[8]

9 HOLD PEOPLE ACCOUNTABLE – DELIVERY IS INDIVIDUAL – CONJUNCTIVE/DISJUNCTIVE TASKS

Whereas leadership is a group activity, delivery is an individual responsibility. The organisational theorist Ivan Dale Steiner analysed group processes and productivity and diagnosed conjunctive and disjunctive tasks.[9] Conjunctive tasks are those requiring the participation of all team members and are often dependent on the least capable performer. Disjunctive tasks are those that are dependent on a single person according to their skill set and can be brought back to benefit the whole group. A headache for CEOs worldwide is trying to break down tasks and work into disjunctive tasks to optimise efficiency and to maximise the role played by diverse people.

It is not, therefore, as is often assumed, that holding individuals accountable is somehow invasive or anti-inclusion. Quite the opposite; holding people accountable and setting clear expectations allows people to demonstrate their unique skill set. Breaking down more conjunctive tasks into disjunctive tasks benefits the individual and the organisation. Distributed problem-solving allows simultaneous investigation, both empowering individuals and increasing the rate of innovation in the organisation. And the more diversity you have in your organisation, the more options for disjunctive tasks abound.

One of the most demotivating occurrences for diverse talent is when the top management sets the right tone but line managers behave badly. It's line managers, not senior management, who influence most people's daily work experience. Leaders should dedicate time and commitment to questioning line management and be actively involved in the talent process. They should also impose consequences for bad behaviour in the form of bonus withholding, compulsory training or simply engage in conversations to make their expectations clear.

Examples of what leaders can do would include demonstrating an authentic interest in the development of all staff and whenever possible requesting to meet and speak to people either individually or in groups.

Request data from HR so that you are updated at all times with relevant statistics, for example attrition rate, who is being recruited and promoted from a gender, ethnicity and LGBT perspective, and results of employee engagement. And, crucially, ask questions of your succession planning process in order to ensure that the most capable talents throughout the organisation are being recognised – namely, there is minimal bias or favouritism.

Merck, Nissan, General Mills, Telstra and ABB North America are among the many organisations that make diversity and inclusion goals part of their managers' performance objectives. 'Each of my direct reports has things that they're going to do personally to help promote diversity, not things that they can assign to their team,' explained Brian Moynihan, CEO of Bank of America. 'I say, "What are you going to do to get involved?" For example, they can mentor somebody individually or sponsor diversity events.' AT&T takes a different approach. 'We benchmark diversity objectives at the senior levels of management, and we have regular meetings around my table about how we're advancing,' said Randall Stephenson, CEO of AT&T. 'A portion of our officers' compensation is based on achieving those objectives.' Many CEOs also reported that managers who embraced diversity were more likely to be considered for promotion at their organisations.[10]

10 CAMPAIGN – INSPIRE PEOPLE AND GENERATE POSITIVE COMPETITION OVER COMPLIANCE

People are inspired by leaders who believe in an inclusive mission. It's more effective to lead by example and show rather than tell. We have discussed how compliance (a Diversity 101 approach) has limited value. It does have value, but it is unlikely to inspire in and of itself. A more effective strategy may be to generate positive, aspirational competition over enforced compliance. This can be a faster, more efficient way to achieving results, a genuine meritocracy and a more inclusive culture.

Ethics matter. Rather than relying on legal compliance, or assuming authority alone will carry the day, ethics can transgress both compliance and hierarchy. They can appeal to self as well as role and form a bridge to out-groups.

Lieutenant General David Morrison

David retired as Chief of the Australian Army in May 2015. In 2013 there was a series of incidents where a group of officers created and distributed highly inappropriate material demeaning women. David could have investigated privately, just taken these men aside and followed due process. He could even, of course, have ignored it, as has happened in the past in many organisations when the victim of discrimination has been moved rather than the perpetrator.

Instead he did something very different, and rather inspirational.

He went on national television and spoke to the entire country.[11] He appealed to ethos and asked others to help him rid the army of sexism by stating, 'The standard you walk past is the standard you accept.' He added, 'If you think that demeaning women is acceptable behaviour then get out. There is no place for you among this band of brothers, and sisters.' If anyone could have commanded it was the General. But he did something far more effective, he co-opted thousands of others to join him in a campaign and in so doing changed the norm far more effectively and sustainably.

11 COURAGE – CHALLENGE BAD NORMS AND DON'T TOLERATE

It takes a brave leader to challenge the norm or go against the herd. It requires courage to challenge myths and conventional wisdom.

The economic research agency YSC was commissioned by KPMG in the UK to produce a groundbreaking report, *Cracking the Code*.[12] This report, based on hundreds of interviews with senior female executives published (and challenged) ten 'myths' around gender equality. For example, it challenged the notion that women were 'less ambitious' or 'more likely to decline travel or promotion opportunities'. When myths remain unchallenged they acquire credibility.

Another example is positive discrimination. One of the main audiences for inclusion work is the proverbial straight white male middle manager who may now think that his promotion prospects are diminished because he's 'not wearing a skirt' (actual quote from a colleague we have worked with). In fact we can show, based on data, that if any positive discrimination is occurring, it is generally in favour of men, who are more networked, more profiled, more in credit with senior decision makers, more aggressive and more likely to leave if they don't get what they want. KPMG was able to show, based on data, that it was not positive discrimination to expect to promote people who were in proportion to the talent available. But more than the data, KPMG needed leaders who would articulate this. So the leadership of many partners was crucial to rebutting the myth of female positive discrimination.

One purpose of myths is to avoid changing the current norm that serves some people very well. Leaders can speak out explaining how transparency is in the interests of everyone, especially those brilliant introverts who may have been previously overlooked. Moreover, they can refuse to apologise for greater competition that is in the interests of a meritocratic ITM system. Diversity is the enemy of mediocrity.

Moya Greene

Moya is CEO of Royal Mail Group. She is a female CEO of a business that, in spite of significant advances in gender diversity, is still 85 per cent male. Upon taking up her position she toured the sorting offices up and down the country. She had a personal, visceral reaction: 'I didn't like what I saw.' 'There was significant diversity at the lowest level but all the managers and above were white 50-year-old men,' said Moya, 'and we looked completely different from the customer base we were serving.'

Moya wanted to inject diversity to challenge current practices. She believes that 'I am the product of affirmative action and wouldn't have had the opportunity I've had without it. I now believe that the threat of quotas is critical in spurring continued action to move forward today.' Moya successfully oversaw the flotation of Royal Mail from the public sector to the private sector and the modernisation and diversification of one of the most traditional organisations in the UK.

Orna Ni-Chionna, Senior Independent Non-Executive Director of Royal Mail, said:

> I have seen many CEOs in action; but Moya is truly distinctive because she is both intuitive and intellectually rigorous. She has used her insights to craft

a vision for Royal Mail's future which helped her to persuade politicians and regulators of the need for radical change within 12 months of her arrival. She has been decisive in the steps she has taken to make that vision a reality; and her exceptional communication skills are instantly apparent to all who meet her. Her style is informal and disarming. Her sparkling use of language to paint vivid pictures makes her a compelling and engaging speaker, whether at shareholder presentations, at industry events or at meetings to inspire women and minorities to seize leadership opportunities. She reaches out to every one of our 166,000 staff, engaging with all and helping them see both the need for change and how to achieve that change quickly.

12 WALK THE LINE

Walking the line is knowing when to push an issue and when to hold steady. If you push too hard, at the wrong moment, you risk being shot down. If you don't push at all, nothing will change. Your judgement call will largely depend on whether the issue had yet ripened sufficiently. Your judgement call will be how to change pace so as to keep progressing but not become the proverbial bull in a china shop. Inclusion is a long game and while short wins should be savoured, they should not be at the expense of more significant long-term goals.

Helena Morrissey

Helena is one of the handful of female CEOs in the City of London. Her role is to run Newton Asset Management. In addition, Helena founded and leads the 30% Club campaigning for more female representation at senior levels. While clearly championing inclusion, Helena has to pick her battles and walk the line on a daily basis. She has to play her role strategically to make a difference. If she intervened on every issue on every occasion it would diminish her political capital and possibly exacerbate stereotypes. So she has to prioritise where and when to intervene on diversity issues to have maximum effect. One key tool is partnering, getting men to speak up on gender parity. Hence the focus on getting chairmen to join the 30% Club and visibly champion the campaign. By partnering with others, and walking the line strategically, Helena has played her role and herself brilliantly to maximum effect.

13 LETTING GO

It is very hard for people who have achieved success using one methodology to adapt and use a different one. But the proverbial 'what got you here won't get you there' is never more true than with reference to inclusive leadership. It cannot be a single egotistical crusade, it has to be a collective enterprise, a group project. You cannot do it all yourself, and the results would be worse if you did. Devolving decision making to the lowest practical level is the way to have efficiency and inclusion.

It is hard for those with exacting standards to let go. But it is the only way to scale the work as well as ensure sufficient buy in.

The London 2012 Games Makers

LOCOG recruited 200,000 people to stage London 2012. It was a physical impossibility to know them all personally, but there were ways in which we could allow self to come to the fore. Basic training covered role material such as health and safety, disability confidence and great customer service. But real customer service came from the explicit permission given to bring your whole self to work. Anyone who experienced the London Games probably recalls a range of characters pouring their personality into megaphones and joking with the public. This was Paul Deighton and other London 2012 managers, Steve included, letting go, and it made for exceptional customer service.

OUTSIDERS

Most of the CEOs we interviewed and have referred to in this chapter, and throughout the book, came from outside their organisation or sector. Depending on where an organisation sits on the Diversity and Inclusion Maturity Model© will determine how much external intervention they require. The Olympic movement required significant intervention and Paul provided it. If there already exists an open and diverse culture then maybe it's preferable to promote from within, as with Sacha at Grant Thornton. Outsiders can exist inside as well as outside. In all cases, inclusive leaders lead from themselves and from the heart. They place their self on the table and adapt their role as necessary in order to achieve the results they seek. In this sense, the background of the CEO, their education, family, early career and their self stand out as significant.

Paul Deighton didn't come from sport and yet he ran the biggest sporting event on the planet. Ronan Dunne didn't come from communications and yet he ended up running the second largest communications company in the UK. Sacha Romanovich was adopted by a Russian father and English mother. Both Pamela Maynard and Karen Blackett are black women who have made it to the top of their respective organisations. Alistair Dormer grew up without a father, Simon Collins is an introvert and Helena Morrissey is a female CEO in a male-dominated environment. Antonio Simoes is the only openly gay CEO in London banking. David Morrison broke with Army convention by going on public television. Moya Greene was a Canadian woman and revolutionised one of the most conservative British male-dominated organisations.

Outsiders offer tremendous value because they come from someone else's out-group. They have given of themselves as well as their role and in so doing act as a role model for others.

COURAGE, CREATIVITY AND TALENT

We hope the inclusive leadership behaviours we have discussed have resonated with you and inspired you. Fundamentally this comes down to courage, creativity and talent.

Courage, because going against the herd is hard. Ask any one of the outsiders. Creativity, because people in HTM worlds are expecting diversity practitioners and advocates to fall in to a Diversity 101 or Diversity 2.0 trap. Talent, because at the end of the day this is the subject of this book, and the objective of our leadership quests.

Let's revisit the questions we posed at the start of the book.

Have you ever wondered why certain decisions were made? Have you ever been frustrated at the promotion of someone who is less able or diligent but performs better in a 'hands up' culture? Have you ever been exasperated at the intransigence of the so-called meritocracy and decided to vote with your feet, rather than take on the status quo?

We tried to answer the first question in Part One and the second two questions in Part Two. Moreover, we have tried to answer them with references to both systems (Chapters 5–7) and leadership. We hope you are now better able to answer these questions. If not, maybe you are part of the problem? Do you bring your self to the table or do you remain in role? Do you consciously include your out-groups or do you remain in your tribe? How inclusive is your leadership style?

SELF-INTEREST AND COLLECTIVE GOOD

Understanding the world from someone else's perspective lies at the heart of the leadership conundrum. As long as people think it is merely charity to do so we remain stuck in a zero-sum world. Think back to the arm wrestle. The male MBA student who spent his 30 seconds beating his opponent and hurting his arm in order to score two points was outdone by the woman who scored 40 points through cooperation.

This exercise and example needs to be scaled up in order to challenge HTM. Systems can do that, but leaders are required to lead the process. We take inspiration from a quote from Rabbi Hillel:

> If I am not for myself, then who will be for me?
> And if I am only for myself, then what am I?
> And if not now, when?
>
> Rabbi Hillel[13]

We have shown there is a series of systematic changes that can be implemented to good effect, in recruitment, promotion and retention. But we end with the most important dependency of all, and that's your inclusive leadership.

KEY TAKEAWAYS

1 The tone from the top carries exponential weight in creating an inclusive culture in the organisation. Inclusion can be accelerated by leaders making themselves vulnerable and revealing something of their self as well as remaining in role and relying on authority.

2 Above words, it is your actions and how you behave that will be the main determinant of whether people believe there is an inclusive culture. Do as I do, not as I say is the best way to bridge cognitive dissonance.

3 Leadership can be taught. Reflecting on your own life experience to date, your own biases and the lenses you use will better equip you to lead inclusively and better understand your own perspective in relation to others.

4 Self-awareness around individual bias will also equip the professional to make more accurate decisions. Additionally, it will help you to recognise and be aware of bias in others.

5 To go against the norm can be a lonely place. To decrease your own exposure, partner and build allies, walk the line and let go so that you are not the sole proponent of change.

NOTES

1 See the contradiction between leadership (conscious inclusion) and nudges (unconscious, systematic inclusion).

2 Pagano, M (2014) Dame Stephanie Shirley: Success has a cost. Women today are so naive, *Independent*, 23 August, www.independent.co.uk/news/people/dame-stephanie-shirley-success-has-a-cost-women-today-are-so-na-ve-9687846.html

3 With thanks to Patrick McWhinney, Young Global Leader, World Economic Forum for the original inspiration.

4 Dyer, WW (2008) *Change Your Thoughts, Change Your Life*, Hay House.

5 Turner, P and Kalman, D (2014) *Make Your People Before You Make Your Products*, John Wiley.

6 See Frost, P (2014) *The Inclusion Imperative*, Kogan Page, for more information about the project.

7 Kelan, E (2014) *Winning Hearts and Minds*, King's College London, www.kcl.ac.uk/newsevents/news/newsrecords/2014/January/Winning-hearts-and-minds.aspx

8 Ignatius, A (September 2015) How Indra Nooyi turned design thinking into strategy: an interview with Pepsico's CEO, HBR.

9 Steiner, ID (1972) Group Process and Productivity, Academic Press.

10 Groysberg, B and Connolly, K (September 2015) Great leaders who make the mix work, *HBR*.

11 Message from the Chief of Army Lieutenant-General David Morrison, 12 June 2013.

12 YSC (2014) *Cracking the Code*, YSC.

13 Rabbi Hillel (2009) Pirkei Avot: Ethics of the Fathers, Merkos L'Inyonei Chinuch, New York.

RESOLUTION

change the system [unconscious nudges]

+

change your behaviour [conscious leadership]

=

inclusion

AFTERWORD

Diversity, inclusion and talent are now established topics in boardrooms worldwide. But the reality still does not match the rhetoric.

Our overriding motivation in writing this book was twofold. First, to marshal the evidence and reframe the inclusion debate in terms of *why*. Second, to offer practical advice on *how* to implement an inclusive talent management strategy. As Emmeline Pankhurst said over a century ago, *deeds not words*.

Having read our book, do you now believe developing and implementing an ITM strategy for your organisation is a business imperative? If so, what are you doing about it?

Beyond the business case, this becomes a question of leadership. If you really believe the business case, and you believe you are an inclusive leader, then you cannot outsource responsibility for diversity to other people. You cannot claim to believe in something you fail to take responsibility for.

Leadership is a team effort, and we have attempted to reframe the issues to help you persuade others that inclusive talent management is in their interests too. But delivery is an individual responsibility. The book is only as good as what you now intend to put into action.

In the final analysis, the success of organisations depends on the contribution, effectiveness and creativity of their people. All of their people. If you are not nurturing the gene pool, then you will become extinct. An ITM strategy becomes an existential strategy.

Orchestras used to interview people as most organisations still do – face to face. Then, in the 1970s, US orchestras tried something different. They interviewed people performing behind a curtain. The only criteria were the sound and the quality of the music. No faces, no names, no accents, no bias. It became so scientific that women who might wear high-heeled shoes were asked to remove them so as to not make a sound that might lead to potential gender discrimination amongst the assessors.

Compare European and American orchestras today and what do you find? Which ones are more diverse? And, by way of logical reasoning, which ones might have the edge in terms of performance?

Just as an orchestra needs many different players to make beautiful music, a diverse workforce is more likely to create a culture of inspiration and engagement. With inclusive conducting, it can also be more resilient, less exposed to risk and higher-performing.

Innovation usually emerges when diverse people collaborate to generate a wide-ranging portfolio of ideas, which they then refine and evolve into new ideas. There may be tension and disagreement but, if properly channelled, this can lead to important fresh and creative ways of doing business.

One of the biggest challenges organisations face is to sustain the implementation of their ITM strategy. We have learnt from our research, our experience to date and our interviews with many different organisations that having a fully integrated inclusive talent strategy can never be taken for granted. Progress is not a given. Regression is a real possibility, indeed a reality for many organisations. To have maximum impact an ITM strategy needs to be consistently applied throughout an organisation.

Based on the internal 2014 NHS staff survey, Professor Mike West recommended a number of strategies to make lasting and pervasive changes.[1] These included:

1 Opportunities to bring about change are more likely to be effective at team level. Teams are more inclusive where they are well structured, have effective processes that include clear vision and values, view diversity as a positive element of the team and encourage all voices to be heard and opinions valued.

2 Implementing D&I policies, procedures and practices in such a way that they can shape and reinforce a culture of equality, fairness and opportunities for everyone.

As human beings we are designed to be aware of difference, the psychological distance people perceive between themselves and others. Professor West describes it as 'the human impulse to categorise others on the basis of the flimsiest of differences, into members of in-groups and out-groups and to discriminate in favour of other in-group members or against out-group members'.

In a business context it is about creating the culture in which difficult topics can be openly talked about without fear of repercussions. Leaders at every level of an organisation need to reinforce diversity of voices, views, skills, experiences and backgrounds to ensure creativity, innovation and good decision-making.

An inclusive leader needs to behave in a way that reinforces the above, not undermines it.

People managers are under pressure. Managing people is exhausting. But if we continue to see diversity as separate from talent, we add to the workload, rather than reduce it. There will never be enough time, there will never be enough resources. However, one thing that is free of charge, in infinite supply and completely within our own control is our capacity for leadership. To a great extent, we can determine how we do things, even within existing time and cost constraints.

Homogeneity triumphs when good people do nothing. So what are you going to do differently, starting today?

NOTE

1 West, M, Dawson, J and Kaur, M (2015), *Making the Difference: Diversity and inclusion in the NHS*, King's Fund

GLOSSARY

BAME Black, Asian and minority ethnic. Refers to members of non-white communities

Big 4 Professional services firms Deloitte, EY, KPMG and PwC

D&I diversity and inclusion

diversity a combination of a person's physical DNA, life experiences and social context

EVP employee value proposition. The mix of characteristics, benefits and ways of working in an organisation

groupthink The tendency of humans to agree with each other in order to prevent conflict

GIS guaranteed interview scheme. A policy to ensure certain minorities are given the opportunity to be seen by employers

hands-up culture the culture that tends to predominate in Western corporate settings, where extroverts are the norm, people who push themselves forward are rewarded and more introverted people tend to be overlooked

HTM homogeneous talent management. Talent management that fails to account for, or benefit from, difference

in-group a person's closest friends and colleagues who unconsciously determines their world view

ITM inclusive talent management. Talent management that takes into account everyone's potential and a culture in place that optimises the contribution everyone can make at all levels of the organisation

LGBT lesbian, gay, bisexual and transgender. Emphasises a diversity of sexuality and gender identity based culture

medical model of disability the belief that disability is predominantly a medical condition, that the lack of ability is primarily an individual responsibility

out-group people who do not form part of a person's in-group, more likely to be people very different from them

real inclusion bringing differences together to add value

role the activity, job or career we choose to do

self our personal characteristics and beliefs

social mobility the degree to which a person's social background enables or limits their life chances and career progression

social model of disability the belief that disability is determined by the environment, that the lack of accessibility in a person's surroundings inhibits their ability

STEM science, technology, engineering and mathematics. An education grouping used worldwide

SWP strategic workforce planning. A widely used methodology to forecast future employee requirements

talent the aptitudes of different people matched to the needs of an organisation

talent management the attraction, deployment, development, reward and retention of people in specific strategic positions or projects

INDEX

Page numbers in *italic* refer to figures and tables.